ESOPs
in Canada

How to Implement an Employee Share Ownership Plan
to Grow and Exit your Business with your Legacy Intact

Perry Phillips and Camille Jensen

 FriesenPress

Suite 300 - 990 Fort St
Victoria, BC, Canada, V8V 3K2
www.friesenpress.com

Copyright © 2015 by Perry Phillips and Camille Jensen
Second Edition — 2015

All rights reserved.

Cover: Tamm and Kit

ISBN
978-1-4602-2666-7 (Hardcover)
978-1-4602-2667-4 (Paperback)
978-1-4602-2668-1 (eBook)

1. Business & Economics

Distributed to the trade by The Ingram Book Company

TABLE OF CONTENTS

FOREWORD
GETTING EMPLOYEE OWNERSHIP RIGHT

Research done across the decades shows that, on average, employee ownership makes companies more productive, faster-growing, and more durable. Employee-owners, on average, accumulate more wealth and enjoy greater job stability than non-owner employees.

But those are averages. Employee ownership does not automatically create better companies, and in some cases it backfires. To reach the potential of employee ownership, and to avoid its pitfalls, you need to know the rules of the road and you need to learn from the experience of other companies. If you are with a Canadian company that is considering employee ownership or that is already employee-owned, this book is the single best way to acquire the knowledge you'll need.

Perry Phillips and Camille Jensen are the leading voice of employee ownership in Canada, and in this book they have assembled the key things you need to know in order to do it right, because much of it is specific to Canada, from law and regulations to prevailing workplace practices. They give you the tools to make sure that all the proverbial "I"s are dotted and "T"s crossed.

But, fortunately for all of us, Perry and Camille do not stop there. Employee ownership is just as much art as it is science, and much of what needs to be done to create a successful employee-owned company goes beyond the legal requirements and best practices for structuring ownership plans. To do the art of employee ownership right, companies need an array of management practices, business literacy training, employee involvement programs, and information sharing systems.

This part of the task gives you a chance to learn from other companies, both in Canada and around the world. Some of my own most inspiring examples of creative ownership come from the country I know best, the United States.

Springfield ReManufacturing has created a company where every employee is involved in managing the financial statements, and where employees generate ideas that create new lines of businesses or even new business entities. New Belgium Brewing has a culture that explicitly develops human potential, a sense of community, and the manifestation of love. Barrett-Koehler Publishing not only practises high involvement management and corporate responsibility, it publishes a compelling lineup of books that helps other companies do the same. Inspiration also comes from other countries, such as Acleda Bank in Cambodia, whose employees actively trade company shares with each other in a daily online internal marketplace.

Maybe the best example of inspiring employee ownership in the world right now is the John Lewis Partnership, a chain of department stores in the United Kingdom. Their incredible customer service, corporate responsibility, participative culture, and history of success have created such a powerful brand that it has become part of that country's political dialogue. All three of the major parties have cited their desire to create a "John Lewis economy" in which more companies become employee-owned. The legislation and regulatory changes adopted in the U.K. created a one-year increase of 9 per cent in the number of employee-owned businesses, and they appear to be on track to reach the Employee Ownership Association's goal of having employee ownership represent 10 per cent of the U.K.'s economy by 2020.

The tripartisan support for employee ownership in the U.K. illustrates one of the unique features of this field. Politicians from the left like employee ownership because it reduces wealth inequality and empowers workers. Politicians from the right like it because it creates a capitalism that has more capitalists. Centrists see a smart policy that creates jobs and roots companies in their home communities. Business leaders, whether their inclination is more libertarian or more communitarian, all find both philosophical appeal and a business case for employee ownership.

Employee ownership is practised in many different forms around the world, and Canada currently has less legislative infrastructure designed to support employee ownership than many other countries. The benefit, however, of employee ownership largely come from improvement in company performance, employee retention, and teamwork, not from tax incentives, and those advantages come from doing employee ownership right.

In this important book, Perry and Camille show you how to do just that.

> **– Loren Rodgers**
> Executive Director
> National Center for Employee Ownership
> Oakland, California

ACKNOWLEDGEMENTS

Employee share ownership encompasses many disciplines. This book couldn't have been written without the contributions of the following experts in their fields.

Thanks to Paul Maarschalk BA; CPA, CA; CBV for providing a careful eye and feedback on Chapter 5 Business Valuations and ESOPs. Dave Clark, a partner with Dale & Lessmann LLP, for his valuable review and recommendations to Chapter 7 ESOP Legal Requirements. Dale & Lessmann LLP also contributed the example shareholders' agreement found in Appendix V.

In Post-ESOP Issues, Loren Rodgers, National Center for Employee Ownership executive director, wrote Chapter 8 Administration and Communication. Dave Tyson wrote on profit-sharing.

Thanks to Alison Anderson, CEO of SuccessionMatching.com, for contributing her expertise and relevant research to Chapter 12 Exit Strategies to Transition Your Business.

We thank these contributors and advise the reader that any errors or omissions in this book are ours and ours alone.

Finally, we'd like to acknowledge our families whose love and support make writing a book like this possible. Perry's wife Helen helped with proofreading and formatting our often idiosyncratic copy. To Perry's daughter Joanna, much thanks for explaining to him how the younger generation thinks and works, and aspires to a meaningful life.

Camille thanks her husband Robert for his unflagging belief in her work and dedication to making the world a better place.

We dedicate this book to the Canadian business owners who have been implementing ESOPs in Canada for more than 20 years. These owners are pioneers, drawn to a new way of doing business for the benefit of society and a better life for all Canadians through ownership.

INTRODUCTION

Since the writing of the first edition of *Employee Share Ownership Plans (ESOPs): How to Design and Implement an ESOP in Canada,* we are pleased to share that awareness of ESOPs and their benefits is starting to take hold.

This is part due to high-profile companies like WestJet implementing an ESOP and experiencing impressive results. More than 85 per cent of WestJet's 8,000 employees participate in their ESOP, and the company is one of North America's most profitable airlines. WestJet's culture of ownership and empowerment has resulted in them being inducted into Waterstone's hall of fame for Canada's Most Admired Corporate Cultures.

Examples like this, along with other Canadian hallmark ESOP companies like PCL Construction and the Flynn Group of Companies brings welcome attention to a workplace solution whose time has come.

For the past two decades, our firm's passion and practice has been the design and implementation of employee share ownership plans for small-and medium-sized business. While many people associate ESOPs with public companies or high-tech firms, ESOPs represent a practical, underused tool for companies working in all industries.

Here are the factors fundamental to all ESOPs:

- Help attract and retain key employees
- Create an ownership mentality because employees are owners

- Recognize and value the contributions of all employees
- Boost productivity and competitiveness
- Give employees a chance to share in the company's success
- Provides a flexible succession plan for the owner

Another boost to ESOPs in Canada came in June, 2015, when the ESOP Association Canada held a national Employee Ownership Conference. This was the first conference in over a decade, helping to raise the profile of ESOPs and build a community among these companies. Seventy people attended the event, including a number of ESOP companies like Friesens, Cando Rail Services, PCL, Flynn, and Protegra.

Also in attendance at the conference were business owners hungry to learn about ESOPs from other business owners. This desire to learn about ESOPs is in part because the majority of Canada's professional advisers are not familiar with ESOPs, and as a result, not quick to recommend the model.

Yet, presenter after presenter, most who were business owners with ESOPs, spoke passionately about the model, the culture it creates, and how important it was for them to know their employees were benefitting from the success of the business.

In this book you'll learn not only the number of practical reasons to embrace ESOPs but important philosophical reasons as well. For example, ESOPs:

- Represent a new way of thinking for an interdependent economy
- Provides a tool for more people to learn business fundamentals
- Represent a real way to narrow the widening wage gap
- Provide an opportunity for capital gain for retirement

This book outlines the processes that are the foundation of an ESOP and some of the nuances that make a plan come alive. It includes case studies and a comprehensive resource directory for more information.

Whether you're looking to attract and retain skilled workers, create a flexible succession plan, recognize the contributions your employees have made to the company's success, or need a method to turn a company around through productivity and morale improvements, read this book. ESOPs present a win-win solution in a world in which it is no longer business as usual.

Within the last 25 years the world has seen an explosion of new ideas, new technologies, and new advances in just about every field of human endeavour. Knowledge is said to be doubling every 13 months — even sooner in some areas of scientific research. How can we actualize our sophisticated systems and increasing knowledge for the good of our society as well as for the good of our country? If we are to harness the abilities and the potential of Canadians in the workplace, we require breakthroughs in methodologies that utilize assets that have been previously underutilized. As shown in the United States, the United Kingdom, and many countries around the world over the last 40 years, a major breakthrough has been made through the use of employee share ownership plans.

Through these plans we can work together to harness the benefits of all the new technologies and new ideas coming forth at this point in time.

One reason ESOPs started in the United States was to address the widening gap between the middle class and the wealthy. Studies have shown that the top 1 per cent of people in the United States owned approximately 80 per cent of the wealth, and it was felt that a continuation of this process would, in effect, be the end of democracy in the United States.

Individuals can create wealth two ways. The first is through their own work effort; however, there are only 24 hours in a day, personal labour can contribute only so much to a person's income. The second method is capital accumulation: the ownership of capital assets that may increase in value without the input of a person's individual labour component. Unfortunately, many people do not have the knowledge, skill, or opportunity to participate in the capital asset growth of a company. ESOPs address this issue by insuring that all employees will benefit by ownership in the companies they work for.

This has tremendous implications not only on the individual employees but also on the political and social fabric of the nation. A wealthier middle class has tremendous implications on many issues in our current economy. It means less reliance upon governments for future pensions. It means a bigger source of income taxes that can be used to help the poor in our society. It means people are more able to take control of their own destinies to attain their specific goals in life.

In times of economic expansion crime rates go down, and in times of economic recession crime rates increase. Would we not be better off as a society to increase the wealth of as many people as possible? Wealth cannot be created by governments; wealth is created by the labour of the workforce. If the employees get the benefits of their work through ownership in their companies, wealth is spread without an intervention mechanism such as higher income taxes. Of course not all people want to give empowerment to the employees. Some people believe that if Canadian employees begin to control their own destinies, governments will have a smaller role in monitoring and creating laws to restrict and focus the allocation of assets within society. We agree that there are winners and losers in implementing ESOPs. The clear winners are the employees who are now able to benefit from another source of income.

This income increases potential for wealth and the ability to control one's own destiny, meaning that employees won't have to rely upon unions, government, or any institutional setting that seeks to control and dictate what their lives should be.

The losers on the other hand are the large institutions that will start to lose control over the very people that keep them in their positions of power. Looking again to the United States, both the Republicans and the Democrats have put into place a very sophisticated level of ESOP legislation, which supports the concept that individuals should have control over their own destiny. Republicans regard ESOPs as a means of empowering individuals, whereas the Democrats see ESOPs as a means of spreading wealth. ESOPs do both, and it is important for Canadians to realize that if we are to compete in the future against countries that have many times our population base and much lower unit costs, we have to utilize our greatest skill:

the ability of our people to innovate and create new ways of doing business.

In this book we will show that ESOPs are effective and do create productivity levels that are necessary for Canadian companies to compete in our global marketplace. However, this is not enough. For breadwinners, no price can be put on the knowledge that their hard work has not only improved their family's life but also created something that is bigger than themselves. They are creating a successful company that will, in the long term, help them to achieve personal and financial goals. This approach has been proven in many countries. In the United States for the last 40 years, in Britain over the last 20 years, and in countries such as Germany, Spain, France, and developing countries, companies are starting to look at implementing ESOPs as a means of increasing the wealth of their people.

Not all private or public companies are suitable for ESOPs. Research in the United States indicates that approximately 25 per cent of companies appear to have the suitable cultural and structural supports to implement an ESOP. However, given that figure, very few companies have actually developed an ESOP plan to both help their employees and the company grow. We believe that Canadian companies must utilize some type of ESOP program if we are to remain competitive on the world stage.

This book was written for those owners and employees who realize that there is no limit to what can be achieved by a team of dedicated individuals. These are the people that can utilize and benefit substantially from an ESOP within their corporation.

To achieve a successful ESOP, it is important to have access to knowledgeable professionals in the area. An ESOP entails many different aspects such as design, communication, law, tax, and valuation, and one consultant alone cannot serve them all. In the appendices you will find contact information for professional firms and associations. While this is by no means an all-inclusive or exhaustive list, it may help the reader to at least begin their search.

HOW TO USE THIS BOOK

This book has been written for readers who are interested in learning about the design and implementation of employee share ownership plans. It addresses three types of readers. The first are business owners of privately-held companies who wish to sell or transfer equity to employees. The second type is the stakeholders of publicly-held companies, both senior executives and their employees. The third type are professional advisers such as accountants, lawyers, tax advisers, and financial planners who want to help clients in implementing and designing employee share ownership plans.

To meet the needs of each group of readers, the book deals with Pre-ESOP issues and Post-ESOP issues. Pre-ESOP issues include ESOP planning, design, and implementation. Pre-ESOP issues also include the period of time during which the ESOP is implemented into the corporate culture of the company. These pre-ESOP processes can take anywhere from three to six months to complete. In many cases in which we have been involved, the idea for the ESOP has been proposed either by the business owners or by the employees as much as three years prior to the time that a designer was brought in to help implement a plan.

For business owners, or for someone who is considering putting an ESOP plan into place, we suggest starting with Chapter 2 ESOP Objectives. The chapter explains the types of candidates who would likely succeed at this type of process, and the process itself, which is key to implementing a successful ESOP. Continue to Chapter 3 Designing ESOPs, which goes into the detail of designing an ESOP and addresses a lot of the issues involved in the administration, communication, and troubleshooting that occurs when putting an ESOP into place in a privately-held company. These two chapters, along with the appendices outlining the types of plans and the appropriate forms, and the communication pieces needed to set the process in motion, will likely suffice for most readers who are interested in starting the process immediately.

Chapters 4 to 7 deal with detailed technical issues around financing, business valuation, income taxes, and legal matters, and although these are important, the business owner must simply understand some of the technical issues to converse knowledgeably with professionals when implementing the design of the ESOP.

For the stakeholders of publicly-held companies, both senior executives and employees, many of the pre-ESOP issues in the earlier chapters are not as important as the post-ESOP issues addressed in Chapters 8 to11. These chapters address the issues relevant to ESOPs for those public companies that have some type of shareholder plan already in place. These issues include profit sharing, the use of open-book management and the proper use of cross-border ESOPs.

For the business owners and employees of privately-held companies, once the ESOP is in place post-ESOP issues occur, usually six months to a year after the ESOP is set up. Chapters 8 and 9 provide useful information for business owners to understand what issues will be coming down the road, in order to start planning now.

We've added Chapter 10 to this edition for business owners who would like to add or have a social or environmental purpose in their business. This chapter discusses the emerging movement and synergies between Certified B Corporations and ESOPs.

Finally, Chapter 12 explores different exit strategies owners can use to transition their business.

For the third group of readers, professional advisers, knowledge of the process is critical for the success of an ESOP. For those readers we suggest Chapters 1 through 3, which deal with the communication, design, and implementation of the ESOP.

– **Perry Phillips and Camille Jensen**
ESOP Builders Inc.

CHAPTER 1
WHAT IS AN ESOP?

Giving all workers a greater stake in the company they work for is a powerful way of aligning the interests of employees with that of the business. A worker who has a financial and personal stake in a company will take more responsibility for its success.

– Norman Lamb, former U.K. Minister for Employment Relations

In technical terms, an ESOP is a formal stock equity plan that can include stock equity, stock options, or phantom stock. The definitions for these terms will be provided later in the chapter. An ESOP can be part of an employee benefits package or a corporate financing strategy.

ESOP MYTH ESOPs exist only in the United States and United Kingdom.

ESOP FACT ESOPs are used around the globe; however certain countries like the U.S. and the U.K have extensive federal legislation to promote the model. As a result ESOPs are more widely used in these countries.

The plan can be open to key personnel or all employees, enabling them to purchase in total from 1 per cent to 100 per cent ownership in the company with the securities acquired through cash payment, profit sharing, bonuses, or services rendered. The equity ownership allows qualifying employees to participate in and benefit from the growth of the company in return for a commitment to stay for the long haul. ESOPs allow employee-owners to share in the company's success through increased share value that can be sheltered for tax-free gain. Favourable tax treatment is available because these gains can be classified not as income earned, but as a capital gain, which is taxed at a much lower rate than income.

That is the technical description. In fact, ESOPs defy easy explanation; every plan is unique. The plan's purpose, participation, and parameters are flexible and tailored to the individual company. In general, though, there are certain common results. When coupled with a corporate philosophy of participative management, ESOPs create an ownership mentality. Employees think and act like owners because they actually are owners. Workplace dynamics shift from a "working for" to a "working with" mentality. The outcomes are improved motivation, communication, productivity, and profitability.

THE THREE TYPES OF ESOP

ESOPs are built with three basic tools: stock equity, stock options, or phantom stock units. A plan may comprise only one, a combination of any two, or all three tools.

STOCK EQUITY

Stock equity is the legal transfer of ownership of a share of stock issued by a company. An employee who owns this share has ownership that may or may not have additional rights attached to it. For example, the share may allow the employee to vote at the annual shareholders' meeting, or the share may be non-voting. Stock equity has the greatest potential for creating an ownership mentality within the company because the employee generally has to pay for the stock. This payment requires the employee to take an investment risk in the company. It is this risk potential that puts the original owners and the new employee owners on the same level.

STOCK OPTIONS

Stock options constitute a contract between the company and the employee to sell equity to the employee at some point in the future, at a price calculated in the present day. At that future date, if the company has increased in value, the employee will be able to purchase company stock at a significant discount and have a real gain in wealth. If the share value declines, the employee does not lose anything because he or she simply does not exercise the option to buy the stock. A stock option can be a motivator and a surrogate for ownership. However, it may not be effective as equity ownership.

PHANTOM STOCK

Phantom stock units mirror *real* stock equity with equivalent rights except the right to vote. There is, however, no legal transfer of ownership, and this tends to be the greatest drawback of phantom stock. It does not create the conditions necessary for true ownership because the employee does not have legal title to any of the assets of the company. However, by adding equity conversion rights to these units, phantom stock can approach true equity plans. The equity conversion allows the phantom units to be converted to real stock equity upon a liquidity event. For example, five years from the time that the phantom plan is put into place, an outside purchaser may buy shares of the company. Employees with the phantom stock units can transfer their units into real *shares* of the company prior to the closing of the acquisition, sell those shares to the acquirer, and realize a substantial gain in equity. Phantom stock units are used when the ownership group is not comfortable with transferring real equity ownership to the employees and does not want employees to have a vote.

The term "phantom plans" is used by practitioners in the field but not when presenting to employees, because the term tends to indicate something false. To avoid this problem, many phantom plans are known as either participation or value-added plans. At ESOP Builders we use the term Equity Value Ownership Plan (EVOP™).

THE IMPORTANCE OF EQUITY TYPES

Stock equity, stock options, and phantom stock may be viewed as a continuum, with stock plans being on the extreme left, stock options in the middle, and phantom plans on the extreme right. The left portion of this continuum represents the maximum changed mindset with regards to employee ownership mentality. In other words, when employees actually own shares in a company, they believe that they are owners, and the process of participation is easier to implement. Participative management in ESOPs will be discussed in Chapter 8 Administration and Communication.

In the middle of the continuum, stock options are less effective in creating an ownership mentality due to the fact that the employee does not actually own anything. He or she merely has the right to future ownership. This right can still be a powerful force in creating an ownership mentality, but it is not as strong as pure equity ownership.

On the extreme right of the continuum are phantom plans. These have limited ability to create an ownership mentality as there is no ownership nor is there likely to be. However, with certain conditions attached to these plans, some ownership mentality can be created. In fact, these plans are still better than no plan at all. In many cases a phantom plan can be a precursor to a share equity or option plan at some future date.

Why do some companies use only one type of plan while others mix and match the elements? The answer lies in the culture of the company and the mindset of the current ownership group. A culture of open sharing of information, for example, will likely go for an equity and/or option plan, while a culture that is secretive will probably favour the phantom plan. There is no right or wrong approach to this design issue. Each plan must meet the criteria as set by both the culture and ownership group's comfort level in terms of sharing ownership. The key to a successful plan is proper identification of the culture and ownership type at the beginning of the assignment so as to create a match. Another aspect that can come into play in choosing the plan type is whether or not the company can legally offer equity and/or option plans. For example, accounting and legal firms may not be able to issue shares and thus have to look at a phantom plan augmented by some participative designs to achieve a successful ESOP.

So first determine your company's culture. For example, if your company tends to give out quarterly financial information, has training programs that encourage employees to understand financial statements, and is open with the communication of these issues, the most effective plan for your company would be a stock equity and/or a stock option plan. If your company is concerned with attracting and keeping your key people only, you may want to look at a pure stock option plan. If your company tends to not communicate its financial positions, does not have a profit -sharing plan, and makes decisions from the top down and not the bottom up, you should probably consider some type of phantom plan to start with.

CONCLUSION

ESOPs represent a win-win, where an employee is motivated to see that the company is a success for everyone in that company. ESOPs are flexible and may be used in many situations for a variety of purposes. Because of their adaptability, no two ESOPs are the same, and each ESOP may be planned and custom fit to a particular culture and type of company. Whether the company is looking at an ESOP for attraction or retention purposes, or for purposes of succession planning, or for higher productivity and value for the current business owners, it is important to assess whether the company is in fact a good candidate for an ESOP.

Because of the expense and the implications of addressing ESOPs and introducing them to an employee group, it is critical that the ownership group determine this as soon as possible.

CHAPTER 2
ESOP OBJECTIVES

When you give employees an opportunity to participate in the success of their company, productivity, customer service, and employee engagement all increase dramatically.

– Paul Douglas, PCL Construction president and CEO

There are well documented benefits to putting ESOPs in place in companies across all economic sectors. ESOPs address key workplace issues such as productivity, competitiveness, survival, succession, recruiting, and retention.

ESOP MYTH   You have to sell 100 per cent of the shares to create an ESOP.

ESOP FACT   An ESOP can be offered to key people or all eligible employees, and can range from 1 per cent to 100 per cent of the company.

From a more philosophical perspective, ESOPs can help address broader societal issues such as the wage gap and the impending retirement crisis by fostering a climate of inclusive capitalism. Inclusive capitalism is the means by which a society distributes its wealth on the basis of a fair distribution without the intervention of government or institutional organizations. It is market forces at work allowing the proper spread of increased wealth to all people who are producing that wealth. It is, in effect, the purest form and the highest level of capitalism that can be obtained.

Surveys and outcomes of ESOP implementation in Canada indicate that ESOPs help attract and retain a motivated work-force and that they help boost productivity and profitability. Although the samplings are relatively small in Canada, the findings are supported by global research. One of the most recent and comprehensive ESOP studies was undertaken by the United Kingdom in 2012. "Sharing Success: The Nuttall Review of Employee Ownership" conducted a comprehensive literature review concluding that several strong themes emerge among ESOPs companies: improved business performance; increased economic resilience; greater employee engagement and commit-ment; driving innovation; enhanced employee well-being; and reduced absenteeism.

Included in this research was a survey conducted by Cass Business School that showed employee-owned companies were more profitable, added more staff and were more resilient during the 2008 - 2009 economic downturn.

In many Canadian companies that have implemented ESOPs, productivity improvements and retention and attraction rates have improved significantly. One high-tech company reduced its employee turnover rate from 30 per cent to 10 per cent after the ESOP was introduced. Another company in a manufacturing field decreased its wasted inventory so much that it increased profit-ability by over 20 per cent. Many other studies are available online from the National Center for Employee Ownership. See the end of the book for a list of websites.

But the mere fact of setting up an ESOP does not automatically transform a corporate culture. It takes more than a shareholders' agreement; employers and employees must embrace the special dynamics of shared ownership and commitment. A shareholder's agreement is simply an agreement between the employees and the owners, setting out the terms and conditions of what it means to be an owner in that particular company. However, when coupled with a corporate philosophy that recognizes the contributions of all workers and stresses participative management, ESOPs become the winning solution they're designed to be. A participative culture and environment will be discussed more fully in Chapter 8 Administration and Communication.

A CONVERGENCE OF TRENDS

We are in a new economy, one of interdependence through mutually beneficial business relationships. The increasing globalization of commerce and cross-border capital flow is changing the standards for business. As a result, regulatory authorities are working to harmonize accounting and auditing practices to formalize global standards and even out competitive advantages and disadvantages. For example, accounting for goodwill changed in the U.K. in 2005 through the combined effects of the new International Accounting Standards. Clearly, a nation out of step with world standards will ultimately be disadvantaged in business. A clear example of this is the lack of ESOP legislation by Canadian government at the federal level when compared to its major trading competitors such as the United States and the United Kingdom. The explosion of technology is being driven by increasing globalization and that explosion has placed a new value on the knowledge-based workforce — it is a key national resource that must be protected. The shift to a global economy has opened national borders and allowed people of different cultures and skill sets more access to more workplaces around the world. The result is employees who are more self-reliant and employers who must reward their employees to get them to stay longer.

Adding to this, the baby boomers are entering their retirement years and will need to transition their businesses. In the following pages we will outline how ESOPs are in sync with the world-shifting paradigms.

ATTRACTING AND RETAINING MOTIVATED WORKERS

People assets do not appear on the financial statements of a company, but the business cannot operate successfully without attracting and keeping key people. There has been a recent change, however, in the United States and Canada regarding who the key people are in an organization. It used to be that only senior executives were seen as being worthy of special compensation packages in options and in equity programs. However, more progressive companies have identified that all people in an organization are key, from the people who answer the phones at the reception desk, up to and including the chairman of the board. Each has his or her own responsibilities and accountability to improving the value of the company in his or her own area of work within the company.

Publix, one of the largest private companies in the U.S., offers an ESOP to all employees who work at the retail grocery store for one year. In an industry notorious for high turnover, on average a 100 per cent, Publix has a turnover rate of 3.2 per cent. Adding to this, Publix is one, if not the most, profitable grocery chains in the U.S.

In the twenty-first century, the demand for key people in all industries is increasing throughout the world. Demand is particularly high in the information technology sector.

A report by the Information and Communications Technology Council (ICTC) entitled "Outlook for Human Resources in the Information and Communications Technology (ICT) Labour Market, 2011-2016" notes that Canadian companies will be looking to hire an estimated 106,000 new employees between 2011 and 2016 for ICT-related jobs. However, the report projects there won't be enough qualified applicants to fill the positions. Many of Canada's most talented and qualified ICT employees are part of a brain drain to the United States. The *Globe and Mail's* Report on Business estimates that 350,000 Canadians are now living in the Bay Area working in technology-related jobs. The global need for skilled workers shows no signs of abating.

While it's increasingly difficult to attract talent, a survey by Rutgers Employee Ownership Fellows Program shows companies advertising as employee-owned should have much more success in recruiting higher-skilled employees. Undergraduates, who were asked to self-report their SAT or ACT scores, were shown two otherwise identical recruitment ads, one that explicitly stated the firm was employee-owned and one that did not. The results show that higher-scoring students were significantly more likely to prefer the employee-owned company.

A second approach in the study looked at a sample of 147 working professionals recruited through Amazon's Mechanical Turk, a crowdsourcing Internet marketplace that enables individuals and businesses to connect to do jobs computers have a hard time doing. The average age of respondents was 36, with 14.8 years of work experience. Twenty-one per cent had experience working for a firm with an employee ownership plan. After completing consent forms, participants were randomly assigned to respond to descriptions of employee-owned firms or non-employee-owned firms. The study found dramatic differences in how participants perceived such factors as empowerment, engagement, job turnover, and other dimensions. On a seven-point scale, employee ownership companies typically rated around a six, and other companies half that or less.

JOBS IN PRODUCTIVITY AND PROFITABILITY

The Organization for Economic Cooperation and Development (OECD) reports in 2012 that while per capita incomes are growing in Canada, productivity has stagnated for decades. Worse, productivity has declined since 2002. Compare this with the United States, where its productivity has grown by 30 per cent in the last 20 years.

We believe this productivity gap between the United States and Canada results from the United States having had a detailed legislated agenda of ESOPs as part of their economic plan for the last 40 years and the fact that one out of 11 American workers own shares in the companies they work for.

ESOPs can foster a corporate culture where a motivated workforce sees the benefit in sharing ideas, trimming costs, and working more productively. The most comprehensive study of Canadian ESOPs was done by the Toronto Stock Exchange in 1986. A comparison of ESOP and non-ESOP public companies showed that ESOP companies had:

- 123 per cent higher five-year profit growth
- 95 per cent higher net profit margin
- 24 per cent greater productivity
- A 2-10 per cent premium on the stock market
- 92.26 per cent higher return on average total equity
- 65.52 per cent higher return on capital
- 31.54 per cent lower debt/equity ratio

Recent studies in the U.S., U.K. and Australia over the past 20 years support the TSE findings.

OWNERSHIP KEY TO FLYNN GROUP'S GROWTH

Doug Flynn, president and CEO of the Flynn Group of Companies, likes to learn by observing. It was in the early 90s as he took over the leadership of his father's building envelope contracting business that he began watching his competitors, who were mostly small, owner-operated firms. Doug admired these businesses and observed some common positive traits among these owners. The owners were passionate, engaged, accountable and nimble. This wasn't a coincidence, thought Doug. As Doug looked to grow his business he knew in order to grow the right way, he would need more owners in the business. He wanted his leadership team, like him, to have "skin in the game," and treat the business like it was their own. In 2000, Doug decided to expand the ownership/leadership base of the company and implement an ESOP for leaders within the company. He arranged financing to make it easier for key people to buy in. While often owners hear the advice to "not give up any equity," Doug looked at it differently. He was happy to give up equity if it meant the pie was getting bigger. The benefit to creating more owners at Flynn is significant. When Doug implemented the ESOP, the company had 100 staff in three offices. Today, the Flynn Group is North America's leading building envelope trade contractor with 4,000 employees, of which 100 are owners, and 25 offices. And growing! From attracting and retaining talent to creating a culture of sharing best practices, the ESOP was a key component in the company's growth, according to Doug.

ESOPS AND SUCCESSION PLANNING

A 2012 report by the Canadian Federation of Independent Businesses noted that in the next 10 years, more than three quarters of all small to medium sized enterprises (SME) will transition. Yet, only 40 per cent of SME owners have an informal succession plan. Only nine per cent have a formal plan.

We believe there is not enough independent capital or independent buyers to purchase the myriad SMEs that could go up for sale in the coming years.

The question for owners ready to retire is where to sell their assets. For many company owners the best solution is to sell to employees, which is why an ESOP can be the ideal succession plan for small and medium-sized business owners and family-run businesses. An ESOP can ensure that the owner gets his or her money out and that the business survives. The advantage in selling to employees is that the owners are selling to people who have a vested interest in continuing the business. It also means that the owners do not have to show their financial information to outsiders who often are competitors. Change can usually take place with a tax-advantageous transfer and at minimal cost. Neither brokerage fees nor complicated legal costs have to be incurred to sell to employees. The major disadvantage is that employees may not have the cash to purchase the company. However, there are now many venture capitalists and sources of investment money that allow employees to complete a buyout. (Please see Chapter 4 Financing ESOPs.)

ESOP HELPS OWNER RETIRE EARLY

President and CEO of DST Consulting Engineers Mike Fabius originally introduced an ESOP into his environmental engineering and consulting firm to recruit and retain talent. However, the ESOP proved so successful he decided to use the model as his exit strategy. He implemented a succession plan and once comfortable with the new leadership group, Mike became a minority owner. He spent one year sharing the president-CEO role as the final part of his transition to retirement. "The ESOP was a great succession plan, it allowed me to retire earlier than I had planned on, and it made it clear for myself," says Mike. (For more details, see the full DST case study in Appendix I.)

ESOPS AND BUSINESS FINANCING

ESOPs can provide a low-cost source of financing for business expansion. They can also assist in securing outside financing. For example, in the United States many venture capitalists require an ESOP to be in place before investing in small or medium-sized businesses.

ESOPS AND RETIREMENT PLANNING

A number of economic indicators suggest that we are headed towards a retirement crisis in Canada. According to the Organization for Economic Cooperation and Development (OECD) in a 2012 report, public (government) transfers to seniors in Canada account for less than 39 per cent of the gross income of Canadian seniors. Compare this with the OECD average of 59 per cent, meaning more Canadians depend on workplace pensions to bridge the gap.

As private pensions are mainly concentrated among workers with higher earnings, the growing importance of private pension in the next decades may lead to higher income inequality among the elderly, the report states.

Adding to this, many Canadians have not saved adequately for retirement. Nearly half of the Baby Boomers are not confident they will be financially secure in retirement, according to BMO Wealth Planning Group in Toronto. That's up 20 per cent from 2006.

Younger generations are facing even direr prospects. BMO notes Gen X and Gen Y are having children at a later age making it more difficult to save. Housing prices have doubled while income has not. Where will the money come from?

The U.S. government recognized 40 years ago that ESOPs would give a broader base of citizens the opportunity to invest in their own futures and accumulate capital. Canada could do the same by changing tax laws and capital-gain provisions to encourage companies to implement ESOPs and employees to buy them.

On a per capita basis, the United States economy is wealthier, has lower unemployment and higher productivity. These factors set it apart from the Canadian economy.

One area that will start to diverge in the future will be the difference between what United States citizens and Canadian citizens will be have to retire on. The implications are enormous as our society ages and needs more funds to take care of its population. ESOPs give Canadians the ability to take care of themselves in the future rather than relying on governments to do this.

A TALE OF TWO SISTERS

Two American citizens, Cathy Burch and her twin sister Deborah Cook, are a potent example of how ESOPs can transform our current system for retirement savings. Cathy and Deborah both applied to Winco Foods, an employee-owned U.S. grocer, more than 20 years ago. At the time Winco had an anti-nepotism policy and hired only one sister, Cathy. Cathy stayed working at Winco for 23 years and at 42, has close to $1 million in Winco stock, enough to allow her to retire immediately. Her sister Deborah, on the other hand, bounced around several jobs and managed to save $30,000 in a retirement account, mostly in stocks. The 2008 financial crises cut her retirement savings in half. This was a huge wake-up call for Deborah, who essentially had to start over. She was able to find a job with a federal agency and figures if she works to 67 she will have a decent pension.

SPREADING THE WEALTH

ESOPs enable a greater cross-section of individuals to build personal wealth, to be recognized for their effort, and to share in the rewards. A broad-based ESOP is an investment in human dignity in that it recognizes and values the contributions of all employees. ESOPs encourage more broad-based stock ownership by giving the opportunity to participate in equity ownership to people who otherwise would not have the means to do so. As such, ESOPs can be an effective lever to share wealth and ownership. This is no small point when you consider that the wage gap has become a chasm in Canada, where Canada's 100 highest paid CEOs made 195 times more than the average Canadian worker and 237 times the average Canadian woman.

Some people can't afford to purchase shares in a company, but even a small investment, given the tax advantages and the growth of the capital value over years, would help each individual towards increasing his or her wealth.

Many owners believe that they owe a large part of their success to the hard work of their employees over the years and want to acknowledge this fact through a program of employee ownership. Employees also believe that the success of the owner had been through their hard efforts over the years. An ESOP is neither a paternal gift nor a right. It is in fact a great challenge that the owner is offering the employee — a challenge to take on a share of responsibility for the company's success and thereby enjoy the benefits of the rewards. With this inevitably comes the possibility of loss. It is critical that the owner not promise blue-sky results but be honest about the risks and rewards and treat the employee-owner with respect. Having said this, there is no question that the rewards generally far exceed the risks. In many cases employees have been able to leave companies with tremendous built-up wealth.

Before getting into the nuts and bolts of how to design and implement an effective ESOP program, let's examine what makes a good candidate for an ESOP program.

CHECKLIST FOR ESOP CANDIDATES

Experience shows that there are key attributes that suggest a company is a good candidate for an ESOP:

- The ownership group is willing to share information and to share ownership.
- The company is in a fairly good financial position and is not in a turnaround situation looking for the employees to bail it out.
- The company has a history of maintaining its profitability and is likely to continue to grow.
- There's a specific need to share the responsibilities with the employees. This need may be to attract and maintain key people, a succession plan for the ownership group, or maybe there's a need to increase productivity within the company.
- For a broad-based plan there should be at least 10 employees in the company; otherwise the ESOP could prove an expensive task for the company to take on, due to the minimum costs involved for legal and accounting fees. For a key-person plan no minimum exists.
- The ESOP may be an opportunity for the company to differentiate itself from competitors. The ESOP may also be a competitive necessity if in fact the company's competitors have ESOPs in place.
- Where there's been a history of employee mistrust of management, as long as that mistrust is not too deep seated, an ESOP may be able to resolve the problem. Once an ESOP is explained

to the employee group and has been put in place with the right intentions, any prior low morale or mistrust will generally dissipate.

- The amount of percentage of ownership that will be transferred to the employees will be defined in the process by the ownership group. It is not necessary to transfer 100 per cent ownership to the employees unless of course a succession plan is being contemplated. The percentage of the transfer is less important than the employees being able to participate in the potential growth of the company.

- Management or the owners must be able to listen to the employees. During the ESOP process management needs to take criticisms seriously and use them in the process to come up with a better plan. If management cannot listen to constructive criticism, the company may not be a good candidate for an ESOP.

- The employees as a group must be interested in this type of scenario of equity compensation and be willing to listen to the presentation of an ESOP.

If the company is a candidate for an ESOP-type plan, whether it be equity, options, or an Equity Value Ownership Plan (EVOP), the next step is to develop a process, which is key to implementing a successful ESOP. On the following page is an overview of our ESOP Transformation Model:

The ESOP Transformation Model

STAGE 1:
Feasibility Audit
The Assessment

Owners Review: a detailed discussion with ownership to define ESOP goals

Employee Review: interviews with key employees to assess knowledge and interest

Corporate Review: thorough review of financials and corporate and tax structure

You will receive a holistic summary of Stage 1, including:

- **Professional Opinion:** our comprehensive recommendation
- **Pros and Cons:** as they relate to stated business objectives
- **Next Steps:** available options and plans
- **Cost Estimate**
- **Critical Path:** proposed implementation structure and timeline

STAGE 2:
ESOP Design, Implementation & Communication
The Delivery

Core Team: establishment of core employees and owners who will draft Blueprint and Shareholder's Agreements

Engagement: employee information sessions

Status Review: a business valuation report

Tax Review: including an Income Tax Summary document

Legal Review: review of legal documents and consultation

Internal Communication: assistance preparing Employee Information Package

Final Engagement: Town Hall Meeting with all stakeholders

Beyond the Plan: optional Ownership Thinking™ program

In some respects setting up an ESOP is much like taking a company public — in fact, you could call the process "taking it private" since the investment is available only to the employee group. The successful ESOP process first establishes the company's goals in implementing an ESOP and then juggles parallel tasks to design and implement and tailor the plan. It is an intensive exercise carried out over at least 16-weeks and requires total commitment from the ESOP team, consisting of the employer or owner, employee representatives, and consultants. Experienced project managers and open communication are key to success.

The work is best conducted in two stages.

STAGE 1: ESOP FEASIBILITY ASSESSMENT

Before diving into implementing an ESOP, it is important to understand the owner's goals for the plan as well as employee interest, and assess whether this feedback aligns with the tangible benefits of an ESOP.

The starting point for an ESOP is a fact-finding, facilitating exercise on the part of the ESOP consultant. A consultant, unlike the business owner, can give an independent third party view of the issues.

In this initial phase, we also recommend the consultant provide the business owner with an approximate value of the business. This ensures that before moving too far along in the process there is agreement by the owners on the approximate value of the company. While the full business valuation will be conducted in Stage 2, it's important to have the owners agree to an approximate fair market value. (Please see Chapter 5 Business Valuations and ESOPs.)

After the ESOP consultant speaks with the owners and employees and reviews key documentation, they will write a report determining the feasibility of an ESOP based on their findings, and recommend a model they think would work best. At this point, the owners can proceed with the recommendations, modify the goals of the ESOP or stop the process, depending on the results of the feasibility audit.

STAGE 2: ESOP DESIGN AND IMPLEMENTATION

Once the ESOP model and strategic goals have been clarified verbally and in writing, the ESOP consultant meets with the ownership group to determine the broad parameters of the ESOP, agree on the composition and design and implementation team, and commit to a critical path.

In terms of planning parameters, there are a number of key discussion points, which will be examined in greater detail later on in the book. For now, we will outline the process and all the things owners need to consider:

- Type of equity — basic tools are stock equity, stock options, or phantom stock units.
- Percentage of ownership to be offered — the ESOP can range from 1 to 100 per cent employee ownership.
- Sources of shares — from treasury (i.e., shares that the company owns but they are not owned by the shareholders) or ownership group (i.e., shares that are owned by current owners and can be sold directly to the employees). If shares are purchased from treasury the proceeds of the investment go back into the company's bank accounts.
- Employee eligibility — there is generally a requirement for a continuous period of employment before a person becomes eligible for ownership.
- Allocation formula — the number of shares available to an individual will typically be a percentage of total shares available, based on an individual's base salary over the aggregate of total salaries. Allocation formulas can be based on different methods, salary being the primary method. Other methods could include merit, seniority, or attainment of target levels.
- Vesting period — where stock options are used, the plan will specify the length of time before they may be exercised.
- Buyout provisions — the shareholders' agreement will specify buyout provisions based on termination of employment, retirement, death, or disability.

- Share acquisition — equity may be sold at Fair Market Value, at a discount, or given to the employee free, but the ESOP is usually more successful when employees purchase shares. Employees take the investment much more seriously when they have to sign a cheque than when they are given something for free. The ownership group may then choose to match share-purchase with gifted options.
- Financing — equity may be purchased outright, granted in lieu of bonuses or acquired through a payroll deduction. The consultant will outline the pros and cons of all options and work with the ownership group to determine which alternative best suits the company.

ESOP CRITICAL PATH	
PROCESS	WEEK
Stage 1 ESOP Feasibility Assessment	3-4
Stage 2	
ESOP Design and Strategy	3-5
ESOP Team Meetings	6-12
Stock Plan	6-8
Financing	6-8
Education Seminar	6-10
Valuation	6-10
Tax Strategy	8-12
Legal Structure	8-10
Questionnaire	8-10
Feedback Loop	12
Draft Blueprint	7-11
Employee Information Package	13-14
Final Employee Info Package	15
Town Hall Meeting	16-18
Closing of the ESOP Transaction	18+

After the initial owner meeting, the ESOP team is assembled, a critical path agreed upon, and responsibilities allocated.

There are formal and informal communication channels built into the process. Employee representatives on the ESOP team bring issues to the table and provide ongoing feedback to their co-workers. Midway through the process the employee group is polled through a formal questionnaire. (A sample question-naire is included in Appendix III.) There are education sessions and distribution of an employee information package. Once the ESOP closes, and the equity and/or options are issued to the new employee-owners, the implementation of the plan sets a new process in action — ongoing participative management. This post-ESOP program is discussed in Chapters 8 and 9.

TIME TO COMPLETE AN ESOP

It is important for the ESOP consultant to have the process under control. In many cases the owners have been promising some type of ESOP plan to their employees for as long as five years and have never done anything about it. The key to creating a successful ESOP is declaring the ESOP and then putting it into place effi-ciently and quickly. Business owners are very busy, and the ESOP may fall by the wayside. Through a process of interviews and cor-porate document research, the consultant will identify the goals and issues that drive the desire to put an ESOP in place. In most cases the ESOP is initiated by the business owner, but an employee group may also initiate it. The latter happens most often in cases of a leveraged buyout or a business rescue. Although ESOPs are usually the result of a practical purpose, there are philosophical implications that should be considered. An ESOP transforms a corporate culture, creating new lines of communication between management and employees. It creates a group of shareholders with a vested interest in the company's plans and decisions. In order to be successful, the plan design and implementation must have an ownership team with a full understanding of all the impli-cations and total commitment from the outset. Experience shows that lukewarm or non-existent commitment will generally lead to a failed ESOP. Therefore, in order to make the plan work, the commitment for success must include the allocation of key people and time to the ESOP project over a short timeframe. That means the owners must invest their own time in seeing their project through. Key employees must also invest their productive time and work closely with external advisers. There also needs to be a general commitment to open communication and timely feedback.

COMMITMENT MEANS SUCCESS

The success of an ESOP is a mixture of tangible and intangible ingredients with common, underlying factors.

- It is a priority to all those involved.
- Employer and employees trust each other.
- Employee input is welcome.
- Immediate action creates results.
- Open and timely communication is achieved.

ESOP TEAM

The scope of the project will dictate the composition of the ESOP team. Generally, the optimum is to have a wide range of input from the ownership group, external advisers, and the employees themselves. The ESOP is a process, and the greater the input at the beginning, the better results at the end.

ESOP TEAM RESPONSIBILITIES

TITLE	RESPONSIBILITIES
Owner	Sets baseline parameters, represents company position and interests.
Employee Representatives (4-8 reps generally)	Voices employee ideas, concerns, issues; reports back to employee group.
ESOP Project Manager (outside consultant)	Determines feasibility, monitors timetable and budget, facilitates plan design and implementation, trouble-shoots based on experience; implements organizational improve-ment and change; drives commun-ication; oversees ongoing plan maintenance
Lawyer	Assures compliance to legislation, prepares shareholder's agreement; acts as trustee, oversees any nece-ssary adjustments to corporate struc-ture, provides basis for employee info-rmation package.
Accountant	Assists with plan, inputs data
Tax Accountant	Prepares tax structures for ESOP; identifies tax effects for owners and employees
Business Valuator	Independently values company to determine share price
Insurance Agent	Responsible for funding of buy-sell employee insurance (this can be a necessity or optional depending on the needs of the company)

OWNERSHIP AND EMPLOYEE REPRESENTATIVES

The ownership side should be represented by at least one or two of the owners, at least initially. The owners can opt to be less involved as the process continues. There should be 4-8 employee reps, depending on the number of divisions and the number of employees in the company. It's important the ESOP team is not too big or too small, generally 3-12 people at most. A team this size ensures conversations take place in a timely manner and there is opportunity for anyone who wants to share feedback to do so. The employee reps may be picked by the ownership group or by the employees themselves, again depending on the culture of the company. The ESOP consultant may also provide input into what attributes make for a good ESOP team member, for example a team player and respected by their peers. It is very important to get a good chemistry on the ESOP team so that the plan proceeds smoothly and successfully with an efficient use of time for both the company and the outside consultants. The employee reps are generally not brought into the loop until after the go-ahead meeting, when the issues have been finalized and the general blue-print has been drawn up.

CONSULTANTS

Finding the right consultants can be a difficult task. The first consultant to be chosen is the ESOP design consultant. He or she will be general contractors for the plan and it is his or her ability to choose the right sub-contractors that will move the plan efficiently forward. It is very important for the legal counsel to have expertise in corporate and commercial work, specifically in the areas of shareholders' agreements, share restructuring, and the ability to propose and help write the employee information document. Consider using the lawyer chosen by the ESOP consultant working with the ownership group rather than the lawyers who act for the company for various reasons:

1. These lawyers tend to be advocates of the owner's position and do not take the employee's position into account.
2. The lawyers may be specialists in certain areas but likely do not have ESOP expertise or commercial or corporate expertise.
3. The lawyers may not have the ability or motivation to ensure the assignment is done on time.

Tax consultants can be chosen either by the ownership group based on people they work with or by the ESOP consultants. The business valuator can again be chosen by the ownership group or by the ESOP consultant in conjunction with the needs and desires of the ownership group. An insurance agent, if key person insurance is needed, is usually chosen by the ownership group.

TIME TO COMPLETE

The ESOP process generally takes three to six months, with the norm about 16 weeks. This time is needed to get the various parties to the table, to have an understanding, to present the education sessions for the employees, and to have everybody, including the outside consultants, the employees, and the ownership group, on side and agreeing to the elements of the plan. By the time the process is finished, a majority of the people buy in, having had input to the process.

TIMETABLE

It is imperative that a formal timetable be drawn up and agreed to, starting with the closing date for the ESOP and working backward.

PRELIMINARY CRITICAL PATH

DATE	DELIVERABLE	ASSIGNED TO
Jan 28	Documents sent to Consultant.	Company
Feb 7	Employee questionnaire developed.	Consultant
Feb 23	Educational Seminar presented.	Consultant
Mar 1	Draft blueprint for review.	Lawyer
Mar 31	Final blueprint for review.	Company

OTHER CONSULTANTS

Depending on the scope of the ESOP, there may also be venture capitalists or other financial representation on the team.

The team, which generally consists of the owners and employee reps in addition to the ESOP consultant, meet at regularly, scheduled times to ensure the integrity of the communication process. Depending on the company and its needs, some businesses choose to conduct the entire ESOP team meeting over the course of a day and a half.

PLAN DESIGN

The core activity at this stage is the preparation of a draft blueprint based on the broad parameters agreed to at the go-ahead meeting. The ESOP consultant prepares a summary of all previous discussions and includes specific action that needs to be taken in formulating the plan. The blueprint also outlines all technical and financial considerations concerning the ESOP. There are three parallel activities in tandem with the preparation of the draft blueprint: the business valuation, the preparation of a tax plan, and legal structuring.

Business valuation is fundamental to the structuring of an ESOP in order to put a price on the shares, especially for privately-held companies. This requires an independent appraisal to establish a fair market value (FMV), a valuation akin to the due diligence required when a company goes public. The valuator reviews the company's financial records, including past performance and future projections. He or she also reviews operations, interviews key managers, professional advisers, and customers, and researches the trends in the company's industry and marketplace economy.

Also important is feedback from the lawyer and tax accountant to ensure that the plan will meet all legal and tax legislation requirements. In order to structure the ESOP in a tax-effective manner, a review of the corporate tax structure and the personal tax positions of the ownership group is necessary. There are also tax implications relating to the financing and acquisition of equity by the employee group. The tax accountant does the reviews and prepares a tax strategy for discussion as part of the ESOP blueprint. The lawyer on the team is responsible for reviewing the corporate structure to determine whether any changes are necessary to comply with legislation. He or she also prepares a template agreement to cover the buying and selling of shares. This template is simply an outline of the initial shareholders' agreement. In-depth discussions of these complex topics follow later in Chapter 5 Business Valuations and ESOPs, Chapter 6 ESOPs and Income Tax, and Chapter 7 ESOP Legal Requirements.

The ownership group and external consultants then meet to review the draft blueprint. This is a blueprint that outlines all the issues relevant to the plan for the employees. There is enough information at this point to completely appreciate the full scope and implication of the ESOP.

COMMUNICATIONS AND FEEDBACK LOOP

The draft blueprint is a structural framework of the technical aspects of the ESOP. Once it is accepted, the creative design work begins to address the unique needs of the company's culture. This is where communications are critical.

ESOPs are organic in that they mould to the company's nature. Input and feedback has to come from the employee base in order to create a true partnership and to engender trust in the process. In order to be successful with the design and implementation of an ESOP, open, two-way communications must be a priority throughout the design process — a continuous circulation and feedback loop.

The primary function of the ESOP team at this juncture is to formalize the communication process with key objectives to circulate information and solicit feedback. A typical information flow would include the following:

- ESOP team includes employee representatives to consider draft blueprint.
- ESOP team drafts and circulates employee questionnaire.
- ESOP team reviews questionnaire results.
- Employee reps relay information between ESOP team and employees.
- ESOP team circulates employee information package.
- ESOP consultant holds employee education/information sessions.
- ESOP team hosts open forum for discussion of all aspects of plan.
- ESOP team accesses employee feedback, revises plan accordingly.

- ESOP team prepares final information for the employee information package, including legal documents, and hosts the town hall meeting and the subscription distribution.

DOCUMENTS

The main documents of the communication plan are the employee questionnaire and the employee information package. The purpose of the questionnaire is to gauge employee interest in share ownership. In addition to ownership aspirations, it also serves to measure the level of knowledge about investments and ESOPs. The employee feedback guides the ESOP team in the technical design of the plan. The feedback also highlights the extent and the need for education sessions around investment. (The readers should review the typical questionnaire found in the appendices for further information.)

Education sessions would normally address how to read financial statements and include discussion of financial planning, tax planning, and the importance of independent legal advice. Other topics could be ESOPs, stock option valuations, etc. The employee information package and the ESOP package is much like that of a public offering, however, it is briefer and much less expensive to prepare. The employee information package includes a profile of the company, its history and its potential. The package also includes the company's financial picture and a summary of the valuation report that gives an idea of the company's worth and is used to help establish a fair market value (FMV) for company shares. The employee information package includes the blueprint as well as the legal documentation.

The culmination of the communication process is a town hall meeting where employees and their spouses can ask questions of the ESOP team in an open forum. Typically, the team outlines the design process, explains the choice of specific plan parameters, and discusses feedback from employees and its inclusion in the plan. In some scenarios, the ESOP team will assess and consider employee feedback from the town hall meeting and makes final modifications to the plan. Often, the town hall is the final meeting where employees receive an employee information package which they can take home and review with their own advisers prior to the closing of the ESOP.

Although the process is driven by the executive team, it is in fact an outline that will be molded and shaped by communication with the employee group so much so that by the end of the process every stakeholder in the ESOP plan will understand the plan and support that plan as it is implemented.

The continuous flow of information between the ESOP team and employees, coupled with the will on the part of the company to welcome input and listen to employee concerns, helps ensure a high subscription rate and a successful ESOP implementation.

TRANSITION TO AN ESOP CULTURE

Once the ESOP transaction stage has been successfully completed, and the original goals of the owners and the employees have been met, the cultural transformation begins. The initial euphoria occasioned by the process has now given way to a time of getting back to work. The goal for the ESOP team during this stage should be to install a participative culture where employees start to act and think like owners.

Employees may now want to start acting like owners but they may be hesitant and uncertain about how to go about this. It is up to the board of directors to channel this new entrepreneurial energy and focus it on the goals of the corporation. At this point, a company must address four areas in the interaction with its employees: ownership, participation, training, and information. These areas will be discussed in more depth under post-ESOP issues in Chapters 8 and 9. To have a successful outcome for the ESOP, it is critical that the process outlined in this chapter be followed.

CONCLUSION

Critical to designing an effective ESOP is understanding the owners' goals for the plan. ESOPs address specific needs within the company, like sharing responsibilities with employees, attracting and retaining key people or a succession plan for the ownership group. Once the ESOP goals are defined, and a plan agreed upon, implementation should become a priority with a clear end date in mind. A good ESOP implementation process builds ownership and participation into the design of the plan resulting in increased engagement, trust and greater understanding of the investment opportunity and risks. The next chapter will discuss some of the key design issues that will arise during the ESOP process.

CHAPTER 3
DESIGNING ESOPS

A good number see employee ownership as complex. It need not be. The company can be much like any other company. What is different is how it is owned.

– Graeme Nuttall, Fieldfisher's Tax Practice Partner

The process outlined in the preceding chapter is essential for arriving at the appropriate ESOP for a company. Design issues are of course critical to the foundation of the ESOP and whether it will be able to grow to meet the needs of the company in the future. Design issues must be reviewed in terms of each company's individual objectives and may have to change depending on the needs of the employee group.

ESOP MYTH In Canada, it's too complex to sell company shares to the employees. Adding to this, employees can't afford ownership and they don't understand what it means to be an employee-owner.

ESOP FACT ESOPs have been successfully implemented in Canada for nearly 20 years and are no more complex than any other cultural change.

WHERE DO THE SHARES COME FROM?

There are two sources of shares. Shares may come from treasury, which means the proceeds go back into the company's coffers, or they may come from the existing ownership group, in which case the proceeds go to the original shareholder. The deciding factor on sources of shares is influenced by the purpose of the ESOP. If the shareholders are looking at the ESOP as a means of liquidating one of their major assets, they will probably decide to sell shares to the employees. That way the owner receives the cash from the employee, the employee receives the shares, and the owner has his or her liquidity. The other alternative, if the owner is seeking not liquidity but working capital for the company, then he or she would issue shares out of treasury. The shares then would be issued from the company out of treasury to the employees, and the money from the employees would go back into the company's bank account.

For example, if an employee bought 1,000 shares at $1.00 a share, the owner would receive $1,000 and the employee would receive $1,000 worth of shares. For our example we'll assume the company had $10,000 shares owned by the owner at the start of the transaction. After the sale to the employee, the owner would have 9,000 shares, and the employee would have 1,000 shares. If, however, the owner issues treasury stock to the employee, the employee would pay $1,000 to the company and receive 1,000 shares. The $1,000 paid by the employee would stay with the company. The company now, however, would have 11,000 shares. They would be made up of the 10,000 shares previously owned by the owner and 1,000 new shares that were issued by the company. Therefore, in this transaction, the owner would have 10,000 of 11,000 shares, and the employee would own 1,000 of 11,000 shares. If the owner wished to allow the employee to own 10 per cent as in the first example, the company would restructure and issue 20,000 shares to the owner for his previously 10,000 shares, and then allow the employee to purchase 2,000 shares from the company, thereby owning 2,000 of the 20,000 or 10 per cent of the company.

SHARES FROM TREASURY

Treasury shares are those that have been allocated through the company's corporate structure but have not yet been issued. Companies that want to use stock options as a means of attracting and retaining staff tend to issue shares from treasury. They do so because the liquidity issue is not a major concern for the ownership group. Liquidity is an issue only when the ownership group wants to take money out of the company. The amount of money raised through ESOPs is not usually significant when the main aim of ESOPs is to attract and retain people. At other times, raising money from the employee share purchase is the main aim of implementing the ESOP. An owner may liquidate a portion of his or her own shareholding with the express purpose of raising capital or for the acquisition of additional assets to help the company grow.

From a corporate confidence perspective, it is powerful to be able to demonstrate to employees that the proceeds from the shares they purchase are staying in the company to help expand and grow the company. Another way to look at this is when an employee is being asked to sign a cheque to actually give money over for acquiring those shares. If the employee realizes that the money is staying in the company and being used to expand the company he is much more confident in his investment. In contrast, if he believes that the owner is just taking the money out of the company and leaving the employee with the risk of expanding the company he may feel less willing to participate. It is important to understand that there is a major difference for ESOPs that are introduced in a public versus a private company. In a public company, if the employees want to purchase shares they can do so through a stock exchange. In a private company, the only shares available are those of the current owners or through the treasury of the private company. Decisions regarding what shares to issue differ tremendously, depending upon whether the company you are investing in is public or private. Public companies tend to *always* issue out of treasury shares and therefore create a dilution when they are looking for additional equity. Private companies, on the other hand, have the option to issue out of treasury or the owners can sell their own shares.

SHARES FROM OWNERS

In cases where an owner's major assets are tied up in the company, an ESOP may be implemented as a means of freeing up some capital for the owner's personal use. Owners do that by selling their personally-held company shares. When employees buy ownership shares, they buy directly from the actual shareholder. This often gives rise to questions about why the ownership group is selling equity or giving any kind of option plan in a company. It is important for the ownership group to allay any concerns employees may have and to recognize that there is nothing wrong or unusual about recouping net worth in the form of proceeds from shares. Eventually the employees themselves will want to liquidate their assets for the very same reasons as the current ownership group.

COMBINATION OF SHARES

An ESOP implemented as a succession or exit strategy must satisfy the owner's financial need in leaving the business and the business's need for ongoing financial health. In such cases, the source of shares may be a combination of ownership and treasury.

DILUTION

Any time shares are issued from treasury, the current shareholders' percentage ownership is diluted. For example, assume there are two shareholders, each owning 50 per cent of a company. There are 10,000 common shares authorized in the company, of which 1,000 have been issued to the two owners. If a further 9,000 treasury shares are issued to employees, the two current shareholders move from a position of owning 500 shares each in the company that had 1,000 shares issued, or 50 per cent of the company, to owning 500 shares in a company that has 10,000 shares issued, which effectively reduces them to 5 per cent ownership of the company. That's an extreme example, but it is important that the ownership group as well as the employees understands dilution. Although the owner's percentage has decreased, the actual value has not because the 9,000 shares that have been issued out of treasury have raised the value of the company because the money raised by selling those shares has gone into the company and therefore increased its value. There's been no change in the value of the owner's shares, only of their percentage.

NUMBER OF SHARES

The structuring of the share issue often highlights the fact that the actual number of available shares is inadequate. More than 90 per cent of the time the corporate share structure cannot support an ESOP. We have seen some private companies that have only three shares issued. Obviously to issue shares to another 100 or 200 people, more than 3 shares will be needed. It then becomes necessary to increase the number of authorized shares, not only for immediate ESOP needs but also to support future growth. Increasing the authorization of shares is not a difficult issue. A corporate lawyer will amend the company's articles of incorporation to increase the number of shares. In some situations, perception may dictate volume of stock. Employees may prefer to get 100,000 shares each valued at 10 or 20 cents a share rather than 100 shares worth $20 each. The decision on how many shares each employee receives is dependent upon the sophistication of the employee group and the feedback received from the employee questionnaires.

STOCK SPLITS

If there is insufficient stock to issue as a company grows, the stock may have to be split. This entails additional legal and accounting fees and a communications effort in terms of explaining the intricacies of a stock split to the shareholders' group. For example, if an employee owns 500 shares of a company and the stock splits 2 for

1, after the stocks split the employee will own 1000 shares of the company but the value of those 1000 shares will remain the same.

CORPORATE STRUCTURE

When discussing the source of shares, additional consideration should be paid to the current ownership's tax position. The tax advantages for owners of a Canadian-Controlled Private Corporation (CCPC) and qualified Small Business Corporation (SBC) will also come into play. A retiring owner will want to take advantage of the $800,000 capital gains exemption currently available to owners of a CCPC and SBC.

This may lead to a restructuring of some of the ownership position, so as to maximize his or her tax position. For example, an owner may decide to capitalize on the capital gains exemption to set up a separate holding company. The new structure should be discussed and evaluated for the impact it would have on the company going forward.

EMPLOYEE ELIGIBILITY

There is usually an employment requirement for a person to be eligible to participate in an ESOP. This can range from immediate eligibility to up to two years of continuous employment, and it will vary depending upon the nature of the company, its culture, and its training cycle. For example, if it will take two years to assess whether an employee will be a real contributor to the company's growth, a lengthy eligibility period is appropriate. Typically, established manufacturing companies require a longer qualifying term. The reason for this is that there is a longer learning curve in manufacturing facilities for both knowledge-based and technical employees. In the high-tech or knowledge-based field where there is a high demand for talented employees, the eligibility norm seems to be between six months to a year. Even within a plan, there needs to be room for flexibility, allowing for variances for key people. For example, if a company requires a senior sales person to start with the company immediately, and wants to issue stock options to that employee, the plan will allow the company to waive the eligibility requirements so that key person could be hired.

Generally, a company wants enough time to determine if an employee fits into the corporate culture. A probationary period also saves the company administrative headaches by avoiding having to collapse shares for employees who are not working out in the corporation.

The eligibility factor highlights the fact that the issuance of stock, stock options, or phantom stock is not a right of the employee; it is a benefit that the company confers on those employees who have put effort into growing the company. The eligibility requirement, however short, establishes that share ownership is not given out to just anyone, but that employees must earn the right to become a partner in the future viability of the company.

ALLOCATION FORMULA

The number of shares allocated to an individual employee will generally be a percentage of total shares available, based on the individual's base salary as a percentage of total salaries. However, there are other ways of allocating stock or stock options. Base salary may be coupled with seniority, level of management within the corporation, or departmental targets. An allocation formula is important for several reasons. It tends to create a level playing field because perceived fairness is important for employees. An allocation formula makes the plan administratively convenient for a company as it can allow new employees to be incorporated into the plan fairly easily. It also allows the employees to do a quick calculation of what they are entitled to, which again reinforces the concept of fairness.

For the majority of companies, the individual's base salary is the most common method of allocation. The culture of the company will define what works best for each kind of employee. For example, if there exists a cadre of people who have been with the company for a number of years, and whose salary would not be a fair representation of the contribution that these employees have made, some seniority component must be put *into* the allocation formula to account for this.

Generally, an allocation formula is the same for all people in the corporation; however, differentiation between different positions or levels within the company is possible by adding or subtracting from the formula. Everyone is treated equally in the sense that the formula is calculated fairly for each person in any particular position. The best way to determine an allocation formula is in the initial meetings with the ESOP team when the particular issues (e.g. cultural) of the company can be discussed and the various formula applications put forward. It is only at this point that you have input from the owners, the advisers, and eventually from the employees themselves, from which you can arrive at an allocation formula that is fair for everybody.

VESTING

Vesting gives employees the right to exercise stock options and become equity shareholders. Exercise price is usually set at or below the fair market value (FMV) on the date the option is granted. The employee is guaranteed that price for a fixed period of time until a specified future date when share options vest in title to that employee. Vesting means that the person has earned a right to be able to exercise the option and buy the shares. Normally, vesting is based on a time element whereby the employee earns the vesting after having been employed for a certain length of time. For example, a four-year vesting period with 25 per cent vesting each year means that for every year that the employee is with the company, he or she earns the right to purchase 25 per cent of the total number of his or her allocated share options. Other means of earning options can be tied into performance so that when certain targets are achieved by an employee or by the company, stock options become vested with the employee. For example, the stock option plan may state that if the company increases its revenues by 30 per cent the employee's stock can be vested at that point. The employee's stock does not get vested until the company has grown revenue by 30 per cent. Performance options are valuable to companies because they do not dilute the company until such time as the company has grown in certain revenue or profitability targets that has some application to wealth creation and therefore some minimization of the dilution factor. Vesting usually takes place at the beginning or end of the year. With cliff vesting the employee receives all the stock options immediately and can exercise them at any time because there is no waiting period involved. This is used fairly selectively, usually to attract senior people to a company. Most companies will have a vesting period ranging from three to five years with the percentage allocation spread over that timeframe. The term of the stock option is usually between five to 10 years. This means that employees have that period of time to exercise their right to purchase the shares at the grant price. If the options are not exercised within that time, the employee loses the option to purchase the shares. There are many tax implications for both private and public companies to the granting of stock options. These are discussed in full in Chapter 6 ESOPs and Income Tax.

BUYOUT PROVISIONS

In a private company the only way the employees will be able to turn their shares into cash is if there are agreed-upon terms in the shareholders' agreement. An ESOP is basically a long-term plan, a method for employees to generate wealth and benefits due to the increase in the wealth of the company. In a public company there are generally fewer problems with liquidity because employees can sell shares on the public market at any time. However, in a private company this is not the case, which is why shareholders of private companies can sell only when a third party purchases a company or when it goes public with an IPO. Given changing circumstances and the volatility of life, not all employees will be around for this liquidity event. One of the key philosophies in an ESOP is that there should be protection for the employees who are continuing to be employed by the company, balanced with fairness to the people who are leaving for various reasons. An ESOP should avoid a situation where many leave, take value with them, and leave the employees who are staying to pick up the pieces.

There will be cases of death or disability, bankruptcy, separation, or divorce, all of which may affect employee shareholdings. There are also retirement circumstances or the case of an employee being fired. Generally for the sake of fairness, employees who are no longer employed due to death, disability, or retirement will receive fair market value for their shares. The question is how to deal with employees who leave for any other reason. Most companies pay a discount anywhere from 25 to 75 per cent of the fair market value and spread the payments over a number of years, typically three to five years. The board of directors always has the authority to overrule the buy-sell provision in special cases. For example, assume an employee is fired within two years of joining the company. This employee has contributed to the company, but because he or she is leaving before the company has fully realized its growth potential it is unfair to give the full fair market value for the employee's shares. This employee may receive 50 per cent of fair market value rather than the 100 per cent received by an employee who stays for a five or 10 year period.

The buyout can be a difficult issue for both owners and employees who have different perspectives. Although leaving, employees may feel entitled to full fair market value for their contribution to the value growth of the company.

For employee owners who are staying, the value that the departing employees have contributed may not be realized through an equity event for many years. Employees may question whether it is fair for people who are leaving to receive fair market value when there is in fact no liquidity to those shares. To balance these opposing issues, companies generally pay less than fair market value when people leave for reasons other than death, disability, or retirement.

Understandably, employees want to know how they will be able to sell their shares in the future. The shareholders' agreement covers this. There is usually a "tag-along" clause that ensures that if the existing majority shareholders agree to sell their shares in the company, the employer-owners have the right to tag along or to sell their shares at the same price. There may also be a "drag-along" clause that states that if the majority shareholders agree to sell their shares in the company, they have the right to drag along the employees or require them to sell their shares at the same price.

The company may also create a minimarket where employees can sell their shares to other eligible employees, usually once a year. This internal market for share trading helps create liquidity for shareholders who are leaving or who want to cash in some of their gains for various reasons. The minimarket is typically supported and managed by the company. Many employers will put a minimarket clause in their shareholders' agreement if they're in the type of company that's not likely to be sold or go public within five years.

Typically the minimarket doesn't come into effect until year two or three, and in some cases longer than that. The result is that employees will have to be with the company for a period of 2 to 5 years to see some liquidity in their shareholdings.

However, if an employee does leave before this five-year period, then the shareholders' agreement applies, and the company is required to buy back those shares at either fair market value or a discount. (The mechanics of the minimarket are described further on in this chapter.)

Generally a company will purchase key person-insurance to fund the buyout provisions of the agreement for key employees such as senior-level executives. For the stock in general, a company may consider some type of modified sinking fund that would be put aside at the end of the year for people who are leaving. A sinking fund is a fund or a reserve into which funds are deposited and available to buy back shares. The key element in any buyout provision is that both the employee group and the ownership group understand that this is a contractual arrangement in which the employees are agreeing to invest in the company, and the company is agreeing to make sure that the growth value will be reflected in some type of liquidity to the employees at some point in the future. The amount to be set aside in a sinking fund is determined by the individual company, and it depends upon their cash flows, future projections of profitability, and what the company needs for short-term and long-term expansion strategies. Without any liquidity provisions in the shareholders' agreement the stock is, in effect, of no value to the employees. This, of course, defeats the whole purpose of the ESOP, the creation of a participative environment, and sharing in the wealth of the company as it grows.

As you can see, clear communication between the employee group and the ownership group and an understanding of the shareholders' agreement and liquidity provisions are critical. However, the ownership group must be very careful to ensure that they are not restricted in decisions about a third-party offer or IPO. The legal agreement must be structured in such a way that the employee group must go along with the original ownership group's decision as to what is necessary for the company. An ESOP does not reduce the fiduciary responsibilities of the board of directors or of the ownership group to increase the value of the company for all employees. For example, if the original ownership group wants to sell portions of their company in the future, the employees generally will have the right to sell the same percentage as the ownership so that they are not disadvantaged. Such legal provisions ensure that the ownership group is not being restricted as to the long-range viability and strategy implementation of the company. The commitment of the ownership group is key to the success of an ESOP and therefore the ownership group has to feel that if it decides the company should be sold in the future, it cannot be restricted from making that decision. However, the proceeds from that sale will be distributed equitably among all employees, depending on their percentage of ownership.

SHARE ACQUISITIONS

Equity may be sold or given to the employees, but an ESOP is more successful when employees are required to purchase a certain portion of shares. The ownership group may choose to match share purchase with gifts. Over the last 40 years, research has shown that there are four elements for an ESOP's performance:

participation, training, ownership, and information. The element that we are talking about here is the ownership element.

There are many plans that comprise only stock options. Certainly, stock options do have the ability to motivate and retain people. Stock options may allow employees to participate in the wealth that they've created. However, in terms of long-range growth and retention and attraction of people, stock options themselves are limited because there is no downside risk to the employee. They do not invest any money in the company. If the company goes up in value, employees make money, and if the company goes down in value, they don't lose money. The employees do not assume a risk position in the company. They do not take that investment as seriously as they would if they had invested money in that company.

True ownership of a company occurs when a cheque has been passed from the employee to the company and the employee owns legal title to those shares. For example, once an employee is actually an owner, participation, information, and training become more real and are approached with more passion. A good analogy is a person who owns a house versus one who rents one. The mindset of the owner is completely different from that of the tenant or even the rental property owner. The same of course holds true in the ownership of shares in the company; the level of commitment is much higher in the ownership of an asset. The actual number of shares that are held is not as important as the fact that the person actually does own those shares in the company.

The ESOP can range from 1 to 100 per cent employee ownership. The percentage that's offered is not as critical as the fact that shares or options are being offered at all. Generally, initial ownership offers of between 10 to 20 per cent of the value of the company are sufficient to create the benefits of an ESOP within a company. As can be imagined, in a privately-owned company, the current ownership group does not want to dilute its ownership position more than it has to. Many owners have struggled and sacrificed for many years to build successful companies. This must be discussed thoroughly with the ownership group so all owners fully understand what's at stake in allowing an ownership percentage to be sold or given through stock options to the employees. Generally, there are opposing forces in this area. The ownership group as a rule wants to give up less and less, and the employees want more and more. If the percentage of shares offered is too low, less than 10 per cent, the employees will regard the offer as being not a true intention by the ownership group to share the rewards of the company. On the other hand, unless the ESOP is being put into place for succession planning, or if too much of a percentage is given out to the employees initially, it becomes more difficult for the owners to keep control of the company and to implement their strategies going forward with the company.

As a general rule of thumb, no matter which percentage is chosen, employee groups will likely pressure owners to increase the percentage as time goes by.

Employees, on the other hand, are coming into a company that has passed its initial risk stage and is into the secondary and tertiary levels of risk. The highest risk for any company is in its first five years of ownership. This is because the company has not established a history with its customers or suppliers and has not created conditions of stability that tend to reduce risk. As a company survives longer, its risk reduces somewhat as it moves into different phases. It has the ability to weather recessions, and has clients and suppliers who have helped it grow while still maintaining a viable operation. Often employees do not appreciate the amount of effort and sacrifice that the original ownership group had to make to get the company to this stage. As such, it seems that no matter what percentage of the company is offered to employees, it is perceived by them as not enough. So a key element of any ESOP plan is to manage expectations and to make sure that the employees understand the reasons for the percentage offered. Most owners tend to pick this number based on what other companies and similar industries are doing, hence the 10 to 20 per cent figure.

FINANCING

Stocks may be purchased outright, granted in lieu of bonuses, or acquired through payroll deduction. The investment is like any other for employees, and ultimately, the onus is on the individual to research, question, and analyze whether it is beneficial to them. The individual must be comfortable with the investment of his or hers hard-earned money in this company. An ESOP investment is just that, a business investment. The major difference, of course, is that the employee has some control over the future growth of the particular ESOP investment. Generally speaking, when financing ESOPs:

- The company may loan funds to employees so that they may invest in the company.
- The employee may use funds from an RRSP or TFSA, or borrow money from the bank and utilize a current RRSP/TFSA to fund this investment (subject to Canada Customs and Revenue Agency restrictions as outlined in Chapter 6 ESOPs and Income Tax).
- The employee may borrow money from friends, relatives, or the bank to invest in the company.
- The company may allow the employee to purchase the shares through a payroll-deduction plan.
- If the company has a bonus plan that has been set up in concert with the ESOP, future bonuses may be used to acquire shares in the company (See the use of bonuses in setting up plans in Chapter 6 ESOPs and Income Tax).
- There are a number of tax implications depending on the type of financing used which are discussed in Chapter 6 ESOPs and Income Tax.

MINIMARKET

The Plan Administrator has the discretion to create an internal market for share trading, referred to as the minimarket. If implemented it would be open to employees who own ESOP shares. It would generally be an annual event, designed to allow some liquidity for employees as well as an opportunity to increase their investment in the company, subject to any individual limits imposed by the company.

Trades would be administered by the company in order to facilitate the buying and selling of shares. The share trading price would be the annual share value, the FMV as calculated by the most recent valuation.

1. This price is not negotiable. Employees cannot make side deals with each other at different prices.
2. About a month before the minimarket opens employees are asked through a form if they want to buy or sell shares on the market.
3. The form states the name of the person, the amount of shares they want to buy or sell and the value of the stock they are buying or selling.
4. The company designates one person (it should be the plan administrator) to collect all the forms and check the value calculations on the forms.
5. The company determines the total number of shares in the buy requests and in the sell requests.
6. If the number of shares available for purchase does not match the number for sale, then shares are allocated for sale using the rising tide method. (See the accompanying chart).
7. The company fills in a two-page proforma share purchase agreement between the buyer and seller, and the board issues a proforma resolution authorizing the sale.
8. The company lawyer will then prepare new share certificates and record them in the company share registry.
9. The buyer and seller will sign the share purchase agreement and the buyer will give a cheque to the plan administrator who will then give the cheque to the seller. Once the cheque clears, the buyer is the owner of the new shares.

RISING TIDE METHOD		
EMPLOYEE	**BUY REQUEST**	**ALLOCATED**
A	$2,000	$2,000
B	$5,000	$5,000
C	$6,000	$6,000
D	$20,000	$18,500
E	$100,000	$18,500
Total Sell Requests		$50,000

ADMINISTRATION

The administration of an ESOP is an area that is not well addressed but is very important to the ongoing success of the ESOP plan. There are two methods for dealing with the administration issues: internal and external. A company may choose an internal person to do the administration tasks regarding new hires and employees who leave. Alternatively, a company may hire an outside, third-party trustee to do the record-keeping and keep the company informed of changes in legislation that may affect their plan. The company must decide whether it has the internal capability for handling the administration or must look to an external source. The items that will help the ESOP team decide on this issue are as follows:

- What is the annual turnover rate of the company?
- Is there an HR person already onboard or will one be hired?
- Are the company's benefit plans taken care of internally or externally?
- How does the company communicate and administrate its current benefit plans?

- Is the current administration of employee benefits and resources satisfactory, or will an external person be needed in the future?
- Does the company like controlling its administration issues, or does it have a history of sourcing them out to third parties?
- What is the cost of using an internal person versus the cost of an external party?

The administrator, whether internal or external to the company, is the "face" of the plan, as far as employees are concerned. The employees will be content with a plan that is administered in a way that provides them with timely, relevant information when they need it. The administrator must respond promptly to all employees' requests and be able to interpret the plan rules. Should employees be unhappy with the administrator, their perception of the plan as a benefit to them may be tarnished. For example, poor record-keeping of employees' allocations can result in misunderstandings and in increased tension between management and employees. This is true especially if the plan has increased in value over time.

A key decision by the ESOP team is to decide whether or not to appoint an internal administrator or go to an external adviser. The advantages of an internal administrator would be:

- A face known to employees
- Already part of the corporate culture
- Faster at responding to employee concerns
- Knowledgeable about the plan
- Most likely a participant in the plan themselves

The disadvantages are:

- Cost
- The valuable HR time needed that can be used in other areas
- The learning curve

The advantages to hiring an outside administrator are:

- Cost containment
- No learning curve

- Specialized administrative advice
- The outsourcing of HR needs

The disadvantages would be:

- Unknown to employees
- Perhaps slower at responding to employee concerns
- Distant from employee concerns as they are not involved in the company

Whether an inside or outside administrator is chosen, his or her tasks will be as follows:

- Is the main contact with employees
- Deals with questions about the plan
- Handles all document approvals
- Deals with reporting and tax obligations
- Advises employees when options are exercised or when shares are redeemed

In our experience over the last 20 years, we've found that nearly 95 per cent of companies choose to have the administration completed internally. It can quite often be done on an Excel spreadsheet and requires several hours per month in addition to a day or two at the beginning of each ESOP year.

CHOOSING ADMINISTRATORS USING AN RFP

It is always best to obtain several quotes if deciding to use an outside administrator. A Request For Proposal (RFP) to be sent to prospective trustees, custodian, and administrative service providers would include:

- A description of the ESOP plan.
- An outline of the company history and future.
- A request for the following information about the administrator company:
    - Their corporate history and experience in providing stock plan administration, including how much of their business resources are devoted to these services;

- A clear description of their system for plan administration in terms of logistics, accuracy, efficiency, flexibility, timelines, and problem resolution;
- Information on the range of investment availability such as whether they can facilitate cashless transactions, diversification, real time trading, and private stock transfers;
- A transition plan.
- Steps they take to educate employees on issues relating to their current stock plan, employee ownership in general, financial planning, taxes, and retirement planning.
- A clear outline of all costs associated with the plan for both the company and the employee, including the billing schedules and out-of-pocket costs.
- References to be contacted during the evaluation process.

An evaluation of the proposal would include both cost factors and intangible factors:

- A cultural fit. The service provider should understand the company's business and be prepared to deal with employees as the company itself would deal with them.
- A clear long-term commitment to the business. The provider must have the financial muscle to remain in the stock option administration business.
- A highly trained staff experienced in stock option administration. The right service provider will have invested substantially in the training and development of its employees.
- State-of-the-art technology. The right outsourcing firm will have superior technology to provide complete administrative services, and the right service provider will have a flexible and extensive technology platform.
- A formal transition process. The right service provider will be able to offer a clearly defined process to transfer records from

the company provider, and minimize the company's involvement in the transition process.

- Well established quality controls. The provider will have a
  system of checks and balances in place to ensure quality
  throughout the administration of the company's stock
  option plan.
- A process for assessing client and employee satisfaction. The
  right vendor knows the importance of company and participant satisfaction.

COMMUNICATION

INITIAL ANNOUNCEMENT

The initial announcement to the employees is a key milestone in
the plan. This signals to the employees that the company is serious
in proceeding with the design and implementation of an ESOP.
Many companies have been talking about implementing an ESOP
for years. The hiring of an ESOP consultant as well as meeting the
proposed timetable will create a sense of excitement and urgency
among the employees. It is important to maintain this excitement
through a serious of communication pieces.

FOLLOW-UP COMMUNICATION

The next major communication piece is the Employee
Questionnaire (See Appendix III). The questionnaire assesses
the level of interest of the employees in the plan and determines
the employees' motivation to join such a plan. In addition,
employees' knowledge in this area can be assessed. The results
of the questionnaire allow the ESOP team to focus on key issues.
For example, how much education will have to be offered to the
employees for them to have an understanding of the plan? What
is the employees' preferred means of financing the plan? Employee
representatives on the ESOP team maintain ongoing communication with the employees. This can be on an informal basis or

through a formal meeting whereby employee representatives brief the employees on the status of the plan.

COMMUNICATION DOCUMENT

The initial stage of the ESOP process produces a blueprint that clearly outlines the proposed plan. The blueprint contains information on all the technical issues concerning design of the plan: is it a share purchase, stock option, or phantom plan? The relevant legal and accounting issues are also addressed. The blueprint is created by the ESOP team and written by the ESOP design consultant. Once the blueprint is accepted as final by the ESOP team, it is given to the lawyer to draft into "legalese." At the same time, it will become the basis of the employee information package, which will be provided to all participants.

EDUCATION SEMINARS

An education seminar is generally provided to the employees concerning the technical aspects of an ESOP in the areas of accounting, law, tax, and valuations. This seminar is usually produced by the ESOP consultant in conjunction with one or more members of the ESOP team. Usually the owner or an employee representative is involved. At this session, the details of the company ESOP are not discussed however the general issues concerning in ESOPs and their impact on employees are explained.

TOWN HALL MEETING

The final stage of communication is the Town Hall meeting, which is attended by all participants and the ESOP team. It is held as a means to explain the employee information package and to answer any questions from the employees. At this stage, the ESOP is about 90 per cent complete. Based on the results of the meeting, the final plan is prepared, and the employees usually have three to four weeks to decide whether or not to participate. Sometimes, however, the Town Hall meeting will be the end of the process, and the employees will take home the final information package at that point.

COMMUNICATION ISSUES FOR MULTI-SITE, MULTI-TARGET AUDIENCES

The communication phase for multi-site, multi-target audiences includes two stages:

STAGE I-COMMUNICATION PLANNING

- Create and finalize communication objectives and project timing.
- After communication topics have been discussed, the team should develop specific objectives with respect to the two targeted groups: the employees and the presenters. The management group might also be targeted separately. Finally, a detailed timeline for all aspects of the project should be drawn up.
- Prepare a roster of the involved presenters. This roster would include the presenters' names, locations, job responsibilities, presentation experience, and immediate support staff.
- Keep an inventory of all corporate benefit communication pieces and production materials.
- Collect available generic ESOP materials. Generic cost-effective ESOP materials are available from the National Center for Employee Ownership. These materials may be integrated into the company's communication program.

STAGE II-IMPLEMENTATION

Implementation planning includes the following:

- Communication Content: The basis of any communication program should, of course, reflect and enhance the objectives of the plan. The content of the communications program will include three general categories: what the plan means, what the plan comprises, and how the plan fits into the company's culture.

- What the Plan Means: This includes a discussion of the philosophy of the plan, why the company adopted the plan, and what it means for the future.
- What the Plan Is: This would include an explanation of how the plan operates and how it benefits participants.
- How the Plan Fits into the Corporate Culture: This would address the impact on the day-to-day operations of the company and the fitting of the plan with the company's business strategy.

- Targeted Audiences: If there are several distinct audiences to whom these objectives will be communicated, the appropriate objectives for each audience should be emphasized in all communication pieces.
- Communication Materials: The first communication piece is a comprehensive written document that forms the basis for all communication materials, which are then directed to the appropriate audiences. The company reviews and approves these pieces prior to the production of any other communication materials. As part of this work, the ESOP consultant will inventory all corporate benefit communication pieces and production materials. This inventory will help determine what information has already been provided and to what extent there should be compatibility of graphic layout and narrative style. In addition, it may be possible to utilize existing artwork in the production process to achieve cost savings.
- Communication Components
  - Slide presentation which would include detailed speaker's notes that each of the presenters would use at each of their respective locations.
  - Question and Answer booklet, which would anticipate questions that the attendees might ask and which could be referred to after the meetings.
  - ESOP brochure, which meets the communication objectives mentioned above.

- Upon completion of the communication materials, meetings for eligible participants would be held in the company's offices. To facilitate these meetings, the ESOP team will:
  - Conduct a meeting with the presenters to review delivery of the ESOP communication program at their respective locations. The meeting will address presenters' questions regarding the ESOP plan, specific program content, and communication techniques in general.
  - Develop an implementation strategy for each location. The strategy will include the number and location of employee meetings and focus on any differences in corporate culture.
  - Assist in presentations as required providing feedback and suggestions to the presenters.
- To facilitate the ESOP process, designate one primary contact at the company for the operational aspects of this engagement. That person will liaise with the ESOP consultant, presenters, and outside advisers. (The company's legal counsel should review and approve all materials for conformity with applicable provincial and federal laws.) The design, implementation, communication, and administration of a broad-based ESOP are a complicated effort involving a number of individuals both inside and outside the company sponsoring the plan.

THE ESOP TEAM

Having the right team will influence the success of the ESOP process. Chapter 2 discussed how the team is chosen and the importance of the team's chemistry. Ownership commitment is also critical; ESOPs initiated by the ownership group have the highest chances of going forward and being successful. However, ESOPs initiated by a lower level of management, the HR group, or from employees, without a strong commitment from management, have a fairly low success rate. Of course control rests with the ownership group, and that group must be convinced that the process will succeed. Therefore, for an ESOP to succeed, the ownership group must have a vested interest in seeing the process go through. Management will follow the ownership group's lead. It is just as important to manage the expectations of the management group as all the other employees within the company.

OWNER MEMBERS OF THE TEAM

The owner, or the owner's representative on the team, will usually set the parameters for the ESOP as well as represent the company's position and interest. This person must have 100 per cent commitment to the employees becoming partners in the company. Obviously, the owner or executive must be a person respected by the employee group, or the process will fail. This trust and respect may not even be there at the beginning, but certainly by the end of the process after having worked as a team the important element of trust will have been built and used successfully in negotiating and in launching the ESOP. Owners who have the traditional mindset of the hierarchy of ownership will find it difficult to implement an ESOP. The hierarchical way of running a company has proven successful — but not with an ESOP. When employees are asked to invest their money, without any change in responsibilities or interest, trust and respect do not result, meaning an inconclusive or a non-satisfactory ESOP. On the other hand, an owner who passes information to employees, shares profits with them, and involves them in decision-making, will find it easier to create an ESOP.

In some scenarios, we recommend an owner not sit on the ESOP team. While the owner always has full control over the final design of the plan, having them sit on the ESOP team could inhibit discussion due to employees' feeling intimidated or wary of disagreeing with the owner's ideas. In these cases, an owner will join the team for the introductory session and then leave the team to go over the ESOP plan and provide feedback with the ESOP consultant. This feedback will be shared with the ownership group who can choose to change or alter specifics of the plan based on employee input.

EMPLOYEE REPRESENTATIVES

The owners are one part of the project team when designing an ESOP. Next are the employee representatives. These people give voice to the employees' ideas and concerns and report to the employee group as a whole. The employee reps are important to the success of the project. They may be chosen by the owners or elected by the employees themselves in a democratic vote.

The method chosen really depends upon the culture of the company. The majority of companies that implement ESOPs tend to have the owners pick the employee reps because the ownership group is more likely to pick a person with the ability to discuss issues both with the ownership group and with the employees to the benefit of both groups. The employee rep must have a good rapport not only with the employees but also with the owners.

In organizations where direct representation from the employee group is required, such as in unionized workplaces, electing the reps is valid. However, if there are three employee reps, at least two of them are likely chosen by the owners. The employee reps are very important to the chemistry of the process. They must have good conceptual abilities, wide experience within the company, and communication skills to report to their peer group. Most importantly, they must have the trust of their peer group. Nonetheless, it is critical not to bring the employee rep into the ESOP process too early. Owners must set their parameters without the influence of employees. That's not to say these parameters won't change over time, and in fact they do, but the owners must be able to speak freely regarding their concerns. For example, such issues as percentages to be transferred, vesting requirements, and the allocation formula, are all critical issues that have to be openly discussed between the ownership group and the ESOP consultant before they are put forward as a position. Employee reps are brought on board after the initial stage of the blueprint has been completed. The owners explain the blueprint to the employee reps who go back and explain it to the employee groups; therein is created the constant feedback loop. This is key to the success of the process. Employee reps bring enthusiasm and

81

issues that are important to the employee group, as well as some tremendous ideas. The ESOP team is always improved by this constant interaction between the employee reps, employees, and the other members of the ESOP team.

EXTERNAL MEMBERS OF THE TEAM

The pivotal player is the ESOP consultant or project manager. The project manager can be either an internal or an external person. However, we believe an external manager is more suited to making sure that the assignment is done on budget and on time and, more importantly, that all stakeholders feel they can talk to an unbiased external person. The project manager facilitates the initial meetings and decides whether or not an ESOP makes sense for the company and whether one can be implemented. The project manager also monitors the timetable and the budget, to bring the assignment in under budget and on time. Every ESOP runs into some obstacles which can be overcome by an experienced ESOP project manager who troubleshoots and gets the project back on track. For example, many times the ESOP project manager has to coordinate a meeting among members of the ESOP team and, without constant calls and focusing on what is important, those meetings fail to take place; documents that have been provided for all parties to review are never reviewed because of workplace pressures. The ESOP project manager not only reviews these documents to make sure that they meet the needs of the ESOP but also ensures that everyone has reviewed them and understands them. An ESOP project manager also implements organizational improvement and change that is used to help drive the ESOP communications. For example, the communication models that are used within the corporation prior to the ESOP may have to be changed to meet the needs of the ESOP. One company implemented webinars so that it could provide the educational seminars and the town hall meetings with its employees across the country. This worked so well that the company is now utilizing this methodology for training programs.

ESOP project managers also provide ongoing plan maintenance such as communicating changes in the nature or conditions
of the plan. For example, a stock split or the need to introduce
a new share or new option program will require additional communication materials, which the project manager is really in the
best position to provide. In Canada, ESOP project managers are
available from

- Large accounting firms such as Deloitte and Touche
  and PricewaterhouseCoopers.
- Large human resource firms and compensation firms such as
  William Mercer and Towers Perrin.
- Smaller specialty boutiques.

The ideal consultant is the one who best meets the company's
needs. Those needs change depending on size, industry, and
project. Some project managers specialize in large public companies, while others concentrate on smaller private companies.
The criteria for choosing the ESOP project manager are similar
to choosing any other consultant, one where chemistry and the
philosophical approaches to the implementation of the ESOP
are critical. When choosing consultants the following questions
should be posed:

- What is your philosophy towards ESOPs, and how do you imple-
  ment an ESOP?
- How many ESOPs have you implemented over the last
  three years?
- What is the nature of the companies that have utilized the
  ESOPs you have developed? What is their size and geographi-
  cal location?
- How do you budget the project? Do you have a fixed fee?
- What other services do you offer such as tax consulting, busi-
  ness valuations, legal services?
- Can you provide three company references?
- What problems can we expect in implementing an ESOP, with
  both pre- and post-ESOP issues?
- What makes your firm unique?

There is a wide variance, *even* among project managers with similar experience, with regard to fees, so it is important to obtain at least two or three quotes.

LAWYERS

Lawyers are a key component of the ESOP team. A lawyer will ensure compliance as well as prepare the various agreements such as the shareholders' agreement, the ESOP agreement, and any trust agreements that may be necessary. Any good commercial or corporate lawyer will be able to provide this service. In addition, the lawyer oversees any necessary adjustments to the corporate structure. It is important to choose a corporate lawyer, commercial lawyer, or a tax lawyer because he or she has the technical skills to help implement ESOP plans effectively from a legal standpoint. Nevertheless, it is important to remember that lawyers are advocates who advocate a client's position. This is fine in an adversarial legal situation. But in an ESOP situation the goal is to avoid an adversarial position, and it is essential to have a balanced approach from all ESOP team members. This means that the lawyer must treat all stakeholders equally, including owners, managers, and other employees. Not all lawyers understand the importance of ESOPs or are willing to learn this process. The owner's lawyers tend to advocate a position for the ownership group, which is what they are paid to do. However, this can cause major problems in terms of delaying the ESOP and creating animosity among the various stakeholders.

The lawyer must agree with the ESOP philosophy. A naysayer will inhibit the process. Before selecting a lawyer, the owner should ask for his or her opinion of ESOPs. The response is usually very clear. To reduce legal costs it is important to bring lawyers in towards the middle or end of the process, after the blueprint has been prepared by the ESOP team. At this point the lawyer can review the blueprint for legal concerns and it can then be discussed with the employee reps.

ACCOUNTANTS

The accountant will assist with the formulation of the business plan, to calculate the impact of the ESOP on the company's bottom line, and help formulate the financial statements to be presented to the new investors. The company accountant is usually best suited for this role. However, the tax accountants required may be either internal to the company or external. The tax accountant must be knowledgeable in the areas of preparing tax structures for ESOPs and have the ability to identify the tax effects for both the owners and the employees. Because tax is such a specialized area, outside tax advisers are generally used. As with a lawyer, the tax accountant must believe in ESOPs. Any reluctance on his or her part can cause delays and create animosity. ESOP consultants can provide names of tax accountants who may be suitable for the ESOP team.

BUSINESS VALUATORS

The value of any public company is established by the public marketplace; not so in a private company. That is why a business valuator is necessary to independently value the company to determine the share price, or to determine the stock option price. Ownership groups often resist having an independent valuation done for ESOP purposes, due to the cost involved. However, an independent valuation accomplishes several things. First, no matter how much the employees trust the ownership, when they are asked to invest in the company, it is better to have the value of the company established by someone who does not have a vested interest in it. Second, there is also a fiduciary responsibility to come up with a fair value, and the ownership group may not be in the best position to provide an unbiased viewpoint. The value put forward by a third party is viewed as having more credibility than one done internally. Third, the owners also must realize this valuation may be used for other purposes. For example, if there is a shareholders' dispute after the ESOP is completed, the valuation may be used as support. Fourth, an independent valuator can help the company set up a formula to value itself for several years. Every third year, it is recommended the company be re-evaluated to reflect any changes in the business and ensure the formula is current.

INSURANCE AGENTS

Last, but not least, is the insurance agent. In roughly one-third of ESOP cases, an insurance agent is needed to oversee the buy-sell agreements for the key employees. The risk, especially for small- to medium-size companies that rely on several key people to grow the value of the company, is a loss of one of those key people. However, this loss can be insured against through the buy-sell agreements. The insurance *provides* funds to help continue the company in case one of the owners or senior people die or are disabled. This insurance is an important part of keeping the company's value if there's a catastrophe involving any of the key people. The insurance ensures the company continues as well as provides the key person's estate with an insurance payout. The buy sell agreement is in effect funded by key-person insurance.

TROUBLESHOOTING

A number of problems may come up during the ESOP process. Knowing what these issues are and being prepared for them will help minimize the impact on the plan. These issues will vary among companies, but others may appear during the process as well.

FINANCIAL HEALTH

If the company is not earning enough money or if it does not have a large enough asset base, asking the employees to put money into the company is seen as little more than bailing it out. An ESOP can be successful in a turnaround situation. In fact, studies in the United States have shown that ESOPs help in nine out of 10 turnarounds. However, it is unfair to ask employees to be involved in a situation where the ownership group is not willing to continue to fund the operation because of the risks associated with the company. A turnaround is a very special situation and should not be undertaken lightly. It should involve turnaround specialists who can assess the likelihood of achieving some kind of growth and value for the company. Turnarounds are outside the scope of this book.

EXPECTATIONS

One has to manage expectations not only among the employees but also among the ownership group and the management. When an ESOP is announced many people, especially if they are in the high-tech environment, think they are going to become instant millionaires. This just isn't the case. There is a risk to investing in any company, and that risk is not diminished by implementing an ESOP. This risk has to be explained and communicated very clearly to all the parties involved. Unless some unusual equity event such as a third-party acquisition, or a liquidity event such as an IPO, takes place, people should not be looking at an ESOP as a generator of instant retirement funds. The type of expectations will differ of course depending upon who the stakeholder is. The owners will expect instant gratification and total gratitude from the employees for having sold them shares. This will not happen; employees will be glad to be part of a company but will not show much gratitude towards the owners for doing something that they feel they deserved in the first place.

Management will also believe that the employees should be grateful for this opportunity and that the owners should be glad that the management is willing to buy into the company. Management will believe that it deserves the majority of the shares being put forward and will in all likelihood feel that whatever amount of shares it received is not enough. Employees' expectations will be of instant wealth as well as instant respectability. All these issues are dealt with during the ESOP process through communication and feedback.

CLEARLY DEFINED GOALS

When the ESOP process is underway, there may be times when there are major disagreements between the groups involved. For example, the ownership could disagree with the employees or the management could differ with ownership on the question of the number of shares that are being allocated to each of the groups. The resolution of any disagreement has a great impact on the success of the plan. Issues are raised because they are important, and they need to be worked out in an appropriate way. This is where the blueprint with the ownership group's clearly defined goals and commitments comes into play. The blueprint can be used to benchmark and set a limit on what is feasible and what is not, which will help solve many of the disagreements that may arise. In effect, the process itself is a dispute-resolution mechanism and allows for disputes to be identified clarified and solved by the ESOP team.

TEAM CHEMISTRY

Although team chemistry has been covered earlier in this chapter, it is a point that bears repeating. The chemistry of the various team members is critical to the success of the ESOP. The team needs people who want to develop a solution that is fair and equitable for everybody involved. With the right team the process flows smoothly, and the results are sound. On the other hand, when there are people obstructing and favouring one particular group over another, problems will result. There is always the risk that either the ESOP will not succeed, or if it does that there will be hard feelings on all sides. Team chemistry is one issue not to be taken lightly.

TIME

The ESOP process needs enough time. It is neither practical nor reasonable to cut the process short. A proper job will take three to six months. As long as people realize that something is being done, and is being done fairly and professionally, they are prepared to give the ownership group the benefit of the doubt. Mistrust arises when owners try unsuccessfully to meet unrealistic deadlines. If a promise is made in an ESOP process it must be done within the timeline.

DISCLOSURE

Nothing will kill an ESOP faster than the discovery of a statement that is untrue. For example, if the owner truly wants to liquidate some of his or her shareholdings because his or her major assets are tied up in the equity of the company, that should be stated to the employees. Although the owner does not have to indicate what those funds will be used for, he or she must indicate that the purpose of the ESOP is to transfer those assets into cash. Employees must be made to understand that there is nothing wrong with that. When employees are asked to become partners and investors in a company they expect and deserve full disclosure.

REALISM

An ESOP is not a magic bullet; it is an investment with risk attached and needs to be acknowledged as such by all parties involved. Companies can't afford to make promises they can't keep. For example, a strategy such as an IPO should not be guaranteed by the management group; there are no guarantees. Rather, an IPO could be put forward as a long-term goal. Realism comes into play because employees want to know how they are going to liquidate their investment so that they can realize the wealth that they may create over the years. It is critical to define the exit strategy for the company, whether there's a third-party sale, whether it is an IPO, or even how long the employees will have to wait for that liquidity event.

EXPERIENCE

Employees may have past experiences with plans that did not go well, but far from being discouraging these experiences can offer valuable insight to avoid the pitfalls of the past. Through the employee questionnaire, the ESOP project manager will elicit the experiences of employees in these areas and see what areas can be improved upon for the current ESOP plan.

PARTICIPATION

Not *everyone* will buy into the plan. Some people will not take any financial risk. Expect this. An ESOP does not need all employees to buy in, but it would be surprising if more than 20 per cent of employees did not buy into a company that offered a well-thought-out ESOP plan. Studies have shown that participation levels in private companies generally are much higher than those in public companies. Public company take-ups usually are in the range of 20 to 40 per cent while a properly implemented private company ESOP will range between 70 to 90 per cent.

CULTURE

Studies *have* shown that a participative culture is crucial to the ongoing success of an ESOP plan. Once the ESOP plan is in place the company needs to be run with employee participation. Management may require training to *develop* a more participative style. (See Chapters 8 and 9.)

ADMINISTRATION

Companies must be practical in administrating the plan. Whether a company chooses an internal or external administrator, the key to a successful plan is always the KIS Principle, "Keep It Simple."

COMMUNICATION

In most cases, employees want more shares than are available to be sold or to be given out. The management group should explain how the number of available shares was calculated and why these shares are being given up. Communication can forestall erroneous perceptions. For example, if employees believe that the plan is too small and has no significance to them, the motivation for retention and attraction that may have been one of the key features of putting a plan into place may be derailed.

Most ESOPs in Canada and the United States will have an ESOP of 10 or 20 per cent of the outstanding shares either through equity or stock options. A company that gives out less than 10 to 20 per cent is running the risk of being perceived as stingy and not being fair to employees.

CONCLUSION

After this chapter, readers know how to determine whether a company is a potential candidate, start the process of designing the ESOP, and look at the communication and troubleshooting issues that will arise during its implementation. These issues, although critical to the success of an ESOP, are basically non-technical issues, in the sense that they do not involve meeting certain legal and accounting requirements. The next few chapters will go into detail of the practical requirements for the plan and how these impact the design issues that have already been discussed in the previous chapters.

CHAPTER 4
FINANCING ESOPS

If capital ownership is good for the rich, it is a thousand times better for the middle class and the poor.

— Louis O. Kelso

There are two major aspects to financing an ESOP. Each depends upon the owners' purpose for the ESOP. This chapter deals with employee financing, in other words, how and where the employee obtains the funds to purchase equity. Then corporate financing is discussed; where the company looks to obtain corporate financing in partnership with the employees if required, for example, in a succession plan or in a management buyout situation.

ESOP MYTH Employees cannot afford to buy into their company.

ESOP FACT There are at least eight different ways for an employee to purchase shares.

EMPLOYEE FINANCING

Options for financing an ESOP are as numerous as the creative minds that conceive them. What underlies them all is the need to instill a sense of ownership and commitment in the employees, ensuring that they make a financial commitment to establish the ESOP either through a cash investment or other financial obligation. Employees are undertaking an investment in the shares of a company that entails a real risk. This investment is similar to any other investment that they may make, and employees should be fully aware of the risk. Let us examine some of these methodologies in more detail.

EMPLOYEE SELF-FINANCE

There are eight ways for employees to self-finance:

1. Cash
2. Bonuses
3. Dividends
4. Bank loan
5. Company loan
6. TFSA/RRSP
7. Payroll deduction
8. Combination of any of the above

Employees who have sufficient financial strength may purchase shares in the company directly, using their own spare cash, loans from a financial institution or from family and friends, lines of credit from their banks, or their TFSA/RRSP funds. In some cases the company itself will set up a method to loan funds to the employees so that they may purchase shares in the company. The shares are held in escrow until such time as the loan has been repaid. Another way that employees may self-finance is if the company allows them to use their bonuses to buy shares instead of taking cash. The tax implications of setting up such a plan are discussed in Chapter 6 ESOPs and Income Tax. Another way for employees to purchase shares is through payroll deductions. This can be done on an ongoing basis where the company deducts money to purchase the shares from the employee's paycheque.

There are two aspects to payroll deduction. The employee may take a one year notional loan from the company, pay it off through payroll deduction over the year and own the shares immediately. Alternatively, no company loan is made, only payroll deduction, and the employee does not own the shares until the year is complete. In the former case, The Canada Revenue Agency views the loan as an employee benefit, usually about 1 to 1.5% currently. The rate changes with the bank rate.

Typically in most share plans the methodology chosen by the employees is based upon the amount of the investment and whether or not this will cause an investment hardship for the employees. Many broad-based ESOPs do not require a significant investment by the employees for the ESOP to be successful. In most cases the investment by individual employees will be anywhere from $500 to maybe $5,000 as a norm. Also to be considered is the complexity created for the company in terms of administration. Obviously, a plan where employees can have a payroll deduction or use their bonuses to obtain the shares will be more complex than one where the employees can either pay by cash or by some loan arrangement with an institution or through friends.

In privately-held companies a useful method to aid the employees in financing the company is called the Freezing technique. In effect, the founding owners freeze the value of the company at a certain date. The value is then converted into preferred shares which are owned by the founding shareholders. However, once the preferred shares are in place a new common stock can be issued which has a nominal value, as all the company value resides in the preferred shares. These common shares are then issued to the founding shareholders as well as the employees. In this way, the employees can own common shares in the company for a minimal cost. As the company grows in value, the increase is attributable to the common shares, not the preferred shares, the value of which remains fixed at the value on the "freeze date." However, the preferred shares can have dividends, which give the owners a means of return on their investment.

Since the freezing technique has many tax implications, the technique and appropriate capital structure should be done by professional tax experts.

The advantage of this employee financing is the ability to participate in growth at a minimal cost. The disadvantage is the tax and legal costs to freeze, and the difficulty of communicating the freeze technique to the employees.

Variations of this technique can be used. For example, it is possible to freeze only a portion of the current value, and thereby issue the common shares at a value greater than a nominal one.

EXAMPLE OF FREEZING AND IMPACT ON COMPANY AND EMPLOYEE

Let's assume the value of the company is currently $5,000,000 and that the ESOP is selling 10 per cent of the company (i.e. $500,000). It's important to note the following equation in regard to value:

$$V = P + C$$

CORPORATE VALUE = PREFERRED SHARE VALUE + COMMON SHARE VALUE.

Without the freeze employees would be buying $500,000 worth of shares. If we freeze the value of the company at $2,500,000 then the owner takes back preferred shares worth $2,500,000. Using the formula above, we get V of $5,000,000 = P of $2,500,000 + C of $2,500,000.

As the employees are only purchasing common shares, they would need to pay $250,000 ($2,500,000 x 0.1 = $250,000) instead of $500,000.

Let's look down the road and assume the company grows to a value of $10,000,000. Using the formula again, V of $10,000,000 = P of $2,500,000 + C of $7,500,000. The employees' investment of $250,000 now has grown to $750,000 (i.e. $7,500,000 x 0.1 = $750,000). The employees have leveraged their investment through company growth.

BANK LOANS AND COMPANY GUARANTEES

The company may make an arrangement with its bank so that participating employees can get bank loans to purchase shares. The shares serve as security for the loans and usually the company guarantees the loans to ensure the best interest rate and encourage the bank to participate. Because shares in a private company are not very liquid, they can serve as collateral security only when the major part of the guarantee is supported by the company. Companies tend to do this in situations where they have substantial dealings with the bank. This loan becomes part of their loan security agreement. To guarantee the loan the company must have a good relationship with its bank or lending institution, and the bank must have experience in loaning these amounts to a number of employees without creating an administrative nightmare for the company with the ESOP. Not all banks or lending institutions want to get into this type of arrangement. Therefore, it is important that the company first discuss this methodology with its bank before discussing it with the employees.

The advantages of this type of program are that the employees are required to obtain a loan and sign a cheque to the company, which serves to ensure that the employee is taking this investment as seriously as any other type of investment. The company must review its own balance sheet to make sure that it could guarantee such a loan and whether or not it is in a position to encourage this type of borrowing from its employees. As a general rule for privately-held companies, management tends to encourage employees to buy shares with their own cash before borrowing through the company.

COMPANY FINANCE

If the company is not using the ESOP to raise capital either for internal purposes or to purchase a portion of the shares, it may finance employee share purchases by means of a note receivable from employees. In this case the note receivable is held by the company, which is taking the place of the bank or the lending institution by loaning money to the employee to acquire the share capital. Employees then repay the company over a set period of time, say for example, five to 10 years. Interest may be charged on the note receivable, depending upon the needs and conditions of the company and the employees. Notes receivable may also be used with employee bonus programs, and the repayment terms may include a mandatory percentage of any future bonuses awarded until the debt has been retired. For example, if the company loaned $2,000 to an employee for a period of five years, and the employee was able to obtain a bonus each year of $1,000 a year, that employee could use a percentage of the bonus, say 50 per cent or $500, to repay the loan, so that way the note receivable is retired, and the company does get equity into the hands of the employee. The company would remit income taxes on the bonus.

If the company wishes to assist the employees to establish the ESOP, but the company does not have sufficient existing resources, external financing will be required. Loans to the company in this type of financing program are similar to those of the bank loans where the company is the guarantor of the loan. If the company is in a strong financial position and is capable of allowing this debt to be held by the company without upsetting its lending ratios, then the company may be in a position to offer this to employees. If the company has a financial position that is somewhat tenuous, or is in a very volatile industry where it may need its credit leverage to raise financing for internal working capital purposes, the company may not be able to risk loaning employees capital to purchase equity. Other issues that must be addressed are buy-back agreements with the employees that would deduct the amount of the loan still payable to the employer from the payroll cheque of an employee who is leaving.

For most companies implementing an ESOP, the most satisfactory method, with the least amount of risk to the corporation and also the lowest administrative cost, is to have employees provide funds to purchase the shares either through their own resources, lines of credit, RRSPs, TFSAs or future bonuses.

SOURCES OF OUTSIDE CAPITAL

In situations where the employees are purchasing shares in the company for an equity buyout it is important to look at some type of partnership with an outside purchaser. Whether a management buyout or a broad-based plan, many employee groups do not have the funds to close the deal. An exception is if the employees are looking at a buyout planned over a number of years. Buyouts may be planned over five or 10 years to purchase the current owner-ship position without going to an outside party, but in many situations, even in a long-term buyout succession plan, some type of third-party investment will probably be necessary at some point.

When sourcing capital the availability of debt and/or equity capital will depend on the financial strength of the company, the industry in which it operates, and the philosophy of the current owners. The following are some of the principle capital sources that can provide the funding needed to partner an ESOP with an employee buyout.

COMMERCIAL LENDING BANKS

As discussed above, a company's bank should be the first consideration for employees obtaining financial assistance in buying shares. When the company wishes to assist employees directly, but lacks the capability of doing so, the bank can provide assistance through loans or through lines of credit to the individuals. Banks tend to respond to a competitive approach and will be generally aggressive in vying for business that they view as attractive. Banks that have a good relationship with their clients will not want an outside bank to provide loans for an ESOP and therefore encroach upon that banking relationship to the company. This gives the necessary leverage to the company to go forward with this type of lending. In a partnership situation, the bank will also be able to look at loaning money on a leveraged basis against future assets of the company.

ASSET-BASED LENDERS

For companies with significant assets in the form of real estate, equipment, or financial capital, asset lenders may provide an opportunity to achieve more flexible financing than can be obtained from commercial banks. An example of an asset-based lender would be the Business Development Bank of Canada (BDC) or Canadian Western Bank (CWB), which will loan based on covenants on these assets. These covenants tend to be less onerous in repayment terms and are more tailored to the company's situation.

SUB-DEBT PROVIDERS

The share equity divisions at the banks and certain specialized financing firms will provide capital that is often referred to as quasi-equity or mezzanine financing. Sub-debt is subordinate to the security interest held by the primary debt holder, which is usually the bank. Higher interest rates are applicable to this type of financing, reflecting the riskier position, and the company is required to issue some form of equity compensation as well, usually in the form of a warrant, which is issued as a nominal amount. A good source of this type of financing is, again, the Business Development Bank of Canada, formerly the Federal Business Development Bank (FBDB) or Canadian Western Bank. A sub-debt provider creates for a company the ability to loan funds at a higher interest rate that is not solely based on assets but also on the future potential of the company to grow and earn income. Because these lenders will loan money based on future potential of a company, a higher interest rate is charged. In return, the sub-debt lender will usually take back preferred stock in the company with the option to convert to common stock at some future event.

INSTITUTIONAL EQUITY SOURCES

These include mutual funds, pension funds, labour-sponsored funds, and insurance companies, as well as the capital divisions of banks and other lending institutions. The capital division of the bank loans money based on the company's future cash flows rather than its asset base position. Each institution has its own criteria for deals, which may include:

- Preferred or prohibited industries,
- stage of development, and
- size of deal.

Generally these lenders are attracted to companies that tend to have excellent future prospects and good management. Institutional equity lenders generally want to be able to liquidate their investment within a short timeframe, usually five years, and they look for an annual rate of return of at least 30 per cent. Although specific terms of the investment and the rates that an investor would enjoy are negotiable, it should be noted that these investors tend to protect their investment in several ways. They usually want board representation with the right to approve fundamental matters such as the annual budget, major changes in the strategic direction of the company, and solicitation of additional investment.

VENTURE CAPITALISTS

Venture capitalists (VCs) are similar to institutional equity sources; however, they tend to want to invest more in earlier-stage companies and start-ups. Venture capitalists will also consider smaller investments, but they generally want a much greater level of involvement and a much higher rate of return on their investment.

PRIVATE EQUITY SOURCES

Wealthy individuals can be a source of capital. However, it is difficult to find these people, and according to their particular risk tolerance, they may or may not want to invest in a particular company. Access to these individuals is generally initiated by the company owners or through brokers or agents.

If the purpose of the company's ESOP is to engage the employees in the participation of the future growth and wealth of the company, and the accumulation of the investment is not of particular importance to the company, the source of the capital will likely be from the employees themselves. However, if the purpose of the ESOP is to implement some type of succession plan for the current ownership group, or to raise new capital for the company for expansion, some type of partnership arrangement between the ESOP and outside corporate financing is more likely.

SPECIAL ISSUES TO BE AWARE OF IN FINANCING

As every ESOP is different for every company, there are special issues that must be tailored to the needs of the company and its employees.

GIFTING

On occasion we have had clients request an ESOP that was a gifting program to the employees rather than an investment. Although this approach goes against our philosophy that employees should have "skin" in the game, it is a valid option for certain owners. The major reasons given for wanting a gifting program by owners is:

1. Volatile industry and the owner does not want employees worried when a downturn occurs
2. Past promises to employees for shares

3. Sweat equity provided by employees both in the past and currently

Gifting can be accomplished through freezing of share values, as explained more fully within this chapter. It can also be done by using stock options with an exercise price of zero. You cannot just give shares to employees at zero value as this will become an issue of an employee benefit. Once gifting is ascertained as a purpose of the ESOP then an appropriate method can be employed which minimizes the income tax repercussions on the employee and the company.

MANAGEMENT BUYOUT

A management buyout ("MBO") is in fact an ESOP, usually restricted to key employees and financed by external sources of capital or by the current owners. It's used when the purpose of the ESOP is to sell the company by the current ownership group. It can be an immediate buyout or spread over a number of years. External sources of capital are used when the need is for an immediate buyout of the owner, while long-term buyout by the key people can be internally financed.

The reason for looking at an MBO is usually that the current owner has decided, either due to health, personal, or business reasons, that the time to exit the business is upon him/her. Sometimes the reason may be that the owner requires growth capital from a venture capitalist and most venture capitalists require some kind of key person participation as part of the deal. From an ESOP perspective, an MBO is just a subset of the ESOP assignment and therefore has the same issues that face all ESOPs, as described in this book.

CAPPING EMPLOYEE OWNERSHIP

A major element of an ESOP, whether it's restricted to key persons within the organization or is a broad base application to all employees, is to involve as many people as possible to become shareholders. The issue that arises in meeting this ESOP goal is the different financial capabilities of each employee. Each person will have a different state of their financial ability to participate. Someone whose great uncle died and left them with an inheritance may be able to purchase the largest portion of ESOP shares available, thus leaving little left for other employees. Others may be mortgaged and in debt and at this point in time cannot afford to buy into the plan at a level they would like to.

The solution is to cap the amount of shares any one person can own of the ESOP shares being offered. As a rough rule of thumb, most of our clients cap the ownership at 5 per cent of the total value of the company. If a person wishes to buy in excess of this cap, they have to apply to the board of directors for permission to do so.

TAX-FREE SAVINGS ACCOUNTS (TFSA) AND REGISTERED RETIREMENT SAVINGS PLANS (RRSP)

A potential source of financing from employees is their personal funds in a TFSA and/or RRSP. There are some difficult issues to resolve in using these plans to hold company shares. The following are the highlights:

1. First and foremost is the concept that a TFSA and the RRSP are for retirement savings purposes. Therefore, from a personal financial perspective employees should not use all the funds in these plans to buy into one stock in one company. If that company goes bankrupt or cannot make the payments then the employee can be seriously hampered in their retirement plans. Basically the concept of not having all your eggs in one basket applies here.
2. The employee and the company must meet CRA rules of eligibility to be able to use the TFSA/RRSP funds to purchase the ESOP shares.
3. The financial institutions require letters of opinion from a tax specialist, a lawyer, and the business appraiser to set up these plans. This can be costly to the company to set up.

4. Many financial institutions will not want to set these up for the company as they do not make any money on these plans in this instance. Institutions that may provide this service are Canaccord, Canadian Western Bank, and Olympia Trust.
5. If one does go this route, there are substantial benefits to the employee from a tax perspective.

EXPECTATION OF AMOUNT TO BE RAISED THROUGH EMPLOYEE FINANCING

The question arises as to what a company can expect to raise through internal employee financing. A rule of thumb we use is that actual employee cash will be around 10 per cent of payroll. For example, if payroll is $1,000,000 per year, then $100,000 in cash can be raised through employees. Each company is different and depending on the pay grid and the fixed versus variable portion of compensation this per cent may vary.

In terms of what employees can afford to pay for the value of a company, again a rule of thumb is about 10 per cent of the company value. This could be made up of cash, payroll deduction, and bonus. To go beyond 10 per cent usually requires loans and external financing sources. Again this will depend on the value of the company.

CONCLUSION

This chapter has outlined the methods employed to achieve financing for employees and for the corporation, depending on the ESOP's objectives. Once the financing is in place, the ESOP can move forward into the technical details. The overriding rule for financing is to make it as simple and easy as possible to allow the maximum number of employees to become owners.

CHAPTER 5
BUSINESS VALUATION AND ESOPS

Erroneous assumptions can be disastrous.

– Peter F. Drucker

The influence of a business valuation on the successful implementation and continuation of an ESOP is immense. Whether the ESOP consists of an equity share, a stock option, or an equity value unit, the employees need to know the value of their ownership in the plan. When employees know the outcome of the valuation, the company may better use participation in the plan for purposes of measurement, motivation, and team-building. It is important that the employees are kept up-to-date on the value of these plans on a periodic basis. Keeping the employees fully informed creates trust between the employees and the original ownership group as it verifies in the employees' eyes that a partnership truly has been formed, creating a strong foundation for the company going forward.

Business valuations are both an art and a science. On the artistic side, business valuations involve business judgment and experience in a real-world setting. The scientific side involves the selection of appropriate valuation methodologies, analysis, and research, which apply to specific industries and the purpose of each valuation assignment. By properly balancing these elements, a business appraiser will be able to arrive at a successful and fair valuation.

VALUATION TERMS

Each profession, be it law, medicine, or astrophysics, relies on jargon to communicate specific concepts. In business valuation, it is important to understand the terms "fair market value," "fair value," and "fair price," as these are central to all ESOP valuation assignments.

FAIR MARKET VALUE

ESOP MYTH Never sell your company to the employees because you will not receive the highest value.

ESOP FACT Many professional advisers assume that the employees cannot match a market offer. In a hot market for companies, this is true; however, in a down market, the opposite is true, employees can outbid the market. In most markets that are somewhere in between hot and down, the employees' offer equals the market offer.

The accepted Canadian definition of fair market value is "the highest price expressed in terms of money, or money's worth available in an open and unrestricted market between informed, prudent parties who are under no compulsion to transact and who are dealing at arm's length."

"Highest price" is the maximum price the purchaser is willing to pay to acquire the shares and the minimum price alternatively that the vendor is willing to accept to sell those shares. Typically when there is a transaction these two price ranges will intersect. It is important that valuations always be viewed from both the purchaser's and the vendor's point of view. If there remains a significant difference outside of what is considered a normal valuation range, the valuator must be able to logically resolve this difference. Normal value range will generally be plus or minus 25 per cent.

The expression "money or money's worth" means that the transaction price is defined in terms of cash or cash equivalents. An example of a cash equivalent would be a note taken back payable at full interest rates and fully secured by collateral assets. It is important to understand that any terms that can be attached to a transaction can have as great an impact on value as the valuation itself. As an example, if a purchaser offers to purchase a company for $1 million, but the terms indicate that the $1 million will not have to be paid for 100 years at no interest, then clearly the purchaser is telling the vendor that the company has little or no value in terms of its current cash value.

Now consider "open and unrestricted market." Fair market value calculations are hypothetical and therefore occur in a notional market. They are not transactional in a sense that company A signs a cheque and cash is transferred into the bank account of the owners of company B. Because fair market value is notional it is assumed that all purchasers have been included in the marketplace. Whether or not there are specific special purchasers in the marketplace must be considered, and if identifiable special purchasers do exist, they must be taken into account in the valuation. Many types of companies have an active market for the sale of their assets or shares of their company. Examples of these types of companies would be cable television, radio stations, funeral homes, or school bus operators, and in this kind of situation special purchasers can be clearly identified through a rule of thumb methodology.

What is the meaning then of "informed, prudent parties?" Fair market value assumes that both the vendor and the buyer have equal knowledge of the financial affairs of the company. The concept assumes that the purchaser, being a rational investor, will base his or her final decision on the sound economic merits of the investment. In the practical world, economic decisions are but one factor in any transaction, and therefore it is critical that the final valuation number makes sound economic and business sense. As an example, a transaction may occur in a company where the ownership group is selling to its major supplier, who, having special knowledge of the industry, will look at the acquisition in terms of not only the economic impact but also the impact that the acquisition will have in terms of its market position, name branding, and relationship to other competitors.

In the world of fair market value the expression "no compulsion to transact" exists; no one is forced to buy or sell. However, for purposes of calculations this does not prevent the transaction from occurring as it is assumed that both parties will eventually arrive at the highest price in the marketplace. This assumption does tend to remove both the bargain-basement sale price and the premium purchase price due to non-economic pressures. Therefore, bargain-basement sales or premium purchases should not be used as comparables when assessing value.

Fair market value also assumes that all parties are dealing at arm's length, that is, between parties who are not related and who have negotiated in good faith to arrive at a price. The reason for this inclusion is obvious since fair market value is done in many cases on non-arm's length transactions, where parties are related by family or common ownership.

FAIR VALUE

Fair value is a widely used term that, unfortunately, has never really been defined. The term is used in various provincial securities acts as well as the *Canada Business Corporations Act*. It has usually been interpreted by the courts to mean fairness to minority shareholders. In this context, no minority discount is generally applicable in a fair value calculation. A minority discount, which will be discussed later in the chapter, is a reduction in the purchase price to account for the lack of control by the minority shareholder. The fair value calculation can be used for ESOPs involved in public companies rather than private companies, since the former are always quoted on the exchange in minority stock values.

FAIR PRICE

There are as many prices for a business or an asset as there are purchasers. However, in the notional market, there is only one fair market value. Real-world buyers or purchasers are able to pay bargain or premium prices due to synergies in the form of value-added profits they bring to the acquisition. For example, if there are four purchasers for one company, each of those purchasers will make a bid that has a different value attached to the shares. The reason for this difference is that each company will have a different economic and non-economic reason for purchasing those shares. One company may want to include this company in its worldwide holdings and believe that this acquisition will increase its public share value. Another company might be able to increase its gross margin by integrating the product line of the company it is acquiring. Another company might be buying out the competition and, therefore, be able to charge higher prices for its products. The fourth company may be buying the company to acquire its workforce. So each company does its own calculation of value and will arrive at a different price. Each of these prices of course are relevant; the vendor will have to decide which of the deals based on the terms and conditions of each offer are in its best interest, both from an economic and non-economic viewpoint.

WHAT IS FAIR PRICE?

The fair price *may* equal fair market value but only by coincidence. Open market transactions result in sales that can be influenced by illness, retirement, lack of motivation of the original ownership group, and in purchases driven by the need for expansion, the desire to manage, or to gain prestige from the acquisition itself.

As an example, many of the values attributable to the purchase of sports teams are driven not only by the economics of the acquisition of the sports team but also by the egos of the buyers who want to own sports teams.

Any open market transaction between arm's-length parties is at a fair price, since a transaction is evidence that both parties have acted in their own interests. Open market values do not normally reflect fair market value; because of this, comparables can be very misleading, and their relevance in reaching valuation conclusions debatable.

The following diagram illustrates the relationship between a fair price and fair market value:

BARGAIN PURCHASE	FAIR MARKET VALUE (FAIR VALUE)	SPECIAL PURCHASER A	SPECIAL PURCHASER B	SPECIAL PURCHASER C
$100,000	$500,000	$600,000	$750,000	$1,000,000

If one knew that a price paid was a bargain, for example $100,000, or was based on a special purchaser concept, for example $600,000, then one could infer fair market value as a sub-set of the price paid, say $500,000.

FAIR MARKET VALUE VERSUS FAIR PRICE

Fair market value or notional valuations are generally used for estate planning purposes and in dispositions upon death. They are not pricing exercises but pure fair market value assignments. No identified special purchasers are taken into account in the valuation process, which is performed to satisfy tax authorities. In the real world, however, every buyer is a special purchaser and tends to pay for an asset based upon particular needs. A real transaction is therefore a pricing exercise, not a fair market value assessment.

Fair market value exists only in the notional marketplace, not in the *real* world. For one thing, fair market values reflect the perfect world, which does not exist; for another, a buyer's perception of value differs for each individual or company. Nonetheless an understanding of fair market value is recommended as a first step towards determining a negotiated price.

In the notional world of fair market value:

- Parties of equal negotiating and financial strength arrive at the highest price available.
- There are no restrictions on the sale.
- Concepts of forced or imprudent sales do not exist.
- Parties are aware of all relevant information.
- Transactions are always at arm's length.
- Transactions occur only on a cash basis or a cash-equivalent basis.
- Non-commercial goodwill is excluded from consideration.
- The market is unrestricted as to who the buyer will be.

In the real world of fair price:

- Parties rarely have equal negotiating strength.
- Prices do not correspond to the highest price available.
- A company may be restricted to selling certain classes of shares.
- Sales can be forced, and imprudent sales are normal.
- Information is never fully known by both sides.
- Non-arm's length transactions are common.
- An all-cash basis is not the norm.
- Non-commercial goodwill can be paid for.
- The number of buyers is limited due to competition and knowledge.

FAIR MARKET VALUE AND ESOPS

Business appraisers use fair market value rather than fair price when calculating the value of companies for ESOPs because ESOPs are, to a certain extent, designed to meet certain tax criteria. The *Revenue and the Federal Income Tax* Act require for purposes of meeting its criteria that fair market value be utilized in any calculations of valuation between arm's length or non-arm's length parties. This requirement holds true for stock equity plans or for stock option plans. Taxation issues will be discussed more fully in Chapter 6 ESOPs and Income Tax.

MINORITY DISCOUNT

The value of stock owned by minority shareholders is different than that owned by majority shareholders because a majority shareholder controls the use and disposition of the assets of the corporation. This control over one's investment makes a majority holding less risky and therefore more valuable.

This factor is at work daily in the public market. Publicly-held shares are constantly traded on a minority-based price. However, when a takeover bid of the whole company is announced, the bid price can be as much as 40 per cent greater than the trading price. The reason for this premium is that the acquirer is obtaining a control position.

There is no specified discount percentage that can be applied to a minority shareholding in a closely-held company for ESOP purposes. Each case has to be examined on its own merits. However, numerous studies in the United States have shown minority discounts generally start at 20 to 35 per cent of the pro-rata en-bloc value and are adjusted up or down from there depending upon circumstances. The en-bloc value of a company is a calculation of the sale price of the company assuming 100 per cent of the shares of the company are sold. For example, a shareholder with a 10-per-cent ownership in a company valued en bloc for $1 million may receive only $70,000 instead of $100,000, because a 30-per-cent minority discount was applied to the en-bloc value.

Minority values are important in the context of ESOPs because most ESOPs are implemented by transferring minority shares to employees. Although in total a significant amount of shares might be transferred, on an individual basis, the number of shares is usually rather small. Therefore, a minority discount may be applied whenever a fair market value calculation is being calculated for purposes of an ESOP, except where the minority shares in total make up a substantial portion of the outstanding shares. Our experience has shown a normal discount rate applied in an ESOP calculation to be around 20 to 35 per cent. This discount results from the fact that in most ESOPs there is a substantial buy-sell or shareholders' agreement in place that defines the liquidity of those shareholdings and allows the minority shareholder to realize some value at some point in time down the road. This tends to reduce what otherwise would be a higher minority discount that could be applied to those shares. The only caveat in this case is that when an employee sells their ESOP shares they do so with no minority discount applied. In an ESOP, no minority discount may be applied if so desired by the board of directors.

CONTINGENT TAX LIABILITY

In completing a valuation, it may be necessary to revalue fixed assets such as real estate, machinery, and equipment that have fair market values exceeding those recorded on the book of accounts. The valuation calculation may also produce a value for goodwill, which is not normally recorded on the balance sheet. The theoretical or potential sale of these assets, including goodwill, gives rise to contingent income tax liabilities. Examples of these contingencies would be capital gains, recaptured depreciation, or terminal losses. The valuator frequently has to assess the likelihood of payment of these taxes and account for them in some manner, in the valuation price.

For example, a company may own real estate that was purchased in 1965 for $500,000 and is worth $2.5 million in today's marketplace. If that property were sold today, the company would have to pay income tax on the capital gain net of any disposition costs, as well as tax on recaptured depreciation. However, since the company is a going concern, it may not sell this property for 10 to 20 years hence. The valuator must decide, based on the facts, what, if any, quantum of contingent taxes should be applied to the asset value of the company.

GOODWILL

There are two general types of goodwill, commercial and personal. Commercial goodwill, by definition, can be conveyed to the buyer and, due to the conveyance, can be said to have value. Personal goodwill, on the other hand, is considered to be specific to a person and therefore when that person departs, he or she takes the value of that goodwill with him or her.

For example, a world-renowned brain specialist in practice would be considered to have personal goodwill since the particular skill that attracted the patients would leave with the specialist. However, an engineering company with a complement of support staff, work in progress, and a large clientele may have both personal and commercial goodwill. The latter would have some value.

The difficulty the valuator faces is separating the personal from the commercial goodwill component. This is done by assessing the likelihood of sustaining revenues, identifying the key persons in the organization, and investigating comparable transactions occurring both inside and outside the organization.

SYNERGISTIC PURCHASERS

A synergistic purchaser is a buyer that, due to special circumstance, will pay more for a business than is justified purely upon the business' economic results. For example, a bank wanting to enter the trust field will pay more for a trust company than would IBM, which could not utilize the synergies that would accrue to the bank through its acquisition. Similarly, an accountant buying a real estate practice would not pay as much as another real estate agent who would obtain synergies by combining the two agencies. The valuator must be alert to the existence of any special purchasers and, when they are identified, must investigate the potential effect on value these buyers would have. For purposes of an ESOP, synergistic purchasers should be considered very carefully and accounted for in the valuation.

VALUATION METHODOLOGIES

There is a variety of valuation methods used to calculate a range of reasonable values. These methods can be broadly categorized into either asset-based or earnings-based approaches.

GOING CONCERN VERSUS LIQUIDATION

To assess which methodology to use, the question is whether the company is a going concern. The methodology used will depend on the answer. From a valuation perspective a going concern is a business that can continue to operate and produce products and services into the foreseeable future. The company has the following attributes:

- The ability to generate profits and cash flows in excess of expenses either currently or in the foreseeable future.
- It is not in bankruptcy or insolvency.
- It can meet its supplier and creditor obligations.
- It can collect its receivables in a normal fashion.
- It does not have material contingent liabilities or lawsuits which could create a bankrupt or insolvent company.

Some businesses are set up as holding companies and may have marginal profitability or losses. This does not exclude them from being classified as going concerns.

APPROACHES TO VALUE

The chart below summarizes the various approaches to value:

METHOD OF VALUE		
IS THE COMPANY A GOING CONCERN?		
	EARNINGS-BASED	ASSET-BASED
NO	LIQUIDATION VALUE	
YES	Capitalization of Earnings	
	Capitalization of Cash Flow	Adjusted Asset Value
	Discounted Cash Flow	

A "no" response results in a liquidation value. A "yes," however, results in two broad-based alternatives, a capitalization approach or an adjusted-asset approach and/or liquidation approach. Many valuators will use several approaches and then compare them. This allows the valuator to check his or her assumptions and reflect on any inconsistencies in the approaches.

METHODOLOGIES

There are basically two valuation approaches. One approach is dependent on asset values and the other on earnings. The earnings approach governs many going concern circumstances because the worth of the company tends to be based on its future earnings. Assets can often comprise the value of a corporation where, because of industry influences and market conditions, the future for a company's earnings can be uncertain.

CAPITALIZATION OF EARNINGS

This model consists of three calculations: First, an estimate of the company's future maintainable earnings; second, the price/earnings multiple or multiplier (P/E multiple); and third, the value of identifiable redundant assets. The difficulty with this approach is determining the appropriate capitalization rate or P/E multiple to use for a given company. P/E multiples are discussed later in the chapter.

MAINTAINABLE EARNINGS

In evaluating maintainable earnings it is important to understand the nature of the business cycle of the company being valued. An investor always purchases future earnings. The past is only an indicator of this future. Therefore, the risk inherent in every appraisal is estimating the quality and preservation of future cash flows.

Earnings quality is dependent upon two main factors:

- The expertise of key corporate management (including not only senior executives, but also key persons throughout the organization including technical, sales, and accounting staff).
- The product or service (including competitive advantages, business cycles, and market penetration).

In assessing key management, an organization chart detailing titles, responsibilities, ages, and length of employment is essential. This chart allows prompt identification of key persons who should be interviewed, as well as organizational weakness due to lack of qualified backup personnel.

The company's dependence on sales from any one individual or group of individuals should be determined. If the results show a material dependence an investigation should be undertaken into whether these people are under contract, and what, if any, is their stake in staying with the company.

The importance of this review of key persons cannot be overstated. Consider the takeover by a large multi-national of a small regional competitor. The multi-national paid a high price for the company but due to different corporate cultures, several key sales persons with the regional competitor left within six months of the acquisition and took one-half of the sales volume. Had this risk been properly addressed, the buyer likely would not have paid such a high price.

The appraiser must also determine the nature of the company's product or service. Is the company in a cyclical industry and subject to severe volatility based on economic growth and recession? Are the products and services price-sensitive, such that increased competition will tend to decrease profitability? Can the company maintain its unique market niche, which will protect premium prices in the marketplace?

Having reviewed the quality of future earnings, the appraiser then looks to its maintainability or, in service sector parlance, its retention factor. Are sales being maintained due to contractual obligations with clients, or are they due to licenses, patents, or trademarks? What rate of new clients is generated each year? What rate of old clients is lost each year? Is the sales and earnings trend increasing or decreasing? Are there any key factors (e.g. a lease agreement on a main street store) that could alter the company's earnings expectations if there is a change? A good example of the importance of the maintainability factor is in the accounting field. Generally an accounting practice will be purchased over a three-year period, and the purchase price will be reduced by the loss of client volume over that period (no retention, no value).

PRICE TO EARNINGS (P/E) MULTIPLE

The capitalization rate measures the rate of return required by an investor for an asset. Its inverse is the P/E multiple. For example, a required rate of return of 10 per cent on an asset equates to a P/E multiple of 10 (1 divided by 0.1), and a rate of return of 20 per cent equates to a P/E multiple of 5 (1 divided by 0.2).

Of the three components of value used in this model, the P/E multiple can be the most subjective element. Due to the subjectivity of this number, appraisers generally use a range of multiples to calculate value. Therefore, P/E multiples of, for example, four to five times are used rather than a single multiple of either four or five times.

The capitalization rate is a function of many risk-related variables:

- The quality and maintainability of future earnings
- Historical and current verbal or written offers for buying or selling stock in the company being valued
- History of trading in stock of the company
- Shareholder buy-sell agreements' definition of value, possibly through a valuation formula
- Tangible asset backing such as real estate, machinery and equipment, patents
- Industry and country economic conditions
- Comparables of public stock and P/E multiples
- Current market for closely-held companies

Assessing these factors is the art of appraising. Each factor can change the risk, which contributes to altering the capitalization rate. An investment such as a Canada bond paying, for example, 2 per cent provides a benchmark as to a risk-free rate of return. This risk-free rate of return defines the capitalization rate for a risk-free investment at 2 per cent. As risk increases due to various factors, the capitalization rate for the business increases as well.

Once the risk factors have been identified, a range of rates of return can be applied by the appraiser. These rates are then converted to their equivalent P/E multiples. An example of a build-up of a capitalization rate follows:

Risk-free rate of return (long term Canada Bonds)	2%
Business risks including quality and maintainability of earnings	5–15%
Industry risk, including volatility of business cycle	5–10%
Rate of return required (2+5+5) to (2+ 15+ 10)	12–27%
P/E multiple (1/0.27 to 1/0.12)	3.7–8.3

REDUNDANT ASSETS

Redundant assets are current and long-term assets such as cash, GICs, and term deposits, which are recorded on the books of the company but are not utilized in its day-to-day operations. Purchasers can withdraw these redundant assets without impairing the operations of the company. Therefore, these assets must be identified and added, net of appropriate income taxes, to the capitalization of earnings value.

For example, if a company is earning $1 million after tax, and a *P/E* multiple of five to six times is used, the capitalization of earnings value is $5 million to $6 million. Assume the same company has $1 million in GICs, which is not needed for working capital or for future capital expenditures. Withdrawing the $1 million from the company results in say $350,000 in income tax and a redundant asset of $650,000, which, added to the earnings value, results in an overall value of ($5 to $6 million + $650,000) $5,650,000 to $6,650,000.

Redundant assets can be hidden through a company debt structure on the balance sheet. For example, a company with no long-term debt but a high asset value would be able to borrow against these assets. As long as the borrowing did not affect the operations or risk of the company, these borrowed assets could be withdrawn.

Privately-held companies generally do not hold major redundant assets, which could disqualify the owner from claiming the $800,000 capital gains exemption on a disposition of their shares.

The capitalization of earnings model is the approach most often used in valuing going concern privately-held companies for ESOP purposes. However, like all valuation models, it has pitfalls for the unwary.

Using a common-sense business analysis of the risks inherent in the target company will help avoid the pitfalls and arrive at a supportable value calculation.

CAPITALIZATION OF EBITDA

Another method, using Earnings Before Interest, Taxes, Depreciation, and Amortization (EBITDA), commonly referred to as the EBITDA model of valuation, is used extensively in mergers and acquisitions. Like any other business valuation model it has its proponents and detractors.

The EBITDA model is made up of three elements:

1. Future maintainable earnings before interest, income taxes, depreciation, and amortization
2. The EBITDA multiple
3. Redundant assets

Normally, to start the calculation of maintainable EBITDA we use the reported earnings before income taxes. To this amount we add interest plus depreciation and amortization. As well, we adjust this amount for any non-recurring revenues and expenses.

The EBITDA multiple is calculated by reviewing various sources of mergers and acquisitions who list the EBITDA multiple (usually expressed as the multiple applied to EBITDA to determine the value of saleable gross business assets) as well as researching specific multiples in public companies in specific industries. The

EBITDA is multiplied by the EBITDA multiple to arrive at a value for the saleable business assets including goodwill. From this value we deduct all short and long-term debt and add redundant assets to arrive at the net value of the business within the company.

For example, Company ABC has maintainable EBITDA of $3,000,000. In its industry, EBITDA multiples are between 4 and 5x. The balance sheet shows short and long-term debt of $2,000,000. In addition, the company has $1,000,000 of marketable securities not needed in the operations.

Fair market value therefore would be $3,000,000 x 4 = $12,000,000 to $3,000,000 x 5 = $15,000,000

for a range of	$12,000,000	to	$15,000,000
Less debt	(2,000,000)		(2,000,000)
Plus redundant assets	1,000,000		1,000,000
	$11,000,000		$14,000,000

Therefore the fair market value range for this business would be between $11,000,000 and $14,000,000. A further calculation of latent taxes payable on a notional sale of the business assets, including redundant assets, by the company would be required to determine the fair market value of the share capital of the company.

CAPITALIZATION OF CASH FLOWS

This method is similar to the capitalization of earnings except in two respects. First, the cash flow method adds back non-cash expenses such as depreciation and amortization charges to arrive at the company's maintainable cash flows. Second, capital expenditures net of their tax shield are subtracted from the maintainable cash flows. Capital expenditures are those estimated capital costs that allow the company to maintain its forecast sales volume, for example, capital acquisition of buildings or machinery and equipment necessary to produce forecast volumes. The tax shield is the tax savings created by the capital cost allowance associated with the estimated capital expenditures.

DISCOUNTED CASH FLOW

The discounted cash flow (DCF) method is used mainly for extractive industries, businesses that have a contractual basis for future sales volumes, or in high-growth industries such as knowledge-based industries. This method calculates the net cash *available* over a finite timeframe (usually three to 10 years) and present values that cash back at a discount rate. For example, an engineering firm has created a new product and estimated sales volume of the new product at approximately $100,000 per year with royalty from the product of 25 per cent after income tax. The company estimates that the royalty will increase by an inflation rate of 6 per cent per annum. The amount of sales for this particular product will last approximately 10 years, generating each year approximately $1 million in sales.

The value using a DCF model would be calculated as follows:

SALES	ROYALTY $	PRESENT VALUE FACTOR AT 10%	PRESENT VALUE FACTOR AT 20%	PRESENT VALUE AT 10%	PRESENT VALUE AT 20%
$100,000	$85,000	.909	.833	$77,265	$70,805
$100,000	$90,100	.826	.694	$74,423	$62,529
$100,000	$95,506	.751	.579	$71,725	$55,298
$100,000	$101,236	.683	.482	$69,144	$48,796
$100,000	$107,311	.621	.402	$66,640	$43,139
$100,000	$113,749	.564	.335	$64,154	$38,106
$100,000	$120,574	.513	.279	$61,854	$33,640
$100,000	$127,806	.467	.233	$59,685	$29,779
$100,000	$135,477	.424	.194	$57,442	$26,283
$100,000	$143,606	.386	.162	$55,432	$23,264
				$657,764	$431,639

Therefore, the value of the royalty would be in the range of $432,000 to $658,000.

ASSET VALUES

The asset-based value approach is used to value holding companies with little active business of their own or when corporate assets do not earn a reasonable rate of return on their capital investment. This can happen when a company is showing a loss or is in a marginally profitable operation. If this situation is expected to continue, an asset-based approach may be appropriate. Under this approach, there are two methods, adjusted asset value and liquidation value.

ADJUSTED ASSET VALUE

Under this method, the company is assumed to be a going concern. However, due to poor earnings or cash flow, its value is related to the potential sale of its net assets (assets minus liabilities).

To calculate value using this approach, each asset and liability is revalued to its fair market value. For assets such as land, buildings, machinery and equipment, one should look to expert appraisers.

Further adjustments to the net assets may arise due to contingent liabilities. Income tax due upon sale of land and depreciable assets is a major contingent cost. These costs include income taxes on capital gains and on recaptured depreciation. The full income tax payable may be used as a deduction from the net asset, or a portion thereof, or no deduction may be used, depending upon the likelihood that the assets will be sold. Other contingencies to be considered include lawsuits, tax reassessments, or warranties.

LIQUIDATION VALUE

The liquidation value method assumes one of two value concepts: either that the company is not a going concern, or that the company is a going concern but has no expectation of future maintainable earnings or cash flow. In either case, the net assets must be valued on their net realizable value. A forced liquidation approach assumes a quick sale, while an orderly liquidation approach assumes a sale over a reasonable period of time, not at rock-bottom prices. The most common approach is an orderly liquidation. However, if there is a severe cash problem or the company cannot continue, a forced approach may be used. In the liquidation approach, all assets are assumed sold and income taxes paid. The result is a company holding only cash assets. At this point, the tax cost to the company to distribute the cash assets out of the corporation must be calculated. The actual deduction can range from nil to the full tax cost. Many appraisers will take the midpoint for fairness to both the buyer and seller's position. Alternatively an appraiser may tailor the amount of the tax cost based on the perceived likelihood of an actual liquidation.

TAX SHIELD

It may be necessary to value depreciable property under the asset-based approach. This occurs because a purchaser buying a depreciable property inside a corporation loses the step up in the cost base out of the depreciable property. Therefore, the tax shield that is lost must be subtracted from the value of the property. This deduction should be made only in situations where the company is a going concern.

RULES OF THUMB

Rules of thumb tend to be used in industries that are service-oriented, and where there are few comparable publicly-held companies. These special industries have, over time, developed rules of thumb for arriving at a company's value. Rules of thumb have several advantages. They can offer a method of comparing intra-industry transactions, price test the marketplace for that industry, give both buyer and seller insight into that industry, and highlight areas that may not have been valued previously. Finally, rules of thumb can test the reasonableness, or lack of same, of each party's value analysis.

Rules of thumb should not be relied upon to the exclusion of proper financial analysis. The industry rule of thumb can be only a benchmark. It is an indication of what the market is likely to do in pricing the business, but if taken out of context, can lead to an extreme mispricing of the business. As well, rules of thumb change with time, and the use of an outdated rule can cause serious pricing problems. Examples of industries with changing rules of thumb include: retailers based on square footage, auto leasing based on number of cars leased at $x per car, cable TV based on number of subscribers, newspapers based on number of subscribers, funeral homes based on annual numbers of funerals, and advertising and insurance agency firms based on gross commissions. The list is endless. Nevertheless rules of thumb in pricing are practical, but *only* if used with extreme caution: the source must be reliable and the data must be current.

CORRELATION OF VALUES

Correlation of values is an important function because different methods use different assumptions. By computing value under several methods, the valuator can assess whether a material error has been made in the assumptions or the calculations. For example, an assessor may calculate the following results:

- capitalization of earnings approach $500,000
- adjusted asset value $250,000
- rule of thumb $1,500,000

Clearly, the valuator would need to do additional work to analyze why the rule of thumb was significantly different from the other approaches.

SANITY TESTS

Sanity tests or smell tests are useful for checking the overall reasonableness of the value. In the end, value is a range that must be based upon sound logic and common business sense. For example, a value for a knowledge-based company in the high-tech field will in many cases exceed its sales revenue. Goodwill values in excess of five years in these areas may also require revaluation.

Current prices being paid for high growth computer companies can be as high as two to eight times annual sales volumes.

Consequently, the valuator must always step back from the calculated value and ask: Is the company truly worth this value, and would I sign a cheque for this amount?

SHAREHOLDERS' AGREEMENTS

A shareholders' agreement is critical to creating liquidity for the employees in an ESOP, and the valuation element is crucial to the success of this document. Generally, there are three common approaches to calculating value for a shareholders' agreement. They are periodic independent valuation, fixed values, and formula.

PERIODIC INDEPENDENT VALUATION

For periodic independent valuation, parties hire an independent *valuator* to calculate the company's value at specific intervals, usually annually. Unfortunately, few business owners take this approach, mainly because of the perceived costs. Advantages of the periodic independent valuation approach are that:

- It is based on the definition of fair market value.
- It is the fairest approach to be utilized by the employees.
- It reduces the possibility of disagreement with tax authorities.

The disadvantages are that:

- It can be costly if the company is changing rapidly from year to year.
- The employees cannot easily calculate the company's value.
- There is no definite value for future funding arrangements.

FIXED VALUE

The shareholders themselves fix a value periodically, usually annually. Shareholders meet once a year and agree to the value of the company. This is formalized by signing a schedule to the agreement with the appropriate value indicated. For an ESOP, the shareholders would be the original founding owners. The advantages of using fixed value are:

- Simplicity
- Certainty of value
- Provision of value for funding

  The disadvantages are:

- Tax authorities may disagree
- May not be fair to the employees
- Needs to be updated regularly, which unfortunately, is after the first few years
- Potential source of shareholder disagreement (the value selected may be arbitrary)

FORMULA

The original shareholders define a formula that is used to value the shares annually. For example, the book value or multiple of earnings may be used as a value. The advantages are:

- No need for outside review
- Less expensive
- Can be calculated in advance by employees

  The disadvantages are:

- Tax authorities may disagree
- Can be unfair to the current shareholding group or to future employees
- Does not reflect changing business conditions

VALUATION ISSUES IN A SHAREHOLDERS' AGREEMENT

TRANSACTION VALUE

The original shareholders provide for a shotgun clause (put call) or right of first refusal within the agreement. Generally, these approaches always favour the stronger shareholder and may not be fair to the employees who are in the minority position.

VALUATION DATE

The date of the valuation can be based on either the latest annual valuation or an interim valuation based on the latest quarter.

MINORITY SHAREHOLDER

How will minority shares be treated upon an employee's exit? Will the value of the shares be calculated by *pro rata en bloc* value or using a minority discount? A decision must also be made as to whether the minority discount will be in place if there is an actual third-party buyout.

INCOME TAXES

A shareholders' agreement should address whether there should be full or partial calculation of contingent taxes.

GOODWILL

Goodwill should be discussed in terms of calculations based on certain circumstances, such as retirement. The shareholders' agreement should indicate if there is to be no goodwill calculation. And the definition of goodwill value should be clearly stated, whether fair market value, or fair value, or fair price.

SPECIAL VALUATION ISSUES FOR ESOPS

One of the most pressing problems for business owners is finding a way to liquidate their equity in a business to provide cash for retirement or other purposes. However, their decision to sell is often more than an economic one. A founding owner develops a strong feeling of identity with the company and a strong sense of loyalty to the employees. In many cases, the owner would like the employees to have a role in the business through an ESOP.

- Will the sale to arm's length employees be at fair market value or below fair market value? Either may give rise to personal income tax consequences.
- Will the sale to non-arm's-length employees come under the Canada Revenue Agency's scrutiny?
- Will the valuation be performed by an independent party knowledgeable in business appraisals so as to create the level of trust with the employees that is critical to the success of the ESOP?
- If additional debt is being acquired by the company to leverage a sale to the employees, what is the impact of this additional debt on the value of the company?
- What minority discount will apply to ESOP shares, and what are the terms and conditions in the buy-sell agreement that will relate to that minority discount?

MAXIMIZING SHAREHOLDER VALUE

All business people know how to package, market, and sell their products and services. Few, however, know how to package, market, and sell their company. This is critical for the ESOP because the employees need a liquidity event to generate the wealth in their investment in the company. Employees need to know how to increase the company's value so the company and its stakeholders will succeed. The following issues should be evaluated in readying a company for sale.

IMPROVING FINANCIAL POSITION

Before selling a company, financial preparatory work is essential. However, personal tax-planning needs must be considered before implementing any of the actions suggested in the following paragraphs.

BALANCE SHEET

Up to two years prior to selling, any weaknesses inherent in the company's balance sheet should be addressed. A company's value can be enhanced through improving the strength of its balance sheet. Detailed ratio analysis comparing industry norms to company norms and identifying areas for improvement should be made. In addition, improving liquidity ratios by reducing outstanding accounts receivable improve the company's balance sheet. A liquidity ratio defines the company's cash flow and determines whether the company has sufficient short-term cash flow to be able to continue operations and provide for expansion. The company should remove all non-operating assets through a tax advantage basis, for example, term deposits. Any non-operating loans that are within the company should be reduced if possible. If the company intends to acquire new technology to create production efficiencies, this should be done before the company is put up for sale. Any contingent liabilities such as lawsuits or past tax issues should be cleared up. Inventory costing, which can impact the profitability of the company, should be stabilized for a number of years.

EARNINGS STATEMENT

The earnings statement can be improved in several areas, which will help the company in terms of its value and in terms of its saleability. Again, a ratio analysis to compare company results and industry norms will identify areas of weakness. The company should reduce non-operating and non-recurring expenses and keep them to a minimum. In addition, the company should start reducing payments to any family and spouses who are not involved in the company. This should be done in any event once an ESOP plan is put into place. The company should reduce excessive interest costs by a commitment to reduce loans outstanding. If there are long-term leases coming due and the company is dependent on its location, these long-term leases should be taken care of. Any bad debts that have been accrued due to improper credit controls should be corrected.

ADMINISTRATION

It is very important that the company have its financial records reviewed on a regular basis. Being able to provide monthly financial statements indicates to potential buyers that the company had its books in order. Any banking relationships that are not sound should be made so as soon as possible, and the company must ensure that its year-end financials are available within a reasonable time period (preferably within six weeks of the year-end).

STRENGTHEN KEY MANAGEMENT

One of the key value components of any company is its management team. When calculating the company's value, buyers will always consider the management team of the company and how long that management team has been with the company. Management positions should have trained backup personnel for all key areas in sales production and finance. The company should also put into place a comprehensive compensation package to reward high-achieving key persons. An outside consultant can help with these training and compensation issues. Creating a board of directors with outside expertise can be very valuable in identifying potential purchasers. Buyers are comforted by the knowledge that the company has an experienced board of directors.

REDUCE INDUSTRY AND COMPANY RISK

There are many ways to reduce industry and company risk. The company should identify its key products and services and assess their long-term potential. In terms of the market curve, are corporate products and services at the beginning of that curve or at the end, and should new products be introduced? The company should plan for the introduction of any new products and services so that the process is underway. Increasing sales to a wider variety of customers will increase a company's value. If a company sells 90 per cent of its *sales* or services to a single customer, the company's value is reduced because the loss of that single customer would be catastrophic. The company should also ensure that it has at least two or three key suppliers for each major raw material required and that several sub-contractor groups are used. The company should identify all other key dependencies including, for example, key pieces of equipment.

CONVERT PERSONAL GOODWILL INTO COMMERCIAL GOODWILL

As we have said, commercial goodwill has value while personal goodwill does not. Therefore, the company should ensure that long-term contracts with customers or suppliers are in place. Any patents or trademarked products or services that have not yet been marketed should be, to give substance and increase value. Any brand products or services in the marketplace should be identified, and key management must be under contract.

SELLING CYCLE

There is a time to sell every business. Having one's house in order does not mean that value will be maximized; the best time to sell is usually when mergers and acquisitions of large companies are in an upswing. Another good signal to sell is a strong stock market, especially for small capitalization companies, which are valued at less than $250 million. Another good time to sell is after the economy has been growing for several years following a down-turn; this tends to create the desire for acquisitions. Lastly, when market activity for small and medium-size companies is strong, demand will tend to increase a company's value.

TAX PLANNING

Because of the high income taxes in Canada it is critical to have proper tax planning before any efforts are made to increase the value of the company. Therefore, some of the following steps should be considered. The company should ensure that it is a qualified small business and that it is eligible for the $800,000 capital gains exemption. At the same time, it should merge or consolidate subsidiaries to help create a sale situation that allows a consolidated view of the company for potential purchasers.

CONCLUSION

Good business appraisals reflect sound valuation techniques as well as good common business sense. Someone once said that the only problem with common sense is that it is not too common. This chapter has given the reader an overview of the valuation techniques involved in ESOPs. The application of common sense is up to the reader. Once the business valuation issue has been resolved, the next key technical area is income tax, the subject of the next chapter.

CHAPTER 6
ESOPS AND INCOME TAX

People try to live within their incomes so they can afford to pay taxes to a government that can't live within its income.

– Anon

Income taxes are critically important in Canada, and any ESOP plan, whether an equity plan, option plan, or equity value plan, must be tax-effective for employees, owners, and future shareholders. The design parameters of the ESOP will, therefore, impose certain income tax implications for the plan participants. Likewise, specific tax laws can influence decisions on the design and structure of an ESOP. This chapter discusses Canadian income tax implications including:

- Types of participation
- Methods of ownership
- Financing
- Taxation of dividends
- Treatment of capital gains and losses
- Disposition of shares
- Going public
- Corporate deductions for ESOPs
- Canadian Controlled Private Corporation (CCPC) status
- Small Business Corporation (SBC) status
- Salary deferral arrangements

ESOP MYTH   Only U.S. ESOPs have tax advantages for employees. Canadian income tax rules are not friendly to ESOPs.

ESOP FACT   The U.S. does have many tax advantages for both the owners and the employees; however, in Canada, there are several very material and effective tax-saving vehicles for employees owning shares in their own company.

---

1. Types of Participation

As stated in earlier chapters, there are three common types of employee participation in an ESOP: stock purchases (share equity), stock options, and equity value units. In addition, share appreciation rights (SARs) and restricted stock shares or units are less frequently used forms of participation. An ESOP may involve one type of participation exclusively or a combination. For example, a combination of stock purchase and stock options is often used to ensure that the employees both have invested their own funds and also have an additional incentive at no additional cost through the stock options.

2. Methods of Ownership

There are three possible methods of ownership of ESOP shares. They are direct personal ownership, ownership through Registered Retirement Savings Plans (RRSPs)/Tax Free Savings Accounts (TFSAs) and ownership through a holding company. There are a number of factors that affect the method of ownership.

3. Financing

There are eight different methods that can be utilized for employees to finance their participation in the ESOP. The overriding factor however is that the ESOP must be easy to finance by the employees so that they can participate. In addition, terms attached to the financing can make it easier or harder for the employees to buy in. We have had clients who wanted to virtually give the shares to employees without cost. Most owners however believe, as we do, that an important element of the ESOP is that employees have some "skin in the game."

4. Taxation of Dividends

Depending upon the specifics of the plan, dividends (or in the case of equity units, unit distributions) may be payable upon certain types of shares offered to employees. Dividends will come from several sources. If an employee has direct ownership of the shares, any dividends declared on that class of shares will be paid to that employee based on the percentage of shares that he or she owns. If the employee had purchased the shares through an RRSP/TFSA, dividends would be credited to the RRSP/TFSA account.

5. Treatment of Capital Gains and Losses

One of the key benefits of owning shares in a company is the ability to generate gains that would be taxed as capital gains rather than as income, income tax rates on personal income being much higher than capital gains rates. The rules and regulations, however, are very specific in this area and require that the plan achieve the best after-tax effects for the employee.

6. Disposition of Shares

The employee will want to dispose of his or her shares. It is at this liquidity event where the employee can increase their wealth. There are several ways in which shares can be disposed of. The company can be bought out by a third party, in which case the employee would then share in any gain on the sale to that third party. The company itself could buy back the shares from the employee, thus triggering certain income taxes, which will be discussed later. Another option that many companies take is to go public or to start an initial public offering (IPO). In this case, shares held by employees have certain restrictions on them that will allow employees to maximize their after-tax benefits.

7. Going Public

A company that goes public is by definition no longer a Canadian Controlled Private Corporation (CCPC). Therefore, steps must be taken to minimize the tax impact on employees.

8. Corporate Deductions for ESOPs

There is limited income tax applicability for ESOPs in Canada as has been described earlier, but there are some tax implications that will be discussed in a more general format.

9. Small Business Corporation (SBC)

The Income Tax Act defines a small business corporation as a Canadian controlled private corporation (CCPC), in which all or substantially all of the fair market value of the assets are used principally in an active business carried on primarily in Canada. The assets may include shares or debt of one or more small business corporations that are connected with the corporation.

10. Canadian Controlled Private Corporation (CCPC) Status

The CCPC status is very important so the employees can achieve the tremendous tax advantages that still exist under the *Income Tax Act*. Again, the plan must be put together properly so as to achieve these results.

11. Salary Deferral Arrangement

In any ESOP arrangement it is necessary to ensure that the plan does not qualify as a salary deferral arrangement (SDA), which will result in unanticipated tax consequences. An SDA is an arrangement where an employee has a right to receive an amount of salary after one year. The main purpose of the arrangement is to postpone tax otherwise payable on salary in the year or previous year. But there are certain statutory exemptions to SDAs.

The chapter will now discuss, in more detail, the income tax implications when a plan is put into place.

TYPES OF PARTICIPATION

STOCK PURCHASE

In a stock purchase-type of ESOP, employees may purchase shares from either the company treasury or from the owners. The major difference between these types of acquisitions is that when an employee purchases shares from the treasury, the number of shares in the company increase and, therefore, the existing shareholders are diluted. When shares are purchased from the current owners, those owners, rather than the company, receive the funds. The maximum number of shares that each eligible employee can acquire is usually determined by a formula developed for the plan. For a cash purchase from treasury, the employee would pay the employer anywhere from zero to fair market value on the specified acquisition date for the shares. This amount will become the employee's adjusted cost base (ACB) of the shares used by the Canada Revenue Agency (CRA) to calculate any capital gains that the employee may have to pay in future. When employees purchase shares from the owner, the ACB will be the paid-up capital (PUC) of those shares. In most privately-held companies, the PUC is nominal.

If the CRA decided that the fair market value at the time of acquisition was actually higher than the subscription price (the price paid by the employee), the difference between the two would be considered an employment stock option benefit. The section of this chapter on the employment benefit deals with the taxation of this benefit.

STOCK OPTIONS

The granting of options to an employee has no immediate tax consequences for the employee as long as the company is a small business corporation (SBC), but the terms of the options granted will have future tax consequences. The employee may be entitled to deductions of 50 per cent of any employment benefit realized.

To qualify for this deduction, the employer must be a qualified SBC and the employee must deal at arm's length after the option is granted. Also, the employee must hold onto the shares for two years, although an exception is made when there is a deemed disposition on death. If qualifying employees of an SBC do not hold their shares for the two-year period, they will not be entitled to the deduction. If an SBC employer goes public or sells out to a non-resident, the deferred employment benefits do not immediately become taxable because it is the corporation's status at the time the option is granted that is relevant for taxation purposes.

EMPLOYMENT BENEFIT

When the fair market value is greater than the amount paid for the shares under the option, the difference is considered a benefit by virtue of employment and, therefore, is taxed in the same manner as salary, wages, or other remuneration in the taxation year in which the option is exercised. However, for the shares of a small business corporation, the benefit and resulting employment income is deferred until the employee disposes of the shares. Transfer of the shares to a registered retirement savings plan (RRSP) is considered a sale for taxation purposes. This issue is discussed in "Ownership through RRSPs."

CAPITAL GAINS EXEMPTION

An employee might want to exercise the option to obtain ownership of the shares, even if an immediate sale is not planned. For example, due to the restrictions inherent in an Initial Public Offering (lPO), it may not be possible to sell the shares right away. Also, in order to obtain the $800,000 lifetime capital gains exemption on a capital gain resulting from a sale of the shares, the employee must hold them for at least two years. Therefore, the employee might wish to obtain current ownership of the shares to be able to use the exemption on a future sale. In addition, current ownership may be desirable for tax planning purposes in the event that the employer were to become a public company or cease to be a small business corporation (SBC). Where the employer is paying dividends on the class of shares, the employee might wish to exercise the options in order to be able to receive dividends. However, not all companies will pay dividends, as the equity may be required for the growth of the business.

EQUITY VALUE PLANS

Equity value plans do not involve issuing any shares to employees. Rather, equity value plans involve payments to employees by the employer that are tied to share value appreciation and any dividends that would have been paid on shares issued. In a typical equity value plan, an employee is granted a number of units in the company. After a set period of time, the employee may dispose of these units. On such a disposition, an amount is paid by the employer to the employee equal to any increase in the fair market value of the units over the holding period.

As an equity value plan does not involve an agreement to sell or issue shares, the stock option provisions do not apply. In addition, the payment by the employer for the fair market value increase in the units would be taxable to the employee as employment income, not as a capital gain or as a dividend. The employer would get a deduction for the amount of the payment made to the employee under the equity value plan.

SHARE APPRECIATION RIGHTS

Share appreciation rights (SARs) are a variation on the equity value plan concept but tied to stock options as opposed to notional shares. With SARs, the employee obtains the benefits of a stock option without exercising the option. The employee has the option of exercising either the share appreciation rights or the underlying stock option. For example, if an employee had a share appreciation right, and the stock increased in value, the employee can notify the company that he or she is exercising the stock appreciation right and get the benefit or the increase of the value rather than going through the stock option methodology. Most SARs are used in public companies or in larger private companies. If the share appreciation rights are exercised, the employee receives a cash payment from the employer in the amount of the difference between the fair market value of the stock and the option price.

From the employee's perspective the payment is treated as a stock option benefit. The employee may also be eligible for the 50 per cent deduction, provided the conditions for qualification are met. For SARs to be workable, there must be a method to quickly turn them into cash, which is why SARs are suitable mainly in public companies that can be traded on the stock market.

METHODS OF OWNERSHIP

DIRECT PERSONAL OWNERSHIP

There are a number of reasons why employees might consider direct ownership of ESOP shares rather than holding them through an RRSP/TFSA. If funds from dividends or the sale of the shares will be required for personal use, direct personal ownership would be the appropriate alternative. The $800,000 capital gains exemption is available only with personal ownership. Thus, if the company qualifies for the exemption, personal ownership may be advisable. The preferential tax treatment on capital gains (50 per cent inclusion rate) and capital dividends are lost where shares are held through the employee's RRSP, as all amounts are fully taxable when withdrawing from the RRSP. A TFSA on the other hand has no income taxes assessed on withdrawals, neither on capital gains nor dividends/interest.

OWNERSHIP THROUGH RRSPS

If funds derived from the ESOP shares are intended for retirement and are not currently needed, an employee may wish to consider holding ESOP shares in an RRSP. This would defer the tax on any dividends or capital gains until such time as funds are withdrawn from the RRSP. An eligible employee can establish a self-directed RRSP to hold the ESOP shares at certain financial institutions. An employee who wishes to own his or her ESOP shares in an RRSP must put them into a self-directed plan.

QUALIFIED INVESTMENTS

If the employer is a Canadian public corporation it is likely that the shares will be qualified for an RRSP. There are additional restrictions on investments in CCPCs by an RRSP. The regulations to the act allow an RRSP to purchase shares of an eligible corporation including those that meet the same test as for a small business corporation (SBC), as long as the annuitant under the RRSP is not related to the corporation and holds (including shares held by non-arm's length persons) less than 10 per cent of any class of shares of the company. If the employee, owning the RRSP and other non-arm's length persons are to own 10 per cent or more of any class of shares of the company, the cost of the investment by the RRSP must be less than $25,000. The SBC test must be met either at the time the RRSP makes the share investment or at the prior fiscal year end of the company. Employees who will own less than 10 per cent of any class of shares and are purchasing their shares for cash may wish to consider using their RRSP to make the investment, if they have available contribution limits or funds available in their RRSP.

TRANSFER OF SHARES TO AN RRSP

Contributions to an RRSP may be in cash or in kind, and there is nothing to stop employees from holding ESOP shares in their RRSP. Provided the shares are a qualified investment for an RRSP as described above, a tax deduction may be claimed for the fair market value of the shares contributed, subject to the normal contribution limits. This assumes that the RRSP does not pay for the shares out of cash already in the RRSP but that the shares are a contribution to the RRSP. In considering whether or not the ESOP investment should be made through an RRSP, the employee should consider all aspects of personal financial planning, including the overall asset mix of the RRSP.

OWNERSHIP THROUGH A TFSA

The same rules that apply above to the RRSP apply to the ownership of shares in a TFSA. However the big difference between a TSFA and an RRSP is that all funds withdrawn from the TFSA are tax-free, while funds withdrawn from the RRSP go into a person's general income account to be taxed at full rates. In addition, the TFSA funds itself with after-tax income, while the RRSP funds itself with pre-tax income.

OWNERSHIP THROUGH A HOLDING COMPANY

It is possible for employees to own ESOP shares through a holding company. There are a number of disadvantages to holding the shares through a holding company. The capital gains exemption is available only to individuals and when the shares are to be sold, the holding company, rather than the employee, would be selling the shares. If the employer company is a qualifying SBC at the time of sale, the benefit of the exemption would be lost unless the employee is able to sell the holding company shares. In addition, the holding company would itself have to be a qualifying SBC and connected with the employer. Thus, a holding company would be a viable alternative in only limited circumstances for significant minority or majority shareholders, for income tax and/or estate planning purposes.

STRATEGIES FOR THE CAPITAL GAINS EXEMPTION

There are difficulties in determining whether or not the shares should be held in the employee's RRSP when the shares could also be eligible for the $800,000 lifetime capital gains exemption. For example, assume an employee has acquired 5,000 shares at $1.00 per share (current fair market value), under a share purchase ESOP. The employee then contributes the shares to his or her RRSP. The shares would have an ACB to the employee and a fair market value of $5,000. Thus, there would be no capital gain or loss on the transfer, and the employee would get an RRSP deduction of $5,000 but would use up $5,000 of the employee's RRSP contribution limit. If the RRSP later sells the shares for $100,000, the gain of $95,000 would be sheltered. This gain would not be eligible for the capital gains exemption because the RRSP, not the employee, sold the shares. On retirement, the withdrawal of the $100,000 would be fully taxable.

In the opposite scenario, assume that the employee did not initially contribute the shares to the RRSP. Two years after acquisition, the shares have a fair market value of $2.00 per share or $10,000 in total and are eligible for the capital gains exemption. If the employee were now to contribute the shares to the RRSP, there would be a capital gain of $5,000 ($10,000 fair market value minus $5,000 ACB) which would be offset by the capital gains exemption. The employee would have an RRSP deduction of $10,000 and use up $10,000 of his or her RRSP contribution limit. If the RRSP later sells the shares for $100,000, the gain of $90,000 would be sheltered. This gain would not be eligible for the capital gains exemption because the RRSP, not the individual, sold the shares. On retirement, the withdrawal of the $100,000 would again be fully taxable. Thus the only advantage in waiting the two years to contribute the shares to the RRSP is to use the capital gains exemption to increase the amount of RRSP contribution if the employee does not wish to use other funds to contribute to the RRSP. The employee has effectively utilized the capital gains exemption to shelter the capital gain which allows for the higher RRSP contribution. If the value increases significantly during the two-year period, the employee may have insufficient RRSP contribution room to contribute all the shares.

FINANCING

BORROWING

If an employee borrows to buy ESOP shares, interest on the borrowing is generally tax-deductible as long as the shares are held personally. However, interest on money borrowed to make an RRSP contribution is non-deductible.

SHARES IN LIEU OF BONUSES

Some ESOPs are structured to allow employees to receive their shares in lieu of bonuses. It is essential that these bonuses not be considered merely an indirect payment of employment income known as "constructively received." Constructive receipt is considered to occur in situations where the employee has an absolute right to a payment or an amount is credited to an employee's account, set apart for the employee, or otherwise made available to the employee. The decision by the employee to receive shares in lieu of bonus must be made by the employee prior to the bonus being determined and declared by the employer to avoid the application of constructive receipt. The employee must not have an absolute right to the bonus or have the bonus determined and available for his or her use.

Companies use different methodologies for their bonus plans; each situation should be reviewed independently to ensure there is not constructive receipt of the bonus. Consideration could be given to the employees deciding to accept shares in lieu of bonus prior to the beginning of the year where the bonus is earned.

Should the bonus entitlement being used for shares be insufficient to cover the acquisition value of the shares, the employee would be required to fund the difference in cash. This financing option allows an arm's length employee of the small business corporation to defer tax that would otherwise be payable on a cash bonus. As mentioned previously, employers are not entitled to a deduction for the value of the shares issued, but they would have been entitled to a deduction for the payment of a cash bonus.

The receipt of shares in lieu of a bonus is taxed as a stock option with cliff vesting and with a zero exercise price. The section of this chapter on employment benefit deals with this issue.

RRSPS

As discussed, an employee's RRSP/TFSA can be used to finance his or her ESOP shares. Funds available in the RRSP/TFSA can be utilized to acquire the shares under a share purchase ESOP, assuming that the shares otherwise qualify.

TAXATION OF DIVIDENDS

DIRECT OWNERSHIP

Dividends received on ESOP shares held personally will be included in investment income of the employee. These dividends would be taxed under the normal gross-up and dividend tax credit rules paid by any Canadian private or public company. The maximum marginal tax rate on taxable dividends will vary depending upon the employee's province of residence.

RRSP/TFSA

Dividends received in an RRSP are taxable as ordinary income only when funds are withdrawn. The maximum marginal tax rate on ordinary income will vary depending upon the employee's province of residence. In a TFSA dividends are tax-free.

TREATMENT OF CAPITAL GAINS AND LOSSES

Where shares are held personally, 50 per cent of any taxable capital gain is included in computing the individual's income for tax purposes. The $800,000 lifetime capital gains exemption on gains realized from the sale of qualifying SBC shares may be available to offset gains. Employees who have not fully used this exemption in the past should be aware of the following points:

- The exemption is available only for shares owned by individuals, not shares held in RRSPs.
- If the company eventually repurchases shares under buy-back provisions of an ESOP, any gain will likely be taxed primarily as a deemed dividend, not as a capital gain, and thus the exemption would not be available. A capital loss is also usually realized.
- If someone other than the company purchases employee shares, the exemption may be available if the company is a qualified SBC at the time of sale.
- The use of the exemption may cause the employee to have alternative minimum tax. Minimum tax is a calculation required by the Canada Revenue Agency to ensure that Canadians pay a minimum level of tax.
- If the employee has a cumulative net investment loss or has made previous claims for allowable business investment losses, the full exemption may not be available. A cumulative net investment loss is the result of past year investment losses which exceed investment income.
- The definition of a qualified SBC share is quite complex, but in essence a SBC share is a CCPC that meets three tests:
  - The shareholder has held the shares for at least 24 months prior to the sale.
  - The company meets a 50 per cent active business asset test (on a fair market value basis) throughout the 24 months prior to sale; and the active business is carried out primarily in Canada.

- The company meets a 90 per cent active business asset test (on a fair market value basis) at the time of sale.

Full review of the capital gains exemption rules is beyond the scope of this publication. Owners of companies are encouraged to consult their tax accountants to see whether they qualify under these rules.

Shares held personally can benefit from the capital gains exemption, but shares held in an RRSP do not qualify for the exemption. Although any capital gain realized in an RRSP is not taxable, this is only a deferral, not an exemption, as funds are fully taxable when withdrawn from the RRSP. One hundred per cent of the gain is included in the income versus 50 per cent if the shares are held outside the RRSP.

DISPOSITION OF SHARES

SALE

On a sale of the ESOP shares to anyone other than the company, an employee will generally realize a capital gain or loss. A gain will arise if the sale proceeds exceed the cost of the shares plus any costs of disposal. A loss will be realized if the sale of proceeds is less than the cost of the shares plus any costs of disposal. In some cases, such as a transfer of shares to an RRSP, any loss will be denied. Any employment benefit not taxed at the time a stock option is exercised will be recognized at the time of sale, as indicated above.

BUYBACK OF SHARES

There may be circumstances defined in an ESOP in which an employee may be required to sell his or her shares back to the company. In these buy-back circumstances, the employee will be considered for tax purposes to have received the dividend equal to the difference between the proceeds and the paid-up capital (PUC) of the shares. This is why it is important to know the PUC of the shares. Capital gain or loss would also be realized, equal to the difference between the ACB and the PUC of the shares. The dividend and any capital gain will be subject to tax. A capital loss will be deductible only against capital gains from other sources, unless the company is an SBC at the time of the buy back. This could result in current income for tax purposes and a capital loss carryover even though no economic gain has occurred. If the company is a SBC at the time of buy back, the loss may qualify as an allowable business investment loss (ABIL) and, as such, a portion of the loss may be deductible from income from all sources. Prior use of the capital gains exemption reduces the ability to claim the ABIL treatment. The PUC of a share is the average of the total PUC of all the shares of the particular class. Shares acquired in lieu of bonus entitlements will not result in any additions to the total PUC of the shares, as described above. PUC additions on shares acquired under stock options may be less than the ACB of the shares so acquired. Consequently, the ACB of an employee's shares will be in excess of the PUC thereof. Thus, employees may realize a dividend and a capital loss under the buy-back provisions of the ESOP.

For example, assume an employee paid $1.00 per share, the PUC is 1 cent per share, and the shares are bought back for $1.50 per share. The employee would have a deemed dividend of $1.49 per share which would be included in income. The employee would also have a capital loss of $0.99 per share, which would be deductible only against capital gains from other sources, unless the company is an SBC at the time of the buyback. Assuming the employee cannot currently use the capital loss, tax would be paid on the deemed dividend. Any capital loss would be carried forward and would be available to offset capital gains.

This result could be avoided if the company deemed it appropriate to have the employee sell the shares to another employee as opposed to back to the company. The first alternative results in tax savings on the proceeds. Generally, the employee is significantly better off if the shares are sold to another employee rather than bought back. Savings would be even greater if the shares were eligible for the capital gains exemption. In order to avoid adverse tax consequences, consideration could be given to having a separate company or a holding company that would purchase ESOP shares from employees, rather than having the employer buy back the shares. Reselling them to employees entering the plan can effectively act as a clearing house for ESOP shares.

Consideration could also be given to using a class of shares separate from that of the original owners for the ESOP. This would avoid some of the PUC averaging concerns, particularly where the principal owners have a large number of shares issued for a nominal amount. The principal owners would have a class of shares with high fair market value and nominal PUC, whereas the ESOP participants would have a second class of shares with a lower value and a comparatively high PUC. In considering this type of structure, the related legal and business issues should be evaluated. This approach would require careful communication to employees, explaining why they are receiving another class of shares.

GOING PUBLIC

Some ESOPs are started in private companies that later go public and, by definition, are no longer CCPCs. As such, gains on shares realized after going public would not be eligible for the $800,000 capital gains exemption. The act contains special provisions that would allow the employee to elect to recognize some or all of the gains realized up to the date of the IPO.

The election is available where an individual owns shares of an SBC that becomes a public company listed on a prescribed stock exchange. The shares are deemed disposed of for proceeds of disposition at the amount the shareholder elects. This elected amount can be anywhere between the ACB and the fair market value of the shares. Thus, the amount of gain realized can be fixed so as to only utilize the amount of capital gains exemption available. This deemed disposition will not trigger the recognition of any deferred stock option benefit. The shareholder is deemed to have re-acquired the shares at the elected amount. Thus, the gain realized is effectively added to the ACB of the shares for tax purposes. This means that the employee has been able to boost the

ACB of his or her stock, reducing the amount of taxes that he or she would normally pay.

CORPORATE DEDUCTIONS FOR ESOPS

In general, where a corporation has granted stock options to employees, there is no deduction for the employer for the benefit realized by the employee.

CANADIAN CONTROLLED PRIVATE CORPORATION STATUS

In order to meet the definition of CCPC, the company must qualify as a private company under the relevant securities legislation. For example, under the *Ontario Securities Act,* the company's articles must restrict the number of shareholders to 50 exclusive of current employees and former employees who were shareholders while employed by the company and continue to be so. The articles must also contain the standard clause prohibiting sale of the shares to the public.

A company may also be designated a public company where:

- A class of the corporation shares is qualified for distribution to the public.
- There are no fewer than 150 shareholders of any equity shares class, and 300 shareholders in any other class.
- Insiders hold not more than 80 per cent of the issue of outstanding shares of that class.

A CCPC status is required for both the deferral of stock option benefits and the capital gains exemption, so the factors listed must be taken into account to ensure CCPC status is maintained.

SALARY DEFERRAL ARRANGEMENTS

As stated previously, in any ESOP it is necessary to ensure that the plan does not qualify as a salary deferral arrangement (SDA). An SDA is a plan where an employee has a right to receive an amount of salary after the year is complete. One of the main purposes of the arrangement is to postpone tax otherwise payable. There are certain statutory exceptions to SDAs.

An equity unit plan might be considered an SDA, which would cause negative tax consequences to the employees. However, a prescribed plan or arrangement is exempt from SDA treatment. The requirements of a prescribed plan or arrangement are beyond the scope of this book. However, it is important to note that the SDA must be taken into account when setting up the plan so as to prevent negative tax consequences to both the employees and the employer. The best way to do this is to consult qualified tax counsel when putting the plan into place.

CONCLUSION

ESOPs are an integral component of compensation for employees in all types of industries in Canada. The income tax issues discussed above provide a general analysis of many of the key factors. These should be reviewed in depth when designing and structuring an ESOP. It is very important to the success of the plan that all tax factors are reviewed and researched thoroughly because the impact that income taxes have on the company, its value, and the ability of employees to create wealth is enormous. Key elements that have to be addressed in any kind of tax analysis are the tax positions of the various stakeholders, the current ownership group, the employees, and the company. It is important to know if any restructuring has to take place in any one of these groups to be able to create a proper tax plan. Another issue that has to be clarified is whether or not the company shares qualify for capital gains treatment as this has a major impact on the employees' wealth creation. To address all these issues it is important that the best tax advice be obtained. In the end, however, no investment should be undertaken solely for tax purposes.

Since one of the goals of all ESOPs is to increase the wealth of each employee, it is important that the employees understand that the best tax planning must, of course, be based on what optimizes the company's business and related value. Consequently, some of the tax planning techniques discussed in this chapter may not be available in a particular situation due to the business considerations. In terms of an investment vehicle, investing in their own company has advantages over alternative forms of investment, not the least of which is the power to influence the growth in value. The next chapter discusses the legal issues involved in designing an ESOP.

CHAPTER 7
ESOP LEGAL REQUIREMENTS

*The minute you read something that you can't understand,
you can almost be sure that it was drawn up by a lawyer.*

– Will Rogers

Legal requirements of an ESOP, whether a share equity, stock option, or equity value plan, are complex and detailed. Each ESOP has its own format and requires its own set of legal considerations both during the pre-ESOP stage and the post-ESOP stage. This chapter provides an overview of the types of plans and the legal issues that will arise depending upon each plan's unique objectives.

DIFFERENT OBJECTIVES—DIFFERENT LEGAL IMPLICATIONS

Each corporation has different objectives in its ESOP, thereby ensuring that no two ESOPs will be exactly alike. For example, each corporation may be in a different stage of development, or more likely, the corporate cultures will vary significantly.

ESOP MYTH	The only ESOPs in Canada are stock option plans.
ESOP FACT	This myth is prevalent among legal professionals, but the hundreds of successful ESOPs in Canada that are not solely stock option plans attest to the falsehood of this myth.

FEDERAL AND PROVINCIAL GOVERNMENTS

Federal and provincial governments provide very few tax incentives for ESOPs. Although there is some limited provincial ESOP legislation, federally there is no legally mandated format for ESOPs. This lack of interest by the federal government has a positive side; Canadian companies are free to devise ESOPs to meet their particular needs and objectives through different legal entities without bureaucratic interference. Examples of these differences follow.

PRIVATE CORPORATION

Perhaps a private corporation wishes to create an ESOP based on a share purchase plan, but has no intention of going public. The plan is to offer stock options to only a handful of key employees. In addition, the corporation is seeking to finance growth by encouraging employees to purchase corporation shares through the ESOP. Note that both plans will increase the number of shareholders. If the corporation intends to remain a private corporation, consideration must be given to the impact of the increase in shareholders in light of securities legislation. For example, shares purchased by the employees, if the shares come out of treasury stock, will mean the number of shares held by the previous shareholders will be reduced as a percentage of the overall number of issued shares, or "diluted." Every share taken up by the option holders will also have the dilution effect on the existing shareholders. Securities legislation requires, under certain circumstances, depending upon the percentage of dilution, the approval of existing shareholders. Also consider that should a corporation sell shares to more than 50 outside shareholders (i.e. non-employees), it is not longer considered a "private issuer," and therefore, must produce a prospectus. Employees are not counted in determining the 50; however, if the corporation does find itself with 50 non-employee shareholders, it may be a costly exercise to implement an ESOP when a prospectus is required under securities legislation.

PUBLIC CORPORATION

In another scenario, assume a public corporation offers both its key employees and all its employees a broad-based stock option program as a non-cash financial reward for outstanding performance and loyalty to the corporation. In this case, perhaps, the focus of the ESOP would be strengthening communication between the corporation and its workers for the purpose of boosting motivation and enhancing productivity by offering employees a part of the corporation's success. This type of incentive-oriented plan represents the most common ESOP offered by larger Canadian employers. The issuer in this kind of plan may have to meet disclosure requirements, or may be exempt. Moreover, because the corporation is publicly traded, the requirements of securities legislation and the rules of the listing stock exchange must also be taken into consideration, both during the set-up and in the subsequent operation of the stock option plans.

PRIVATE GOING PUBLIC

Consider now a corporation seeking to establish an ESOP as a first step in a complex restructuring program. One possible example is a small, private enterprise that has decided to change its corporate status by making an initial public offering ("IPO"). The purpose of the proposed ESOP is to provide an injection of capital to cover the cost associated with the ESOP. In addition, the corporation hopes to set up a plan that will be attractive to its employees so that they may benefit from the corporation moving from a private corporation to public corporation status. This change in status would require the corporation to address a host of legal issues in establishing the share purchase plans. One major issue to be addressed is the number of share options or stock options that are given to employees one year prior to the IPO. Stock exchanges limit the amount of stock that can be issued during this period. Another major example would be the amount or the price paid for the shares or for the options by the employees in that period prior to the IPO. There are tremendous implications to the corporation and to the employees if the securities regulator deems that the shares were offered at below fair market value to the employees.

EMPLOYEE BUYOUT

The last scenario is an employee buyout of the corporation, one that is much less common during periods of economic growth. This scenario usually occurs when the owner or owners have decided to transition out of their majority position and do not want to sell to a third party. This type of buyout usually requires some type of outside financing to assist the employees in accomplishing the transition. In some cases the owners may self-finance the buyout by way of notes or loans to the employees.

SPECIFIC LEGAL ISSUES RELATED TO AN ESOP

Most legal issues respecting an ESOP are covered in an ESOP Shareholders' Agreement that all employee shareholders are required to sign if they wish to participate. The employees should always be encouraged to obtain independent advice about their proposed investment, including independent legal, tax and investment advice. Frequently, corporations arrange for independent advisers to assist employees in such matters.

Some of the things included in ESOP Shareholders' Agreements are as follows:

RIGHT TO REPRESENTATION ON THE BOARD OF DIRECTORS

This element is likely to be a more significant factor in situations where the ESOP is intended to affect an overhaul of the corporation's culture. There is no clear answer to whether or not employees that are part of an ESOP should have a right to representation on the board of directors. ESOPs generally state there is to be no employee representation at the board level until very significant ownership is obtained by the employees. In many cases the decision results from the corporate culture and the trust between the various stakeholders in the corporation. In a unionized corporation, the unions usually require that representation, if they are to look at an ESOP as a means of supplementing wage concessions. However, where ESOPs are put into place not as a methodology to restrict the employees but as a means to allow them to participate in the growth of the corporation, there is a tendency to develop, over time, the right of the employees to representation on the board of directors. Studies in the United States have shown that a majority of corporations do not put an employee on the board of directors in the first few years of the ESOP. However, after five or six years of operating the ESOP, corporations tend to appoint employees to the board of directors, as all stakeholders begin to understand and respect the issues that are involved in running the corporation, and trust each other to do what is best for the growth of the corporation.

VETO RIGHTS

The ESOP should spell out whether the participating employees will have the power to veto corporate transactions and what transactions would be affected. Veto rights would be considered only when the employees have a substantial voting block of shares in the corporation (probably 33% or more) and, therefore, a substantial say in the operation of the corporation. The following list is illustrative of key veto elements for consideration:

- New issues of treasury shares by the corporation
- Amalgamations and mergers with other corporations
- Sales of significant assets
- Material acquisitions
- Certain material business decisions as defined or specified in the agreement
- The recruitment of the corporation's executive officer

TAG-ALONG RIGHTS

The ESOP must indicate what rights the participating employees will have in the event that the principal shareholders were to agree to sell their shares in the corporation to a third party. The key issue is whether the employees have the right to participate in the proposed share transfer. Can they tag along and sell their shares at the same prices as the principal shareholders?

DRAG-ALONG RIGHTS

The plan must also indicate whether the principal shareholders have the right to require the participating employees to sell their shares to a third party for the same price as that agreed to by the principal shareholders. Most plans have drag-along rights, at a minimum, and often both drag-along and tag-along rights as well.

CONFIDENTIALITY RIGHTS

Generally speaking, employees participating in the ESOP plan will have access to financial information about the corporation that was previously available only to shareholders. In that case, the issuing shareholder should consider including a confidentiality clause in a shareholders' agreement prior to launching the equity-based compensation plan.

PUT OPTIONS

The ESOP should state whether or not participating employees have the right to require the employer or principal shareholders to purchase all or part of their shares, at a specified price, following specified triggering events. Examples of the triggering events include death, permanent disability, and termination of employment for any reason.

CALL OPTIONS

If applicable, the ESOP should state whether the employer or principal shareholders have the right to require the participating employees to sell all or part of their shares, at a specified price, following a specific triggering event. Again, examples would include employee death, permanent disability, or termination of employment for any reason.

PRE-EMPTIVE RIGHTS

The ESOP should specify whether the existing shareholders are entitled to maintain their existing percentage ownership, following the issuance by the corporation of additional treasury shares. For example, if the corporation wishes to raise interim financing for an expansion phase, and does this through issuing treasury shares to a new investor, all existing shareholders will have their existing percentage ownership diluted. Some ESOPs require that shareholders have the right to maintain their existing percentage ownership and thereby avoid dilution, but this would require the existing shareholders to put up more money in most cases.

RESALE RIGHTS

This element is of particular importance in private corporations because aside from any mechanisms contained in the ESOP shareholders' agreement, there is no market for the shares. The ESOP shareholders' agreement must state what rights the participating employees will have to sell their shares, and hopefully realize a profit from the ownership interest they are to acquire, whether the shares are to be sold back to the issuing employer, or whether the employer will undertake to arrange a sale of the shares to other employees. This issue has important tax implications to the employee, which were discussed in Chapter 6 ESOPs and Income Tax. In addition, if the employer undertakes to sell shares to other employees, a minimarket would be required within the corporation.

FINANCIAL ASSISTANCE

Under the *Canada Business Corporations Act* (Canada) (CBCA) and the *Business Corporations Act (Ontario)* (OBCA), a corporation may provide its employees with financial assistance whether through a loan, guarantee, or otherwise in order to facilitate the purchase of shares under an ESOP. Corporations in other jurisdictions across Canada should check with the local legal authorities to determine their provincial regulations. However, the corporation must meet the solvency test outlined in the applicable legislation. Essentially, there must not be any reasonable grounds for believing that the corporation is, or would be after providing the financial assistance, unable to pay its liabilities as they become due. Nor must there be any reasonable grounds for believing that the realizable value of the corporation's assets, excluding the amounts of any financial assistance provided, would be less than the aggregate of the corporation's liabilities and stated capital of all classes. This requires that a corporation cannot put the corporation or the employees in a situation whereby loaning funds for the employees to purchase shares in the corporation will put the corporation's creditors at risk, as well as the employees at risk for potentially investing in an insolvent corporation.

OWNERSHIP ISSUES

If the issuing employer intends to remain a private corporation, retention of control in the hands of the corporate founders is likely to be a major concern. This tends to give rise to special legal considerations such as share ownership in the event of the employee/shareholder's death, or in the event of a family breakdown. In either of these two cases, the shares owned by an employee could constitute a valuable asset and may become the subject of a family law dispute. At the same time, the other shareholders and the corporation itself will want to be able to control the ownership of corporation shares, even when faced with the division of an employee/shareholder's property. As a result, most ESOP shareholders' agreements contain a restriction on the transfer shares as well as specific provisions to cover what happens to the shares of an employee in the event of death or a family law dispute.

PRIVATE CORPORATION RESTRICTIONS

Transfers of the shares of a private corporation require the approval of the corporation directors or the shareholders. The most common way of addressing this matter is by means of a detailed shareholders' agreement, which generally includes rights of first refusal and some type of buy-sell clause. Although most ESOPs create the situation of having minority shareholders, it is possible that for certain classes of shares that have been issued by the corporation in a previous restructuring that certain employees, although part of a minority group in the ESOP, may actually have majority control of certain types of shares. Corporate legislation expressly allows a corporation to repurchase issued shares, which allows a corporation to fulfill the terms of the shareholders' agreement under which the corporation has an option or obligation to purchase shares owned by a director, officer, or employee of the corporation.

TRANSFERRING AND ASSIGNMENT OF SHARES

As employee shares have been issued as part of the ESOP, the issuing corporation would not want these shares to be held by persons other than employees. One reason for this would be, for example, if the corporation has plans to do an IPO. It would be very difficult to quickly find all the shareholders if the original shareholders have transferred their shares to unknown third parties. Therefore, most ESOP shareholders' agreements should stipulate that the employee shareholder must sell/transfer his or her shares to another employee within a specified time period following a triggering event, failing which the shares would be purchased by the corporation for cancellation.

ESOP LEGAL DESIGN ISSUES

The precise structure of each proposed ESOP can be completely unique. Perhaps the most obvious distinction is between a share purchase plan and a stock option plan. ESOPs and stock options offer two very different kinds of investment vehicles, and each gives rise to a unique set of legal issues. The choice between establishing an ESOP that includes a share purchase plan or a stock option plan, or both, and the overall decision on which employees will have access to the plan, will generally also be a function of the underlying motivation for establishing the plan in the first place. If the intention is to enhance employee loyalty, enthusiasm, and productivity all the way down the production line, the choice is likely to be a broad-based plan with a share equity component. On the other hand, if the intention is to keep a lid on the cash portion of escalating executive salaries, perhaps a key person stock option plan would form a significant part of executive remuneration. Obviously access to such plans would be restricted appropriately.

Generally, an ESOP sets time limits for a participating employee to purchase stock and/or options. The employee would be required to make periodic investments into an account over a set amount of time, and the funds would be withdrawn from the account to purchase shares. By contrast, a stock option allows its holder to acquire the option stock at a pre-determined price at the time of the holder's choosing. For the holder of a stock option, purchase of the stock is essentially risk-free, because the holder will exercise the option only when the stock price has risen above the fixed price for which he or she can buy the stock. If the stock price falls below that option price, the holder will not exercise the option and therefore has no investment in the corporation.

Changing market conditions and the changing fortunes of the issuing corporation over time will lead to gains or losses in the value of its stock. Unlike the holder of a stock option, an employee participating in an ESOP with a share purchase plan has no control over the share price. Investment specialists would be quick to point out a decline in the stock price for the employee even though its paper loss would have to be explained and communicated to the employees. This would tend to be counterproductive in the case of an ESOP designed to boost employee morale. As a result, the issuing corporation may elect to set up a matching investment scheme to boost the participating employee's overall return. Alternatively, it might establish a protection scheme such as a guaranteed share repurchase clause, a type of "put" clause that establishes the minimum value at which the shares can be sold back to the corporation. For example, if the employees invest in the corporation at $10 a share and at some point in time designated by the corporation, the employee could then "put" those shares back to the corporation, the share price is guaranteed so that no matter what the value of the corporation at that point in time, the employees would always get at least their $10 per share. The advantage to the employees is that they have tremendously reduced their risk in terms of their investment. The disadvantages to the corporation are that if the corporation does have a decline in value of a substantial amount they may have a liquidity problem in trying to meet the "put" from various shareholders. One way around this is to put a cap on the amount of puts in any one year.

The issuing corporation may also provide employees with optional financial assistance in order to help them participate in the ESOP or the share option plan. In the case of outright equity ownership by means of participation in an ESOP, however, leverage purchasing increases the investor's potential risk. Again, issuing corporations may be tempted to provide a "quick-fix" solution for the participating employees in the event of the downturn of the value of shares, through a mechanism like loan forgiveness.

Both sides of downside-protection schemes — guaranteed share repurchase and loan forgiveness — give rise to a number of significant legal and tax considerations. Loan forgiveness, for example, is similar to a guaranteed share repurchase clause because the corporation basically has loaned the money to the employee to purchase shares and, in certain circumstances, does not ask for the loan to be paid back. For example, if the employee borrows $1,000 to buy shares in the corporation and is required to pay back that loan by the third year, the corporation in the third year could forgive that loan, thereby reducing the employee's risk in terms of investing in the corporation.

DOWNSIDE-PROTECTION SCHEMES

Any outright equity investment involves the risk of loss. The inevitability of cyclical market performance and unforeseen changes in consumer trends all add potential risk for an equity investor. ESOP participants are not immune to these risks. When an equity plan is part of an ESOP, the employees must understand that they are investing in a corporation that has risk. Arguably, the very nature of corporation-wide ESOPs increases the possibility of an investor being taken unaware by the sudden drop in the value of his/her shareholdings. This is because enrolment in an ESOP generally involves a standard form agreement by means of which the employee subscribes to a periodic investment program and a series of payroll deductions. Although ESOPs are intended to be long-term investments, there is rarely any investment advice sought by the employee, or provided by the employer at the time of enrolment. Although ESOP companies may ensure that this investment advice is available to employees, they usually don't take advantage of that advice. The forced savings of periodic investment into an ESOP is attractive to lower-income employees, and for some, the ESOP might well represent their only form of savings. All of these factors increase the possibility that a sudden downslide in a corporation's performance and a corresponding tumble in share value could convert the ESOP from a source of employee loyalty and heightened morale into employee alienation, which is, to say the least, a human resource liability. Most companies would prefer to avoid such unnecessary strains on the employee/employer relationship, and they do so by instituting a downside-protection scheme. It should be noted that payroll deductions, although popular, are not the only way for private companies to institute an ESOP, especially if the amounts involved are within the capabilities of employees to pay through other means.

GUARANTEED REPURCHASE SCHEME

One option is a guaranteed share repurchase right contained within the terms of the ESOP. This right functions like a "put" option in the hands of participating employees whereby they have the right to require the corporation to purchase their shares at a specified minimum price. (Note that this scheme could be a taxable benefit in the hands of the employee.) The employee benefits through this scheme because he or she has limited the downside risk by being able to obtain a minimum price in future if conditions warrant.

LOWERING THE AVERAGE COST OF SHARES

Another option would be for the employer to advance a one-time "bonus" of additional shares at the current depressed prices in a quantity in proportion to each employee's previous shareholdings. This would shore up the employee's paper losses due to a deterioration in the share prices. As a result of the increased number of shares being held by the participants plan, each employee's per share cost would be averaged down. The lower average price would, in turn, allow the employees to recover their losses more quickly as the value of their shares rebounds. From the employee's perspective, the advisability of lowering the average cost of the shares would depend on the likelihood of the corporation regaining its share values in the future. Such a procedure could have tax consequences because the "bonus" may very well be treated as income from employment for tax purposes.

LOAN FORGIVENESS

Loan forgiveness is a common downside-protection scheme in situations where the corporation plans to offer financial assistance to participating employees. This scheme may provide additional incentive for employees to participate in the proposed ESOP or stock option plan. Loan forgiveness is generally structured such that whenever shares decline in value, the corporation, which is either the lender or the guarantor, will forgive or repay the outstanding loan. The Canada Revenue Agency deems the loan forgiveness to be a constructive receipt of an asset, which is taxable in the employee's hands. The amount forgiven would constitute a taxable benefit to the employee because the employee has received a benefit without paying for it.

POTENTIAL FOR NON-EMPLOYEE SHAREHOLDER OPPOSITION

In devising a downside-protection scheme, such as those outlined above, it is important to consult with existing, non-employee shareholders. If the overall package appears too generous in their eyes, it could lead to unwelcome consequences. For example, the other shareholders could sue the corporation if they believe there was a deterioration in the asset base due to the loan-forgiveness arrangement.

SHAREHOLDERS' AGREEMENT

As noted previously, perhaps the single most important component of any ESOP development process is the ESOP shareholders' agreement. The agreement should include all the rights and obligations of the employees or shareholders, the employer, and its principals. The shareholders' agreement is a key element to protect employees and outline their rights and obligations to the corporation and the rights and obligations of the corporation to them. (See the Appendices for a sample agreement.)

ESOP HOLDING COMPANIES

The ESOP holding corporation is important for purposes of income tax considerations where the employee, by selling shares to the holding corporation, can benefit in a private corporation setting for the capital gains exemption. In addition, some companies would rather deal with one trustee representing all the employees than have individual employees directly owning shares in the corporation.

CONCLUSION

The legal matters involved in setting up an ESOP are fairly complex. This chapter is not meant to be an exhaustive overview of the legal issues involved in the design and implementation of an ESOP. It is important that legal representation be obtained by any corporation putting an ESOP into place.

CHAPTER 8
ADMINISTRATION AND COMMUNICATION

The single biggest problem in communication is the illusion that it has taken place.

– George Bernard Shaw

ESOP MYTH   Never sell shares to your employees because they will want to run the company.

ESOP FACT   A successful ESOP requires open communication. Studies have shown that participative ESOPs that are fully and clearly communicated enhance employee engagement (rather than their desire to control the company) leading to high productivity, increased profits, and increased wealth for all.

Employee ownership works. It makes companies, on average, better, faster, and stronger. The typical employee-owner stays with his or her company longer, and many of them come up with the kinds of creative ideas that can push expenses lower than managers thought possible, or that open up new lines of business.

Overall, the statistics show that, on average, everyone comes out ahead with employee ownership.

You may have noticed that I have emphasized the phrase "on average." Not surprisingly, some companies do far better than their peers, and some employee-owned businesses do not get any performance benefit at all, or may even do worse.

What separates the companies that outperform from the ones that underperform? A lot has to do with the way the employee ownership plan is structured, and the other chapters in this book can help make sure that you do all of that right. This chapter looks at what may be the most overlooked aspect employee ownership. What happens after the deal is done? Once the company has become employee-owned in fact, what does it take to start acting employee-owned in practice?

Before we get to some best practices, let's take a look at what can go wrong.

PITFALL 1: THE SIGH OF RELIEF

Imagine that you start working on making your company employee-owned, and the deeper you get into the project, the more complexities you find. You stick with it through the barriers and the unexpected challenges. The process keeps going forward, but you blow past the deadlines you had set for it. You work late and weekends, and eventually it all pays off. You sign the papers that make your company officially employee-owned. You breathe a big sigh of relief.

You may organize a celebration and maybe after that, you think, you'll take a few days off. So you and your team announce to the workforce that they are owners of the business. People cheer, and everyone is excited about the opportunity.

But tomorrow, work goes on. Projects have deadlines, bills need to be paid, supplies need to be purchased. You may have fallen behind on other important projects, so you shift your focus to them. Everyone is still feeling good about being owners, but no one is quite sure what they ought to be doing differently.

Maybe they shrug their shoulders and get back to work. Over the next few weeks and months, the idea of employee ownership gradually slips lower down the list of things they think about at work, until people just are not really thinking about it too much.

Or maybe they do try to do things differently. Maybe they approach their supervisors with process improvement ideas that they've been sitting on for years. But the supervisor isn't sure what to do with those ideas. No one told them, so they say thank you, and eventually those ideas fade away too.

The problem here is that company leadership stopped working once the deal was done. They failed to create structures, systems, and expectations so that people would be able to do things differently. Everyone may like the idea of ownership, but in the long run, people only feel like owners when they act like owners. Feelings follow behaviour. If the company fails to provide any ways for employees to take ownership actions, eventually their excitement about ownership dwindles.

PITFALL 2: JUST PRESS PLAY

A similar problem can occur for a different reason. Some management teams inform the workforce that everyone is now an owner, and then they step back to wait for the entrepreneurial transformation.

Ownership is such a powerful concept that many people doubt they need to do any explaining at all beyond telling people that they are now owners. Owners take responsibility, they worry about customers, they go beyond the call of duty, they care. Everyone knows that, and it's so obvious that explaining it would be patronizing, right?

It's true that everyone understands ownership, but especially when it comes to ownership of a business, they do not necessarily have a common understanding. Ownership may make some people think about the start-up entrepreneur and expect complete autonomy in how they work. Others may think of Gordon Gekko or Wall Street and equate business ownership with being rich. Others may think of burning the midnight oil, or of long golf vacations, or

175

of the riskiness of the family farm. You may well have some people start showing up to work expecting to join the next board meeting, others starting to work unpaid overtime, others asking to see the bank statement, and others worried about whether they have personal liability for the business.

Ownership means so many different things that it's impossible for it to be a unifying force unless someone takes the time to define what it means in the specific context of this specific company. Ownership needs to be operationalized. People need to know what they can expect and what they should not expect. They also need to know what the company expects of them.

PITFALL 3: THE SALES JOB

Now suppose you are passionate about employee ownership, and once those papers are signed, you call a meeting and you give people an inspiring speech. You tell people what's going to change. People are going to be empowered to make decisions, the books will open up, everyone will join together as a unified team to unleash the incredible value of shared entrepreneurship. Stock will grow in value, people will come to work every day happy, and everyone will retire with seven-figure ESOP accounts.

And maybe the company's performance does improve. The problem is that people's expectations are now so high that better is not good enough — they are expecting a fundamental transformation of the company. The danger of an aggressive sales job on employee ownership is that it makes people feel disappointed when improvements are less dramatic than they expected.

The sales pitch that details how wonderful life as employee-owners will be also tends to skirt the issue of responsibility. The future is only going to be bright if we all work hard and think creatively.

Employee ownership is not a no-strings-attached gift; it is an opportunity, and it will only be what people make of it.

And think about how the inspiring speech sounds to the middle managers and supervisors in the audience. What they are hearing is that the company leader has invited people to start taking away parts of their jobs. They feel blindsided and unprepared. They are being asked to help the company build a new culture and way of working, but they have no idea if their jobs are secure or how their roles are changing. They are not likely to be the most effective advocates for employee ownership.

PITFALL 4: MARGINS ARE TIGHT

Most people in North America have misconceptions about how business works and relatively low levels of business literacy. Most businesses, unfortunately, do very little to change that. As a result, most employees have inflated expectations for how profitable their companies are, and that can cause problems when they become owners. People who think that their company's profit margin is 50 per cent may not see any reason not to provide raises to all owners.

Employee ownership can make companies stronger, but it cannot take them out of the market. In fact, it brings the ups and downs of the market directly to every employee-owner. Before they had an ownership stake, people had a degree of insulation from the market, but when the value of their stock changes depending on what's happening in the market, they begin to face some of the difficult trade-offs that companies wrestle with. This can be difficult, and it may make some people uncomfortable, especially those who may prefer to remain in a non-owner employee role.

PITFALLS IN CONTEXT

These pitfalls may be discouraging, and you may recognize some patterns from your own company. Remember that employee ownership works. Your company is starting with an advantage, because people do instinctively understand many things about ownership that are helpful and powerful.

Even if you started off on the wrong foot, don't be discouraged. Many of the most successful employee-owned businesses in North America have fallen into some (or several!) of these pitfalls. In fact, one of the most powerful things a company leader can do is admit that something did not go as well as it should have and ask for help to do better in the future. If your company is in one of the pitfalls above, people know about it. Talking about it out loud does not reveal any secrets, but it does get everyone on the same page, and it creates the transparency you may need to get people to join you in taking a chance to realize the potential of employee ownership.

With that in mind, here are some ideas and best practices to help your company capture more of the potential strength of employee ownership.

1. Understand the Plan

If people are going to think and act like owners, they need a basic level of understanding of the plan through which they have their ownership. Some of the things your company might want to do to build understanding of the plan include:

Have large-group meetings: Bring everyone together to announce the plan and to cover some of the most common questions about the plan. Do not go into detail — the time for that is later.

Have written materials: Everyone has different learning styles, so provide information about the plan, in written format for the people who need to see things in black and white. You may also want to send these materials home so employees' spouses read them as well.

Let the plan sell itself: Most employee ownership plans are good deals for workers. If they trust the information they receive, they will likely come to their own conclusion that the plan is a good thing. If they feel like someone is sugar-coating or emphasizing the positive, they are less likely to trust the information and more likely to have doubts. No one expects utopia, but people usually recognize a good thing when they see it, so show it to them accurately.

Have small-group meetings: Set up a peer-to-peer training group. These people can be elected or invited to join a group and given the time and resources to create a training program. The most successful groups have the active support of the CFO, who can make sure that they have accurate information and can answer all of the group's questions. These communication groups often talk with other committees at other companies so they can share PowerPoint slides, handouts, and agenda items.

Target "just in time" information: People learn best when the learning is digestible and repeated. Young employees who have just joined the company do not need to know all the details about the timeline on which they will be paid out when they leave the company, but they probably do want to know the eligibility rules.

Use examples: Not much is as persuasive to human beings as stories. Talk about people who have retired from your company with substantial value in their ESOP accounts, or, if your plan is newer, use examples from other employee-owned companies. When your plan is new, tell the story of why it became employee-owned. What were the other options? Why did the company choose employee-ownership over those other options?

Use statistics: Some people prefer to see the numbers, so don't hesitate to show them the research highlights on the implications of employee ownership. One good source of data on American companies is the NCEO (National Center for Employee Ownership) at www.esopinfo.org.

2. Rights and Responsibilities

People inherently associate ownership with rights. Psychologically, ownership implies the right to information about whatever it is they own, the right to have a say in what happens to it, and the right to benefit from profits made by whatever is owned. These rights need to be translated into the context of your business.

But rights are not enough. Ownership is also responsibility. Owners are stewards of whatever they own, and that stewardship implies a series of responsibilities. If I want the right to have input in the direction of the company, then I need to accept the responsibility to ensure that my input actually results in better decisions. If I want access to information, I have a responsibility to use that information for the benefit of the company. If I want the management team to be held accountable, I have a responsibility to accept being held accountable myself.

One of the most powerful things companies do to build cultures where people think and act like owners is to consistently refer to rights, responsibilities, and think of the inherent link between them. We all want to enjoy rights in the place where we work, and those rights are only sustainable when people accept the responsibilities that accompany those rights.

Companies create statements of rights and responsibilities, which they may post around the workplace. They refer consistently to those rights in meetings, when making decisions, and in performance evaluations. Here is one example from Padilla, an employee-owned marketing firm.

RIGHTS	RESPONSIBILITES
To share in financial success of the company	To contribute to the financial success of the company
To question business practices that you do not believe are in the company's best interests	To help find solutions and not just point out problems
To have access to the information that illustrates how your actions and decisions affect company profitability	To evaluate your actions and decisions from an ownership perspective

3. Business Literacy and Open-Book Management

People who act like employee-owners make decisions that benefit the company. To do that, they need to understand what the company's interest is. Is it more important to get this order out today, or to give it one more quality check? Would we rather receive payment sooner or get a slightly higher price? Is it worth spending an extra billable hour to exceed the customer's project specifications?

Many employee-owned companies practise open-book management (OBM). It's a deceptively simple term, by which some people simply mean that the CFO discusses the year's financial statement at an annual meeting. Other companies, such as Springfield ReManufacturing Corporation (SRC), have woven the numbers into the day-to-day jobs of all employees. There, all employees gather by department for weekly "huddles," where they plan the week ahead by filling in a prospective income statement for the week. The person responsible for sales may say she expects to do 5 per cent better than budget, and that number is entered in the table on the whiteboard. Based on that, the purchasing agent may revise his estimate for materials.

The employees at SRC not only know exactly how their department is doing, they also know what they individually need to do to ensure that the upcoming week is as successful as possible.

Open book systems often go hand-in-hand with suggestion systems. NCEO member companies have a variety of ways of gathering ideas. One employee-owner found a way to replace a disposable machine part that cost a dollar with a retail Q-tip that reduced cost by 98 per cent. Others have had ideas that led to entirely new lines of business for their companies.

4. Be Predictable

Social psychologists say that the root of organizational trust is predictability. Surprise is the opposite of predictability, and although it is impossible to eliminate surprises, company leaders should make it their personal goal to never be the source of an unnecessary surprise. Companies can reduce surprises and be more predictable in a number of ways, all of which have the impact of increasing levels of trust.

Communication cycles: Many employee-owned companies communicate in a series of interlocking cycles. They send weekly (or daily) email updates about the state of the company. They have monthly department meetings, quarterly newsletters, and annual shareholder meetings. They have elections every July for their employee committee, a guess-the-stock-price contest every May, and a state of the company address from the CEO every February. The information itself is useful, but maybe even more important, these cycles become expected, and when people's expectations are met, trust builds.

Open-book management: The better people understand the business, the less likely they are to be surprised. Teaching business literacy and sharing key financial information not only makes people feel like insiders and helps them manage their day-to-day decisions, it also lets them better see the road ahead.

Anticipate problems: Some ESOP companies have built business contingency plans. These plans specify what a business downturn looks like and what the company will do when one happens. Such a plan may define, say, a "stage 1" downturn in terms of a specific threshold of revenues, EBITDA, projects "in the pipeline," or product development. A "stage 2" downturn would have more ominous triggers, and both stages would say what actions the company would take in that stage. If business is soft, having a business contingency plan will let people know that we're in stage 1 and what to expect. They also know what needs to happen to the numbers to get out of stage 1, and what the warning signs are that the business may be approaching stage 2, or worse.

5. Support Middle Managers and Supervisors

As discussed in pitfall 3, these employees are in the most difficult position in an employee-owned company. When the

NCEO does surveys of employee-owners, this is the group that nearly always has the highest levels of cynicism about employee ownership. These misgivings make sense. Middle managers and supervisors almost never have a role in designing the ownership plan or in operationalizing it. Their specific job responsibilities are often the ones most threatened by increased employee involvement. People ask them questions about the plan, but no one has given them a way to know the answers. Senior leaders expect them to build support for employee-ownership among their reports without having given them a reason to support it themselves.

Companies with strong ownership cultures have actively brought middle managers and supervisors into the planning process. They may use middle managers and supervisors as a focus group to test and give feedback on communications or training programs. They may recruit "middles" to company-wide groups that are working to define or operationalize employee ownership.

6. Manage for Ownership

Building an ownership culture takes concerted and consistent effort. It will be much easier to sustain that effort if you have specific goals against which you can measure your progress. No measure of an ownership culture is perfect, but some companies use employee surveys to gauge how much employees feel like owners. Others use proxy measures, such as the number of process suggestions submitted, the number of people who attend the annual shareholders meeting, or even the number of people wearing company logo clothing on any given day.

Another way to manage for ownership is to build it in to the company's job descriptions and performance evaluations. Many traditional job descriptions can be gently modified to reflect an ownership approach, and some employee-owned companies have created a set of "ownership behaviours" that they expect from each employee. For supervisors, that may include the ability to gather input from the people who report to them, a level of familiarity with the business's strategy, or having periodic meetings with the people they supervise to cover ownership issues.

7. Keep the Faith

It can take a while for ownership to take hold at your business. One pattern a number of companies have seen is that they begin with senior leaders excited and ready to jump into the new culture. Middle managers may be resistant, and non-managers are holding their cards to their chest as they wait to see what things look like in practice. After a few months, non-managers are starting to see how this could be a good thing, but by then, maybe senior leaders have gotten discouraged that change did not happen as quickly as they wanted. The rest of the company may now be ready to join them, but they have moved on to other things.

One challenge with ownership culture is getting all groups to be ready to move at the same time, and in practice that usually means that senior management has to be patient and not lose the faith.

It's also good to remember that not everyone at your company may ever turn into a flag-waving employee-owner. It's OK if you have a number of good employees who just want to be employees.

Many successful employee-owned businesses operate very well with a large minority of their workforces actively engaged in employee ownership at any given time. Just like our civic democracy, a strong, vibrant company needs broad participation, but it does not need everyone to be actively engaged at every moment.

CHAPTER 9
POST-ESOP ISSUES

Share your profits with all your associates, and treat them as partners. In turn, they will treat you as a partner, and together you will all perform beyond your wildest expectations.

— Sam Walton

PROFIT-SHARING

ESOP MYTH Sharing profits will create dissension among employees.

ESOP FACT Sharing profits and information will create more profits and more accountability.

An ESOP is a long-term plan through which wealth is created over several years. During a short-term timeframe, however, many employees prefer a more immediate monetary reward. Profit-sharing can be used as a short-term reward system complementary to the ESOP. Profit-sharing works with the ESOP to motivate employees to participate in the ongoing wealth creation of the company.

We will discuss the types of profit-sharing plans and how profit-sharing can be utilized in conjunction with an ESOP to achieve corporate objectives.

DEFINITION AND TYPES OF PROFIT-SHARING PLANS

Profit-sharing is a compensation program that makes payments to employees over and above their base salaries or wages. These additional payments are determined by the level of the corporation's profits. A classic example is the profit-sharing plan at a small manufacturer of architectural woodwork and cabinetry, which distributes 27 per cent of before-tax profits among the employees, prorated to their base salary.

In Canada, there are three major types of profit-sharing plans:

- Cash
- Deferred profit-sharing plan (DPSP)
- Combination plans

CASH

All payments are made to the employees in cash, which is treated as income and is fully taxable. The payments are deductible for the employer, and there is no limit on the amount of the deduction. However, the income tax must be withheld at source. Cash plans are the most common type of profit-sharing plans in Canada.

DEFERRED PROFIT-SHARING PLANS (DPSP)

DPSPs are established under the authority of the Canada *Income Tax Act*. The employer makes contributions to a trust fund on behalf of employees up to a certain maximum, similar to employees contributing to a self-directed RRSP. The act limits in two ways the amounts that can be contributed:

- The total contribution made by an employer and an employee to DPSPs, registered pension plans (RPPs), and Registered Retirement Savings Plans (RRSPs); and
- The total contributions made by the employer to a DPSP. For a DPSP, the employer would set up a trust fund at a financial institution. Within the limits set out by the act, all contributions are deductible expenses for the employer. Taxes on the earnings and capital gains of the trust are deferred until they are withdrawn, just as for RRSPs. Although there are some restrictions, the fund can be invested in most types of Canadian securities.

COMBINATION PLANS

A company can set up a profit-sharing plan that combines any two of the above options. For example, in a plan that is part DPSP and part cash, the company would pay the maximum allowable under the *Income Tax Act* to the DPSP and pay any amount left over from the employer allocation in cash. Another possibility would be to pay half of the company's contribution to the DPSP and half in cash. The major features of any combination plan will depend on the exact proportions of the major components.

CONDITIONS REQUIRED BEFORE STARTING

When designing a profit-sharing plan, it is very important that the company's senior executives or owners ensure that the following are in place:

- Reasonable employee relations. Do the employees trust the executive team to put a profit-sharing plan into place that will benefit the employees?
- Base salaries that are at least externally competitive and internally fair.
- A high probability that there will be some profits to share. To the extent possible, this should also be true of the next year or two, which is why a profit-sharing plan is a good partner to

an ESOP. Profit-sharing plans give immediate compensation to employees for achieving targeted goals and in years where there may be no profits, due to expansion or for other reasons, the ESOP will continue to have value to the employees.

- There should be some stability in the company since introducing a profit-sharing plan is itself a form of change.
- There should be good communications between management and employees on a regular basis using dependable channels of communication.
- Management must have a commitment to operate the plan but also be prepared to deal with employees who want to be involved.

STRATEGIC ISSUES FOR MANAGEMENT

There are several issues that should be discussed prior to creating the plan or talking with the employees:

- Objectives of the plan
- Type of plan
- Employee involvement
- Employer contribution

OBJECTIVES OF THE PLAN

Management must have a clear idea of what it wants to achieve with a profit-sharing plan. Although plans can perform a variety of different functions, the choice of plan objectives will influence every design decision made later on.

For example, a private company that wants to attract high-quality employees may have to make the waiting period to join the plan very brief or eliminate it entirely. Profit-sharing plan objectives should be coordinated with the objectives of the ESOP, so both meet the company's goals.

A profit-sharing plan should be seen as a complementary employee incentive, not an equivalent for the benefits generated by the ESOP. Profit-sharing plans share many of the same issues as the ESOP, in process and design elements. An effective profit-sharing plan will satisfy employees in the short term while the ESOP will keep the employees engaged in the long term.

TYPE OF PLAN

Many employers know the type of plan they want before they start the design process. Others believe that profit-sharing is a good concept but have not determined the specific type of plan they would like. Those employers are well advised to seek their employees' input. However, experience indicates that virtually all employees prefer a cash plan if given a choice. Therefore, for employers who know they want something other than a cash plan, that decision should be communicated.

EMPLOYER CONTRIBUTION

Before establishing an employee committee, the size and definition of the company's profit-sharing contribution must be decided. Other issues to address are definition of profits, the proportion that will be available for distribution to the employees, the type of formula used to determine the employer contribution, and the timing and frequency of the payments.

Profits can be defined as either net profit before or after tax. Most companies use net profits before tax, because it is easier to calculate the amount of profits that are available for distribution on a before-tax basis. Some companies use operating profit that is calculated before extraordinary items and before overhead items such as interest and foreign exchange gains and losses. Should the plan include extraordinary gains or losses? Examples would be gains or losses on the sale of a building or other investment. Before making this decision an employer should determine whether the employees have significant influence on the activities in question and, if so, include them in the process.

A plan can use either a "discretionary" or "specified" formula. Discretionary means the employer decides each year what proportion of profits will go into the plan, while specified means that the percentage of profits contributed by the company is declared at the outset of the plan. A discretionary formula should generally not be used for a broad-based employee profit-sharing plan because the company is trying to build a trust relationship with the employees. Employees understand that if they meet certain target levels there will be an amount of profit distribution based on a formula. The formula can be a straight percentage of all profits, such as 10 per cent of net profit before taxes. Alternatively, it can be a specified percentage above a certain minimum level of profit. For example, it could be 15 per cent of net profit over $200,000 after taxes. A formula can also be graduated so that the percentage of profits to be paid out increases at various points. It could provide for 10 per cent of the first $1 million; 15 per cent of the next million, and 20 per cent of any profits over $2 million. The final decision is actual percentage used. The most common are 8 to 15 per cent of the net profit before taxes.

Although these percentages are used as a general rule of thumb in the industry, employers should consider their own requirements for capital and cash flow. Alternatively, the employer contribution can be a percentage of the cash payroll. A rule of thumb is that any payment to employees should be at least 5 to 10 per cent of their base pay, otherwise they won't notice. However, this is a very rough guideline; employers just starting their profit-sharing plan, and who are not sure about what percentage of profits to contribute, should start low. The percentage can always be increased later, but it is very difficult to decrease the level of contribution if the company is unable to sustain the plan.

EMPLOYEE INVOLVEMENT

One of the most critical decisions to make at this stage is the extent to which employees will be involved in the process of designing the profit-sharing plan. Some employers sit down alone or with a couple of trusted advisers, design the plan, and then announce it, expecting the employees to be both surprised and grateful. Frequently, however, they are shocked to find that employees are surprised but also very suspicious and even hostile.

In these circumstances, employees will question every design decision made. The only way to counter this is to get the employees involved in the process. This is the same process advocated for the ESOP, and for the same reasons. An employer must build up a level of trust with the employees. Having put an ESOP into place with the participatory process described earlier in this book, it would be foolish for the management group to try to implement a profit-sharing plan without taking employees' concerns into account. Therefore, by far the best way to carry out the planning is to form a committee comprising a representative cross-section of employees. When forming the committee, choose employees who are viewed as opinion leaders by the group they represent, able to understand the concepts involved, and willing and articulate enough to act as spokespeople for their group. It is preferable that the employer select the committee members so as to obtain the characteristics mentioned above. If an ongoing committee to help administer the plan is required, employees could be elected to that.

OPEN-BOOK MANAGEMENT

Open-book management (OBM) programs are useful both for ESOPs and for profit-sharing so that employees can understand the plans and be motivated by the benefits.

OBM can get everyone in the company "up to speed" to build a better business, one that works well and increases in value. OBM involves clear, relevant, and open communication throughout a company, to create the link between what an employee does day to day and the objectives of the company as a whole. In order for OBM to succeed, top management must be engaged and onside first. If owners and management are reluctant to share financial information with their employees, an open-book management policy is difficult to implement. However, financial information is readily available through several sources, including the Internet. We can usually determine a competitor's salaries by simply asking people who work there. Overhead is a little trickier but can be extrapolated by elimination of information. Certainly, there are risks in disclosing financial information. The question is whether management wants to exchange those risks for the benefits of OBM. By adopting OBM, the company can develop something their competitors may not be able to match, a highly motivated, knowledgeable workforce within the entire company, working towards the same goals.

However, it is important that the ESOP be implemented first, so that the employees become owners of the company, and are eager to implement an OBM policy to learn more about the company, achieve results, and contribute to the increase in the value of the company. Because OBM answers all their questions, employees tend to be very receptive to this type of program. OBM can be applied in small private businesses or in large public companies. It applies to unionized and non-unionized businesses alike, and across the full range of industries.

OWNERSHIP THINKING

There are a number of programs that build on the principles of OBM and provide clear pathways to engage employees in thinking and acting like owners. Ownership Thinking™ is one such program, and was developed by Brad Hams over 18 years ago in the United States. Hundreds of companies in the U.S., Canada, and Australia have used this program to improve employee engagement and profitability.

The basis of the success of this program lies in moving employees from thinking about themselves to thinking about the whole company. We want to move their thought process from "me" to "us." To do this requires work on four elements in the company:

1. Right People

It may seem self-evident but too many companies have non-productive and even counter-productive employees. Some studies estimate that as much as 20 per cent of the workforce fall into this category. It's important to remember the dictum to hire slowly and fire quickly.

2. Right Education

Many company employees are well trained in their area of expertise, whether it's sales, administration, operations, etc. but few have any business financial literacy. It is imperative that employees learn about how a business makes and loses money. The best way to learn this is through an understanding of how a balance sheet, income statement, and cash flow statement work.

3. Right Measures

What you measure gets changed. With no measurement, expect no behaviour change on the part of the employees. Measurements must be relevant, simple, and calculable. Ownership Thinking™ proposes that a company must identify Key Performance Indicators ("KPIs"). These KPIs are actions that will lead to the most success for the company when implemented and the most failure if not achieved. There are two types of KPIs which many companies do not identify as such. The first are Lagging KPIs which are financial KPIs that are reported after the fact. The second are Leading KPIs which are operational measurements that occur prior to the financial results. Focussing on the Leading KPIs will bring the most success and profitability to the company.

4. Right Incentives

The final and equally important element of Ownership Thinking™ is to create the right incentive program for the employees. Most incentive plans are failures because they are not linked directly to an employee's self-esteem. Incentive plans must be self-financed otherwise they are just expenses with no self-improvement requirements.

5. Ownership Culture

Ownership Thinking™ propositions that the best companies in the world have three common characteristics:

1. They care deeply about their employees and their community.
2. They want to have fun. The workplace is innovative and full of opportunities for employees to shine.
3. They have high expectations in performance both for the employee and the employer.

Does your company have these characteristics? If not, it is time to change your culture. To learn more about Ownership Thinking™ visit www.esopbuilders.com and click on the Ownership Thinking tab.

TRANSITION ISSUES FOR THE ESOP

An ESOP is organic; it will grow and change to meet the changing needs of the company, its culture, and its employees. These changes may come quickly or slowly — but they will come. Once the ESOP has been put into place transition issues will arise. These issues are

- Expansion of the company
- Contraction of the company
- Dilution
- Change in nature of the workforce
- Liquidity event
- Repurchase liability
- Apathy

EXPANSION OF THE COMPANY

Whether it is a high-tech company growing at 25 to 50 per cent or more per annum or a more traditional company growing at 5 to 15 per cent per annum, growth brings its own issues for the

ESOP plan. Although the plan will have projected growth rates for at least the first three years of the plan, the company may grow faster than assumed. Therefore the allocation of the shares or the options may have been taken up sooner than expected. This creates a demand by the employees for more ownership percentage above and beyond that initially anticipated by the original ownership group. How the ownership group responds to the demand for more share issues will determine how the ESOP will grow from that point onwards.

Various industry studies show that the percentages given to employee groups have grown substantially over the last several years, starting out in the range of 10 to 20 per cent and moving up as high as 30 to 40 per cent in some instances. Depending on the company, the original ownership group may not wish to increase the percentage ownership among the ESOP, due to a number of factors. First, as the value of the company grows, giving up a bigger percentage of the company means a large amount of money given up by the original ownership group. Second, as the company is expanded it will need additional capital. It may need to obtain interim financing or raise additional capital, therefore diluting the current owners' percentage. The ownership group may be very concerned that it could potentially lose control of the company by giving up too much ownership percentage to the employees at this point in time. There is however, usually a compromise level that will satisfy both the employees and the ownership group. Otherwise, eventually, the ownership group will have to decide whether it wants to dilute its percentage ownership to the point of losing control.

The key to having a winning compromise is to be conservative with the initial share allocations, increase them on an annual basis, and communicate the reasons for the share allocations and why the percentages that were chosen are correct for the company going forward. It is not so much the quantity of the shares that are owned by the employees that matters, but that the shares or options are given out on a fair basis, and that the plan must take into account the contributions of the key management team and compensate them accordingly. Failure to address these issues as the plan grows can cause problems among the key management group, eventually having a negative influence on the growth and value of the company.

CONTRACTION OF THE COMPANY

A contraction can occur from either internal causes, such as a market, product, or service that was no longer competitive, internal disputes, and lawsuits or external causes such as economic or industry-wide downturns. U.S. studies have shown that most companies with ESOPs do better at protecting themselves in a contraction than non-ESOP companies. Contractions can be very stressful times for employees who sense that sales and profitability are down, may be worried about their jobs and the future of the company. ESOPs can be used to advantage in a contraction, if the proper foundations have been laid and communication is effective.

One large engineering company in Canada found itself in a major downturn and was facing bankruptcy proceedings. The company was 100 per cent ESOP-owned, and the employees decided that they were going to make this company successful through wage rollbacks and tightened their belts to get the company through the recession. Two years later, the company was back on track. Three years on, the company completed a public offering in which many employees realized gains of hundreds of thousands of dollars on their investment. A senior vice president of this company we interviewed stated that she believed the only reason that the company was able to get through the recession and avoid bankruptcy was that the company was employee-owned.

An ESOP-owned trucking company knew it was going into a severe downturn and had to lay off about 30 per cent of the workforce. Company management, having set up a proper ESOP plan with open communication, took the problem to the employees. It was the employees themselves who decided who would be laid off. The company was able to survive the recession, come back stronger than ever, and within two years hire back 90 per cent of the people it had laid off.

Using an ESOP successfully means communicating the company's problems in an open and forthright manner. The employees are now stakeholders in the company; decisions that are taken for the benefit of the company, even difficult decisions, will be taken in the spirit of cooperation.

DILUTION

Dilution occurs when the company needs to attract external investment and has to sell a portion of its treasury stock. Dilution also occurs when stock options are given out to either employees or third parties for services rendered. Dilution means that a current shareholder who owns 5 per cent of a company for example may be diluted down to 3 per cent if additional treasury shares are issued from the company. Again, dilution is not necessarily a good or a bad thing — it is a fact of life. The company must explain why dilution is taking place, what the company hopes to achieve by diluting the shareholdings, and obtain the understanding of the employees for the necessity of the dilution.

CHANGE IN NATURE OF THE WORKFORCE

Once an ESOP has been in place for several years, many ESOP companies experience a change in their workforce. Inevitably, a certain percentage of employees are not comfortable with an entrepreneurial environment. This can range from 5 to 10 per cent of the workforce that decline to participate in any kind of share scheme or stock option plan. These people are risk-averse and virtually nothing can induce them to participate. Over time, a portion of these people, seeing the results of the ESOP, may decide to participate and become part of the plan, due generally to peer pressure. However, a certain percentage will never be comfortable in an ESOP company. These people tend to drift away from the company, and people who are entrepreneurial in spirit and want to be part of an ESOP company are attracted to the company. So the general nature of the ESOP actually strengthens over time.

Although this is a transition for the company, it should be regarded as a positive growth of the ESOP culture within that company.

LIQUIDITY EVENT

The number-one question asked by employees considering joining an employee share plan is how they are going to get their money out. The liquidity event is the key event that will allow the employees to liquidate their investment and see a return on their assets. Because ESOPs are a long-term incentive plan, this may involve planning over a five, 10- or even a 15-year time frame. Examples of liquidity events are companies going public, a third-party buyout of either all or a portion of the company, an acquisition or merger with another company, and an employee buyout of the company. The liquidity event is unique to each company. In the high-tech community many employees look forward to an IPO as their liquidity event. However, IPOs are dependent upon market forces, which most companies cannot control; it is more likely that a company that has been properly managed and is growing will receive an offer at some point by a third party. At this point, the company has to be prepared to decide whether it is ready to sell. The employees must be constantly apprised of any potential liquidity events that are planned for the future. However, a liquidity event may never occur.

REPURCHASE LIABILITY

The repurchase liability can have a dramatic impact on the cash flow of a company. A repurchase liability is a liability of the company to purchase back the shares that employees own when they leave the company through death, disability, or termination. Generally, the repurchase price and the terms of that payment are stated in the shareholders' agreement. The company must review the demographics of its workforce and be aware that there will be a time when it may have to start repurchasing shares from its employees. There are various mechanisms to account for this repurchase liability. Some companies will plan a liquidity event to fund the repurchase liability. Others will look at setting up a sinking fund so that they can retire a certain portion of shares each year and plan for that retirement.

APATHY

The major issue that the ESOP can present for both the employees and for senior management is apathy: the longer the ESOP has been in place, the more it is taken for granted. Although this is human nature, it is important that the excitement and the original intent of the ESOP be perpetually renewed through various means and mechanisms. For example, shareholder meetings can be made into an event where shareholders are treated to a banquet, party, or awards ceremony that allows them to celebrate the company's achievements. Changes to the ESOP can be made periodically to keep it current. These must be communicated through a two-way process; it is only with continual effort from employees and employers that the original reasons for and objectives of the ESOP remain valid. If these objectives have changed, the ESOP may have to be modified and re-energized. If the ESOP is no longer achieving its objectives, or if the employees feel they have achieved their goals through the ESOP, it may be time to liquidate the ESOP and look for other means of motivation for the employees.

CONCLUSION

As the ESOP grows and matures with the company, more sophisticated design issues may occur. For example, the acquisition or start-up of offshore branches will mean hiring employees in those countries and bringing them into the scope of the original ESOP plan. Cross-border ESOPs are very much a current topic, as even the smallest companies have representation and employees in various countries.

CHAPTER 10
ESOPS AND B CORPS

I think B Corporations will make more profits
than other types of companies.

– Robert Shiller, Nobel Laureate in economics

ESOP MYTH For employees, an ESOP is only about a financial return.

ESOP FACT Many employee-owners not only want to see a
financial return but also feel connected to the
greater business vision of the company.

Well documented throughout this book are the business benefits
of ESOPs. In our opinion, backed by decades of research, ESOPs
combined with participative management provide companies
with a competitive advantage.

However, we believe there is a larger transformation taking
place in business that ESOPs also tap into. This business transformation hinges on a company's social license to operate.

More than ever consumers and employees are expecting businesses to not only make and offer great services and products,
but also generate a social or environmental return. This evolving
expectation of business goes far beyond traditional corporate
social responsibility (CSR). Traditionally, CSR is a small and

isolated department of the business that through donations to charity or staff volunteering aims to make a positive impact.

As business thought leader Michael Porter shares the next big opportunity for business is what he calls "shared value," which involves creating economic value in a way that *also* creates value for society by addressing its needs and challenges. According to Porter, businesses must reconnect company success with social progress. The timing for an evolving vision for business couldn't be better. The world needs business to help solve problems that government and non-profits alone cannot resolve.

There are a number of practices and models a business can use to make a positive impact through its core business but this chapter will focus on one of the largest and most widely-used models – Certified B Corporations, or B Corps for short.

Since B Corps were first created in 2007, more than 1,300 companies in 41 countries have been certified. In Canada, there are now more than 130 B Corps including popular companies like Hootsuite, Bullfrog Power, Beau's All Natural Beer, Ethical Bean Coffee and Trico Homes. Thousands of articles have been written about these companies and how they are demonstrating a new and successful model for business.

Most recently *Fast Company* published "20 Lessons of Innovation for 2015" and concluded that while B Corp was once seen as a fringe movement, this is no longer the case. With three of *Fast Company's* most innovative and high growth businesses being B Corps, *Fast Company* concludes "the model can scale."

Nobel laureates, even former U.S. president Bill Clinton, are recognizing that B Corps offer a more holistic business model at a time when capitalism is facing a number of challenges.

What's more, B Corps are a natural fit with an ESOP company. In fact, if a company has employee ownership they already have an advantage when going through the B Corp Certification process.

In this chapter, we will explain the driving force behind the creation of the B Corp movement, how to become a Certified B Corp and the business benefits B Corps experience. Plus, you'll hear from employee-owned companies why B Corp is valuable.

It is our belief that business owners who implement ESOPs already share many of the values that the B Corp Certification embodies. We hope this chapter will encourage more ESOP companies and B Corps alike to learn how each of these models can better their business.

INTRODUCING B CORPS

What if the energy and innovation that drive corporations to maximize shareholder value was equally driven towards benefiting employees, community, and the environment?

This was the guiding vision behind the creation of B Corps, and it came from two business owners who not only proved this vision was possible but also experienced what happens when a company is reduced to focusing solely on maximizing shareholder value.

Jay Coen Gilbert and Bart Houlahan were co-founders of AND1, a $250 million basketball footwear and apparel business. Throughout the 1990s, the founders pioneered socially-responsible practices such as paying higher wages to their factory workers in China and giving 10 per cent of profits to local charities.

As the company grew and competed with Nike, it was put up for sale. Under pressure from private equity partners, AND1 had to unwind its social commitments to fulfill its legal obligation under corporate law to maximize shareholder value.

This, to the chagrin of the founders who were proudly demonstrating that business could make a profit and achieve social and environmental goals.

This compelled Gilbert and Houlahan along with their friend and colleague Andrew Kassoy, a former Wall Street investment banker, to begin exploring how AND1's situation could have been different. They wanted to find a new model for business that would allow and validate companies to achieve a larger purpose than just generating profits.

The outcome was Certified B Corporations, a new type of company that has a mandate to maximize "stakeholder value," which includes employees, community and the environment, in addition to shareholders. B Corps are certified by the non-profit B Lab.

To become a B Corporation, a company must complete the B Impact Assessment, a rigorous and comprehensive assessment of a company's social and environmental impact. The 90-minute Impact Assessment focuses on four areas of your business: employees, community, the environment and governance. The assessment measures everything from the difference between your highest- and lowest-paid employee to how many independently-owned suppliers you use, whether you have implemented energy efficiencies in your office building to whether you practise open-book management. Companies must receive a score of at least 80 points from a total of 200 to become certified.

Completing the B Impact Assessment is highly recommended even if you don't plan on becoming a B Corp. The results can provide your company with a baseline against dozens of best practices on employee, community, and environmental impact.

While 1,300 companies have become certified, more than 20,000 have used the tool to measure and improve their business practices. Certified B Corporations also amend their articles of incorporation to say that managers must consider the interests of employees, the community, and the environment instead of worrying solely about shareholders.

WHERE ESOPS AND B CORPS MEET

When creating the B Corp standards, the founders were well aware of the important role employee ownership played in creating a business that is a force for good in the world. In fact, one of the key stakeholders in the B Corp's Impact Assessment is the employees.

A company that offers employee ownership can earn points in two areas of the assessment, the first being Operations. In this section, if a company offers employees ownership they can earn 7 to 10 points depending on the amount of ownership offered.

The second half of the assessment focuses on what is called "Impact Business Models." The Impact Business Model section rewards companies who are solving environmental or social problems directly through their products or operations. Examples of Impact Business Models include a solar panel company, a business owned by a non-profit organization or one of the recent one-for-one companies, such as Warby Parker, where they match every pair of glasses purchased by a customer with a pair of glasses to someone in need. Another equally important Impact Business Model is majority employee ownership, according to B Lab co-founder Houlahan.

"We're trying to award impact created for your stakeholders and your business and one of the stakeholders in your business is the workers, whom you employ. In fact they are a critical stakeholder", he says.

"We know no other profound way to create impact for your workers than the ESOP model."

Companies where employees own 51 per cent or more of the company qualify as a Impact Business Model, earning a total of 40 points, half of the 80 points needed to become a Certified B Corporation.

Recognizing majority employee ownership as an Impact Business Model pays tribute to the fact that wage inequality is one of the major issues of our time. In the United States, the richest 400 Americans have more wealth than nearly half of the country's population, 150 million Americans. Many think the wage disparity is a problem only in the U.S.; however in 2014 the *Globe and Mail* ran a series of stories on our own wealth paradox. The *Globe* reported that in Canada, incomes among the top 1 per cent have climbed 80 per cent since 1986. This is compared with gains of 19 per cent for the bottom 90 per cent of earners. The Conference Board of Canada gives Canada a "C" grade for inequality, ranking it 12th out of 17 peer countries.

With a widening divide between the middle class and the wealthy, The *Globe* concluded that income equality is threatening to erode a cherished Canadian value: equality of opportunity for all.

BETTER YOUR BUSINESS WITH B CORP AND ESOPS

B Corps are receiving widespread attention because they are profitable, growing and making a positive impact using the tools of business. While companies acknowledge a number of advantages to being a B Corp, below are the most common advantages cited.

RECRUITING AND RETAINING TOP TALENT

There is a war for talent, and that talent's motivations for work are changing. According to Harvard Business Review, millennials, which represent roughly 50 per cent of the global workforce, want work that connects to a larger purpose. As an independent third party certification, B Corp Certification demonstrates to new recruits that your company is committed to doing business better.

The certification process, which requires a re-certification every two years, is also a great tool to engage employees. At Gardener's Supply, an employee-owned company that became a B Corp in 2014, the certification process provides an easy tool to get employees involved in their greater business mission.

"B Corps became compelling because we were a socially-responsible business before that became a buzzword and we wanted a way to measure how effective we are," says Jim Feinson, Gardeners Supply CEO.

"We've always had an ESOP Committee, and an active green team, but we were making that up as we went along. B Corp was a way to put some structure around that and to engage employees around those questions from either completing the assessment or implementation."

Companies with highly engaged workforces display a number of well-researched benefits including, on average, having 3.5 times more job applications and 20 per cent higher productivity performance scores.

TRUSTED BRAND

B Corp Certification also provides a level of transparency and credibility as a result of being a third-party certification. B Corp co-founder Gilbert likens B Corps to Fairtrade or LEED certification. These certification labels are easily identified by the public who understand the label represents a higher commitment to either social or environmental outcomes.

This credibility is something consumers are increasingly looking for. A recent report by the Business Development Bank of Canada entitled "The Socially Conscious Consumer: Opportunities for Entrepreneurs," states that consumers are increasingly concerned about how their choices impact the environment, their local community and their own well-being. As such, they expect companies to be greener and more ethical, and to provide healthier, and more Canadian, products and services.

The report highlights three key trends: nearly half of Canadians are inclined to buy environmentally-friendly products, nearly one third of Canadians are willing to pay a premium for ethically-made products, especially those that are certified, and 90 per cent of consumers would stop buying from a company using irresponsible practices.

It is for these reasons that the B Corp seal can provide your company with a marketing edge over your competition.

Co-operative Home Care Associates (CHCA) is a worker-owned co-op in the South Bronx, New York, and they became a B Corp largely for the marketing value it would bring. CHCA president and CEO Michael Elsas recalls looking over the certification criteria to become a B Corp. The worker-owned co-op that began in 1985 with the goal of making the job of a health care aide into a reputable career already embodied most of the B Corp values.

"When I looked at the criteria for B Corp and started checking each of the items that we had it became very clear to me that there was a synergy there that what B Corp was promoting was many of the elements that the co-op had established," says Elsas.

In the increasingly crowded marketplace for health-care services, CHCA became the first company in its industry to adopt the

B Corp Certification, differentiating itself from its competitors as a company committed to making a real social and environmental impact through its work.

B Corp Certification also opened the doors to a community of new potential customers.

"One of the advantages (of being a B Corp) is to do business with other B Corps, who treat their workers well and have the same mindset and similar culture," says Elsas.

LEAVING A LASTING LEGACY

So B Corps can help you recruit and retain talent and elevate your brand to one of trusted distinction, but what about when it's time to exit?

As discussed earlier in this chapter, it was the B Lab founders' original experience of selling their business that compelled them to create B Corps. B Corps were primarily established to protect a company's social or environmental mission when growing or selling the business.

B Lab, the non-profit behind B Corps, realized that for some companies certification wouldn't be enough so they also created a legal mechanism to provide enhanced protection to companies who may be pressured by investors.

Called benefit corporations, this new corporate structure provides a higher level of clarity and legal protection to a company's directors and officers, who have a duty to consider employees, community and the environment in addition to shareholder value when they make operating and liquidity decisions.

Since first being passed in Maryland in 2010, benefit corporation legislation has been adopted by 31 U.S. states with more than another 10 states introducing the legislation. The benefit corporation as a legal entity does not exist in Canada yet, although a group is exploring the model's feasibility.

According to Ryan Honeyman, who wrote *The B Corp Handbook*, the expanded legal protection for a company's mission is particularly relevant in succession planning. Some entrepreneurs who built mission-driven companies are using benefit legislation to ensure that once they step down, the company's mission is not only protected but elevated by law, meaning any new investors or CEOs will be obligated to consider the company's wider stakeholder base when making decisions in the future.

Patagonia, the popular maker of outdoor clothing and gear, became a benefit corporation in 2012. Patagonia founders Yvon and Malinda Chouinard credit their legal incorporation as a safeguard that enabled them to retire knowing their company's environmental mission, which has been pivotal to their success, was protected.

"Patagonia is trying to build a company that could last 100 years," Yvon said in a *LA Times* article.

"Benefit corporation legislation creates the legal framework to enable mission-driven companies like Patagonia to stay mission-driven through succession, capital raises, and even changes in ownership by institutionalizing the values, culture, processes, and high standards put in place by founding entrepreneurs."

It's for this same reason — protecting a company's mission and legacy — that ESOPs will be appealing to some B Corps as a potential exit strategy. B Lab founder Gilbert wrote an article on exactly this: "'B' a Better ESOP: Why the Marriage of B Corps and ESOPs Makes Sense."

In the article Gilbert notes that while B Corps may differ from traditional companies, every business owner needs an exit strategy. What makes ESOPs more appealing is their likelihood of preserving the mission and values in the long run when compared with other options, for example selling to a third party, participating in a merger, or going public.

He cites Dansko, the Pennsylvania-based footwear company, as an example. Dansko already had an ESOP and later became a B Corp. Both changes were aligned with the culture and vision of the owners. In 2012, the company fully transitioned to 100 per cent employee-owned, allowing the husband and wife founders to fulfill their mission-aligned exit.

Employees are more likely to share the vision and values of the owners, and they have a vested interest in the business succeeding. For B Corp owners looking for an exit, research shows the business is more likely to succeed in the long-term when employee ownership is part of the succession strategy.

A MODEL FOR THE FUTURE?

We know the positive results an ESOP can generate for companies with the right mindset and culture. Now we are seeing B Corps as one more catalyst for building a successful and long-term business that engages employees and customers alike in your mission.

To quote Jim Feinson, Gardeners Supply CEO, "There is an amazing alignment between being a B Corp and being an ESOP." That's because both models are about business sustainability and helping the larger community succeed.

In our opinion, B Corps are common sense. B Corps recognize that capitalism works best when it's interdependent. The health of all stakeholders, most notably the middle class and the environment, are vital to the health and wealth of capitalism.

B Corps also appeal to the left and the right by offering a market solution that is profitable and scalable while solving social and environmental problems.

If we want to build capitalism for the long term and a thriving society, B Corps and ESOPs are potent tools. We look forward to watching these two movements grow and cross-pollinate in the years to come. A healthy future depends on it.

CHAPTER 11
INTERNATIONAL ESOPS

The ultimate resource in economic development is people. It is people, not capital or raw materials that develop an economy.

– Peter F. Drucker

ESOP MYTH Only certain fringe companies, usually small, can benefit from employee ownership.

ESOP FACT Some of the most successful companies in the world, including those with 20,000 to 40,000 employees, use ESOPs as a cornerstone of their success.

Many Canadian companies find that to grow and prosper they have to export their goods and services, mainly to the United States. In the high tech field as much as 90 per cent of sales can go to other parts of the world. This has led many private companies, both large and small, to establish offices in the United States, Europe, and Asia to take advantage of the sales opportunities in other parts of the world.

When a company sets up facilities in other countries, it is important to create a compensation scheme that is attractive to the local employee base so that the company grows and prospers for all of its employees. An ESOP can present an equitable plan for all employees of multinational companies by attuning employees throughout the world to the goals of the parent company. By achieving the company's goals the cross-border ESOP can increase value to an even greater extent for all the employees involved. One example of a successful cross-border ESOP is Cisco Systems, which has ESOPs in well over 20 countries.

SPECIAL ESOP ISSUES

- Legal, accounting, and tax issues vary significantly from country to country. The culture of a company can have a big impact on the nature of the plan that is put into place. Americans are more likely to look favorably at an opportunity to buy into a company than Canadians, who tend to be more conservative investors. People in the United Kingdom, because they are more familiar with ESOPs due to their longer history there, tend to be somewhere between the conservative nature of Canadians and the more aggressive nature of Americans.
- Long distance communication of the nature of the plan is an issue to be dealt with, especially when most of the workforce is in Canada; the satellite businesses may not have the full impact of the communication that exists in the company's home market.
- Finding competent and experienced practitioners who can implement cross-border ESOPs is not easy. The designer must be able, through either internal capacity or external connections, to service the client in a cost-effective manner. The cost of a cross- border ESOP will generally exceed that of a domestic plan because of the complexities involved.
- The ownership group's tax position can play a role in the final structure of a cross-border ESOP. For example, if the ownership group has holding companies through which the shares in the offshore companies are held, the tax structure of the holding companies must be considered when designing the overall plan for a cross-border ESOP. Therefore, it is crucial that the structure in Canada be put in place before the cross-border ESOP, to prevent tax structural problems for the ownership group.

- Language questions, even with the Americans and British, can create difficulties because the terminologies used in certain forms may differ and will have to be researched and understood thoroughly.
- Administration for a cross-border plan is more complex and may require a more costly structure to be efficient.

APPROACHES TO CROSS-BORDER ESOPS

There are several approaches to setting up a cross-border ESOP, each with advantages and disadvantages.

HOME-COUNTRY FOCUS

Canadian content should be the basis for the cross-border plan. The cross-border component will fall into place as a translation of the Canadian content.

Setting up a home-focussed country plan is cost effective. The plan benefits the majority of employees and can be maintained at a reasonable administrative charge on an ongoing basis. The disadvantage of such a plan is that the tax implications to the non-Canadian employees may be substantial. For example, Americans residing in the United States who own stock options in Canadian companies will have to pay higher taxes than their Canadian counterparts due to the income tax laws in the United States. Although the gains realized by those non-Canadian employees may still be substantial, they will not be as great as with a country-specific plan.

COUNTRY-SPECIFIC PLANS

A second option is to create separate plans in each country to take into account the tax laws of each country and capture the indigenous benefits that exist for ESOPs. For example, one Canadian company that has subsidiaries in Spain and the United States has a plan that takes advantage of the tax laws in each country. However, even though the plans are country-specific, they were coordinated to be as close as possible to the Canadian plan so that there was no advantage or disadvantage for each employee.

To take a country-specific plan and set up separate plans results in increased costs for both the administration and ongoing maintenance. The advantage that may offset these costs is that each employee will maximize the after-tax return on his or her investment. A second benefit is that the employees realize that these plans are specifically designed for them.

OFFSHORE TRUST

It may be advantageous to set up an offshore trust to hold the shares of the company, in which case there are no concerns about multiple tax jurisdictions, only the jurisdiction of the off-shore country.

An offshore trust means not having to worry about the specific tax laws of each country. The administration is fairly straightforward; however, there is a large up-front fee for creating an offshore trust, and some of the tax issues are fairly complicated, increasing the maintenance costs on an ongoing basis. Also, if a company will be raising interim financing eventually, it is much more difficult to invest in an offshore company than in a company registered in the United States, the United Kingdom, or Canada. The reason is that if the deal goes sour it is much more difficult for the investor to reclaim its investment in an offshore jurisdiction.

PLAN SUITABILITY

Home-country-focussed plans should be used by companies where a vast majority, 90 per cent or more, of the employees are situated in that company. An exception to this position would be if the location of the vast majority of employees changes quickly from one country to another; in that case the plan may require a separate plan to be established in the second or third country. If a company has a majority of its employees in one country but has subsidiaries that are clearly business entities unto themselves, it may be in the interest of that company to set up separate plans by country: the benefits to be derived from having a global employee mentality may not exist. If a company is in more than three countries and of a sufficient size, it should look at the offshore trust, which will allow a more efficient utilization of a global ESOP as well as minimization of tax issues for all employees.

The preferred method for most companies is to set up a plan that meets the needs of the majority of employees. The plan can be adapted at later stages and adjusted if circumstances change.

CONCLUSION

As the global economy expands and more countries are able to compete in the world market, long-range planning should include an international ESOP. Although an ESOP may not be designed for several years, management should plan by communicating and educating its workforce and by strategizing for that eventual day.

Understanding some of the concepts of employee ownership in Canada, the United States, and the United Kingdom will assist in developing a plan for a cross-border ESOP. The U.S. is a major trading partner for Canada, and it has more than 35 years experience with ESOPs. The U.K. has been utilizing ESOPs for the last 20 years, and is regarded by many Canadian companies as an entry into the European market.

This chapter gives you an overview of the main issues when designing an international ESOP. However, designing an international ESOP is complicated and requires expert advice to understand each company's specific circumstances and needs. You can find contact information for international ESOP experts in the appendix.

It is beyond the scope of this book to discuss ESOPs in Asia, South America, and Europe.

CHAPTER 12
EXIT STRATEGIES TO TRANSITION YOUR BUSINESS

There's a trick to the Graceful Exit – it begins with the vision to recognize when a job, a life stage, a relationship is over – and let it go. It means leaving what's over without denying its value.

– Ellen Goodman

ESOP MYTH The best way to exit a business is to sell to a third party.

ESOP FACT Only 50 per cent of sales to third parties are successful, while 80 per cent of sales involving employees as buyers are successful.

TRANSITION PLANNING

One of the great business paradoxes is that business owners are great at planning the future of their privately-held companies, but lousy at planning both the transition and their eventual exit. Multiple studies in the U.S. and Canada show that 70 per cent of all SMEs (small to medium-sized enterprises) will undergo ownership transition in the next 10 years, yet less than 10 per cent of owners have any type of formal transition plan. The reality of this lack of planning is brutal. Only 20 to 25 per cent of SMEs up for sale are sold successfully. The other 75 to 80 per cent actually end up winding down the company through a liquidation.

There are nine exit strategies that can be employed by owners of privately-held companies:

SALE TO AN ESOP

Selling the company or a portion of it to the employees has these advantages:

- No disclosure of financial information to competitors
- An ESOP creates a culture of employee engagement on a wide scale, thus increasing value
- The owner has flexibility as to when he can make the transition
- An ESOP creates an additional cadre of motivated purchasers when the time comes to sell the rest of the company

There are some reservations to an ESOP. An ESOP is suitable only for a gradual exit over time; not for when an owner needs to sell quickly. The change in corporate culture may be difficult for some organizations. Advisers to business owners are often anti-ESOP, cannot envision the benefit to the company of shared ownership, particularly as it is their client who must give up something to achieve it, and will discourage the owner from pursuing this path.

SALE TO EXISTING SHAREHOLDERS

Selling the company or a portion of it to other shareholders has these advantages:

- Again, there is no need for disclosure of financial information to competitors
- The owner has flexibility as to when he can make the transition

As with an ESOP, selling to shareholders is suitable only for a gradual exit over time; not for when an owner needs to sell quickly. The change in corporate culture may be difficult for some organizations.

MANAGEMENT BUYOUT (MBO)

Selling a portion of the company to key persons has similar advantages:

- No disclosure of financial information to competitors
- It creates a culture of employee engagement, thus increasing value

An MBO will provide a quick exit. It does not allow the owner any flexibility in timing. The change in corporate culture may be difficult for some organizations.

SALE TO A THIRD PARTY

There are advantages to selling to a third party:

- The owner can access the cash relatively quickly, as the deal usually closes within 12 to 18 months
- In a strong economy, demand due to the increased number of buyers can achieve a high valuation

The disadvantages:
- Opening up the books to potential competitors
- The loss of control over the business legacy that the owner has created
- The founder may have difficulties dealing with the new owners
- The potential for loss, of both customers and employees, during the transition
- Difficulty finding a buyer
- Buyer may require flexible financing options. According to CIBC World Markets, 310,000 Canadian businesses are currently considering transitioning their business. Due to supply of businesses and the demand for buyers, business owners have an

increasing need to become more flexible with the third parties buyout or payment terms.

SALE TO FAMILY

Selling to family members means that the owner's business legacy can continue, while providing them financial security. On the other hand, it can create or increase family discord. Often, family cannot afford to pay for the purchase. Businesses passing to second and third-generation owners have a proven lack of success.

For example, 88 per cent of current family business owners believe the same family or families will control their business in five years, but succession statistics undermine this belief. Only about 30 per cent of family and businesses survive into the second generation, 12 per cent are still viable into the third generation, and only about 3 per cent of all family businesses operate into the fourth generation or beyond.

NO SALE – REFINANCE

In refinancing or recapitalizing the business, the owner maintains equity in the business while at the same time taking some money off the table. The disadvantage of increasing debt in the company increases the risk of bankruptcy should there be an economic downturn, and there are more external reporting requirements and compliance rules. Also, refinancing does nothing to diversify the owner's personal financial planning risk, as they still are carrying all their eggs in one basket.

SALE TO PUBLIC WITH AN INITIAL PUBLIC OFFERING (IPO) – GOING PUBLIC

The cash realized from the sale can be used for growth. If the stock is actively traded, the owner's shareholdings now have liquidity. Also, company value increases as valuation multiples for public companies tend to be higher due to increased liquidity. The disadvantages are:

- The expense of a prospectus is such that few SMEs can afford the cost.
- If the market ignores the company so that it is orphaned or thinly traded, liquidity vanishes.
- The owner loses all control.

DEFER SALE – HIRE PROFESSIONAL MANAGEMENT

In this temporary solution, the owner maintains equity and control, but can be absent from the business. A potential buyer is created for the eventual sale of the business. The disadvantages are:

- The owner receives no cash or liquidity.
- The difficulty of finding adequate management externally.
- The postponement of the inevitable decision to transition.

SALE OF ASSETS

The advantage to liquidating the assets of the company is that the process is relatively simple and fast. The disadvantages are that liquidation values are minimal and many owners experience feelings of failure at this loss of their business legacy.

CONCLUSION

Having business owners cognizant of the timelines and expectations required for different exit strategies can greatly increase the success rate of a business succession plan. Similar to ESOPs, all exit strategies demand time, foresight, planning and proper execution.

APPENDICES

APPENDIX I
CASE STUDIES

This section features three Canadian ESOP case studies. All three of these ESOP plans were created by ESOP Builders.

For a wider array of case studies on ESOP companies, visit the National Center for Employee Ownership (NCEO) at www.nceo.org and other ESOP Associations listed in Appendix VI.

DST CONSULTING ENGINEERS

President and CEO of DST Consulting Engineers Mike Fabius was facing a problem. After years of 20 per cent revenue growth, his company's growth appeared stifled. Mike knew in order to boost sales he would need to hire experienced leaders who could take the company to the next level. However, he was finding recruiting talent the traditional way — head hunters and advertisements — ineffective.

That's when Mike realized that offering key employees an ownership stake could be DST's competitive advantage. He asked his lawyer to draw up a shareholder agreement which he enthusiastically presented to four of his senior employees.

To his dismay, they weren't interested.

"It turns out the lawyer had written the agreement one-sided (to favour the owner), and I hadn't realized it at that time," he said.

Despite not getting the reception he'd intended Mike continued to explore Employee Share Ownership Plans (ESOPs), and learn more about who was offering these services.

Mike found ESOP Builders Inc. and met with their president Perry Phillips. Perry shared that it was crucial that the future employee owners be involved in creating the ownership plan in order for it be successful.

DST hired ESOP Builders and created an ESOP team comprised of key employees. Perry facilitated the creation of the shareholders' agreement with the employees. It took a number of visits over a period of 18 months to finalize the plan.

"It took a while to find something everyone was comfortable with, we were meeting about every 2-3 months and eventually got something that everyone was happy with," recalls Mike. "We even retained independent legal advice for employees."

Starting in 2001, the plan offered shares at Fair Market Value (FMV) less a 25 per cent minority discount to key employees who were deemed eligible by the board. The plan ensured share liquidity and that only employees could own shares.

Initially, only four employees became shareholders. The ESOP experienced slow uptake for the first three years while people became comfortable with the plan and began to see returns. Then, it took off, once it became obvious that the annual return on investment was consistently exceeding 40 per cent.

The ESOP proved to be successful at attracting talent.

"Working for larger firms, they (the employees) have no chance of ever becoming major owners. It was an attraction to come to us as we were a young company," says Mike.

Based on the success of the ESOP, DST expanded the plan to include all employees. After one year of working with the company, any full time employee would be eligible to purchase a select amount of shares.

"What became apparent to me early in the game was that a broad-based plan would fit in with our culture of employee engagement rather than control," recalls Mike.

"It didn't matter if you were a key person; if you were a contributor to the company you should be an owner. The variable is the more you contribute the more you own."

Furthermore, Mike added an annual minimarket to allow share transfers between owners providing employees with some liquidity.

While the ESOP achieved its desired goal of recruitment and business growth, it also precipitated another important event – Mike's succession plan.

It turns out the employee owners were much more concerned about Mike's exit strategy than Mike himself. Mike assumed he'd continue selling his shares and slowly remove himself from the company. But the employee owners wanted more details: how many years would he continue as CEO, who would be his successor? This compelled Mike to create a formal exit strategy.

Mike became a minority owner in 2007 when he was comfortable with the new leadership group. In 2011 he spent one year sharing the president-CEO role as the final part of his transition to retirement.

"The ESOP was a great succession plan, it allowed me to retire earlier than I had planned on, and it made it clear for myself," he says, "I still enjoy my role as a director."

When asked to reflect on the challenges of being an ESOP company, Mike says it was the realization that everybody relates to ownership in different ways. For some employees, the ESOP is purely an investment, for others, ownership is much more emotional.

He recommends being open and transparent and sharing financial information with employee owners. Ensuring employees pay for the shares at FMV is also a key concept, so that they have "skin in the game."

When creating the plan, some people can get stuck in what may seem small details. Mike underlines the importance of having someone like ESOP Builders, which is seen as an independent adviser, to work with the employees. "There were some rocky meetings along the way as the succession details were developed, but Perry's vast experience helped us resolve the issues," he says.

"I'm convinced it was a good idea, a great way for me to divest, and in the end we are a better company for it."

FACT SHEET:

COMPANY NAME	DST Consulting Engineers Inc.
INDUSTRY	National environmental, geotechnical and blast engineering consulting firm
REASONS FOR IMPLEMENTING AN ESOP	Continue growth via recruitment and retention of leaders
THE PLAN	Key person ESOP that expands into broad-based ESOP within 5 years
ELIGIBILITY	Full-time employees are eligible after one year
ALLOCATION	Based on contribution as deemed by leadership team and as approved by board.
FUNDING	Employees could fund up to 80% of their investment through payroll deduction, bonuses and company guaranteed loans.
PRICE	All shares issued and sold at FMV less 25% minority discount. Formula independently established every 3 to 5 years.
OWNERSHIP CULTURE	Sharing financial information, quarterly owner newsletter, annual AGM in Toronto.
RETIREMENT POLICY	Before age 60, full value is paid out over 4 years. At age 60, employees

required to begin selling their shares back to the company. The philosophy is to keep ownership in the hands of employees who are working at DST.

MINIMARKET   Yes, implemented in year 5

RESULTS:

- 40% ROI for past 10 years, both in FMV and annual payments
- Share value increase from $0.25 to $5.40
- Improved recruitment and retention
- Employees increased from 40 to 140, one third of whom have become owners
- ESOP provided owner with exit strategy

ROSS VIDEO

The technology industry is one of the few sectors where employees owning company shares is a well-used practice to attract, retain and incent employees.

So it was no surprise to David Ross, owner of Ross Video when some of his employees began asking if they could purchase company shares.

Ross Video was and remains a family-owned company, which David had taken over from his father in 1997. While David was interested in the idea of having employees own company shares, he was troubled by what it implied. Many technology companies have an exit in mind, to be either sold to a third party or to go public. But those options weren't in the foreseeable future for David, who was in his 30s and had ambitions to grow the company for the long term.

As a result, David felt it was unfair to sell shares to employees knowing there would be no liquidity exit for them in the next decade.

David's perspective on employees owning shares changed after he attended an introduction to employee share ownership plans

(ESOPs) by Perry Phillips. It was during that session he learned about valuing privately-held companies and the potential to allow employees to sell some of their shares annually in an internal minimarket.

"The light bulb went off that you could let employees be part of the company's growth, especially if you're a big company, and at least give them limited liquidity," says David.

With this new understanding, David hired ESOP Builders to design and implement an ESOP for Ross Video. David knew he wanted an ESOP that wasn't just for the executive team but instead would allow anyone working in the company to become an owner if they so desired.

The company has a diverse workforce, with employees working in roles ranging from engineering to manufacturing. Its workforce is also international, with Ross Video having an Ottawa office in addition to offices in Singapore and the U.S.

The company implemented a broad-based ESOP, which allows anyone who had worked at Ross Video for six months to purchase an almost unlimited amount of shares, which is capped at 10 per cent of the company's shares.

"A lot of people think an ESOP is only for management but people working on the factory floor really appreciate being part of the company", says David.

As part of the ESOP process, and to make perfectly clear the company's intentions, Ross asked everyone who invested in the ESOP to sign a form indicating that they were aware that this was a long-term investment and the company wasn't going to be sold or go public.

At the same time as implementing its ESOP, Ross Video introduced a BHAG, which stems from Jim Collins book *Built to Last* and stands for Big Hairy Audacious Goal.

Ross Video's BHAG was to more than double the company's size in five years. The goal was audacious because the company was coming out of three years of barely positive growth. "It seemed impossible at the time," recalls David.

With the ESOP and a stretch goal in place, Ross Video began to see momentum. The company experienced 20 per cent year-over-year growth the first year. Ross Video hit its goal of doubling in size in two and a half years instead of five. Since implementing the ESOP, Ross Video has experienced 5 years of consecutive 20 per cent year-over-year growth.

During this time, the number of employees multiplied from 225 to 600. The share price jumped from $3 to $9 per share.

While growth can be challenging, David says the ESOP strengthened the company's team mentality by creating a reward for everyone's hard work and contribution.

Before and after implementing the ESOP, Ross Video shares its financials quarterly. However, before implementing the ESOP, David likened the company-wide financial update to an academic exercise that employees largely didn't relate to.

This changed after implementing the ESOP, where suddenly employees were meaningfully engaged in understanding the financial information as owners wanting to know how their investment was doing.

"If employees are engaged as owners I think all boats rise, it positively impacts the morale of people around here," says David.

The company uses a simple formula to determine the value of the company, after learning from Perry that employees should be able to calculate the value "in the shower."

Ross Video offers employees the opportunity to purchase shares with cash or payroll deduction. If an employee chooses payroll deduction, they commit to buying shares at next year's share price once they've saved enough funds through payroll deduction.

Ross Video implemented a minimarket in year 2, which allows employees to sell shares if needed. David says on average $200,000 is traded annually, providing employees with liquidity and allowing others to increase their investment.

When asked what is the most challenging part about having an ESOP, David says the only real difficulty can be when a large shareholder leaves and the company is tasked with re-purchasing the shares. However, he concedes that this inconvenience is only because the ESOP has been successful in growing the size of the company and its share price. David adds that critical to an ESOP's success is nurturing a culture of trust and open communication.

"In an ESOP, for people to want to invest it has everything to do with trust," he says. "So, if the management team is secretive, is elitist, or doesn't share strategies, why would employees choose to invest?"

FACT SHEET:

COMPANY NAME	Ross Video Ltd.
INDUSTRY	Production technology
REASONS FOR IMPLEMENTING AN ESOP	Employees asking for ownership, owner's desire to increase engagement, recruitment and retention
ELIGIBILITY	Full-time employees are eligible to participate in ESOP after working for six months
ALLOCATION	Open allocation. Employees can purchase as many shares as they desire, assuming the shares are available and don't exceed the total ESOP share pool of 10%
FUNDING	Cash and payroll deduction
PRICE	Shares sold at FMV
OWNERSHIP CULTURE	Financials shared quarterly, open communication
MINIMARKET	Yes, implemented in year 2

RESULTS:

- 20% year over year growth for five years
- Share value increased from $3 to 9$
- Increased employee engagement
- Company grew from 225 to 600 employees

CHANT LIMITED

Implementing an employee share ownership plan (ESOP) is often new territory for business owners. However, this wasn't the case for Ted Chant, president of Chant Limited, who previously worked at an ESOP company and was aware of both the benefits and challenges an ESOP could bring.

Prior to starting his own project and construction management company, Ted worked for Peter Kiewit Sons, which offered shares to key leaders within the organization.

Ted recalls how at first Kiewit's ESOP wasn't highly coveted by new employees. That all changed when a series of business opportunities resulted in the share value jumping considerably, an outcome that was repeated over a number of successive years. Much wealth was created for employees and more importantly, the ESOP was suddenly a major benefit of working at Kiewit.

Senior team members would work harder and longer hours knowing the ESOP would reward their efforts.

"I always saw that owners are more engaged, and that if the program becomes successful, people want to become owners, which creates a virtuous circle," says Ted.

In addition to seeing the benefits an ESOP could create, Ted also experienced the potential pitfalls. One of Kiewit's subsidiary companies also had an ESOP. However, the company wasn't performing and people weren't seeing returns.

As a result, the ESOP wasn't desirable and the firm experienced higher turnover and lower enthusiasm in general than that of Kiewit.

Going in with his eyes wide open, Ted decided to implement an ESOP at Chant Limited with the goal of attracting and retaining talent. Ted says he viewed the ESOP as an essential part of engaging his key people "out of the gate."

"I saw it as fundamental to our approach to attract and retain good people in a competitive marketplace. The objective was to have a differentiator by allowing key managers to be directly connected to their net impact on our corporate performance," says Ted.

Chant Limited hired ESOP Builders to facilitate the process and create a plan that met Ted's main goals. The ESOP would also incorporate a valuable lesson learned from Ted's Kiewit days: the plan had to not only be fair, but be perceived as fair by employees. A key component to creating a fair ESOP was transparency in the design, implementation and management of the plan.

The company decided to implement a broad-based ESOP for all of its employees. The number of shares an employee would receive each year was determined through a simple formula based on salary. Higher paid employees (assuming the company got that part right) were likely to be in a position of making the larger impact on financial results.

A salary-driven formula meant the higher paid employees would receive more shares ensuring key people would be properly compensated with a large component of the compensation tied directly to their and the company's performance.

Ted also recognized the importance of starting strong out of the gate. While the company was struggling with profitability, the ESOP was structured (through a separate share offering) so employees would participate directly in a single large payout Chant believed it would be receiving from an outstanding claim. The claim was successfully resolved.

"It was exciting times, people saw a payout right away," recalls Ted.

In the following years, the ESOP achieved its main goal, which was to attract and retain employees. While many of the firm's competitors were large and multinational, people were drawn to Chant Limited by the opportunity for greater participation in a mid-sized, local and employee-owned business.

"It helped with retention, (our company) is hands on and a lot of people feel they can directly influence both the overall corporate and their personal outcome," he says.

As part of building an ownership culture, Chant Limited held annual general meetings where they would share financial information with employees. Ted says having to report openly on the company's earnings was a powerful component of the ESOP.

"Our shareholders participate directly in the EBITA outcome of the business and as such, they are entitled to know everything that drives that result – good and bad," Ted explains.

However, in the early to mid-2000s the project and construction management company saw its industry change dramatically, resulting in decreasing growth for Chant Limited.

Through the downturn, Chant Limited kept its ESOP in place but Ted admits he stopped paying real attention to it. In his mind, the ESOP wasn't an important strategy seeing it was not generating returns for shareholders.

"I dropped the ball in terms of being the driver of our ESOP," says Ted. "Had I remained the champion of it, I'm a firm believer that we as a company could have done better."

When the company implemented the ESOP, Chant Limited was about 50 people. In 2015, the company was closer to 20 employees.

And yet despite the ESOP not being resoundingly financially rewarding for employees to date, Ted says he still hears from the management team and even junior employees the value of being shareholders.

"If I listen to the feedback of my people, even though it's not yet lucrative and it's not lining their wallets, there is something very intangible about being a real owner in your place of work."

Ted recommends the model to other business owners.

"All of the reasons I thought would be complicated, they are just not there," says Ted.

"I do think it's been important, creating the 'golden handcuffs.' The biggest challenge is we've had a tough time as a business constantly creating shareholder value."

Ted directly controls 70 per cent of the company's common shares while up to 30 per cent can be made available to employees Over 12 per cent of the common stock is currently in the hands of employees and 18 per cent of the common stock is held in treasury under the plan for ultimate distribution to employees. No employee can own more than 10 per cent of the company.

While exiting the company isn't on Ted's radar yet, the ESOP will provide one possible support strategy either allowing the company to recruit someone from outside or to promote from within and start a process of transferring total common stock ownership to his successor group.

FACT SHEET:

COMPANY NAME	Chant Limited.
INDUSTRY	Project and construction management services primarily to the energy sector
REASONS FOR IMPLEMENTING AN ESOP:	Owner's desire to increase performance through employee engagement, recruitment and retention
THE PLAN	Broad-based ESOP
ELIGIBILITY	Regular and contract employees are eligible to participate after one year of full-time employment.
ALLOCATION	Shares allocated based on an individual's base salary as a percentage of total salaries against an annual share offering.
FUNDING	Cash and payroll deduction
PRICE	Shares sold at FMV

OWNERSHIP CULTURE   Full financial and performance disclosure at AGMs, flat organizational chart with open-door policy

RESULTS:

- Increased employee engagement
- Improved targeted employee recruitment and retention outcomes
- ESOP provides owner with a potential exit tool

APPENDIX II
LETTER OF ENGAGEMENT FOR AN EMPLOYEE SHARE OWNERSHIP PLAN AT
COMPANY INC.

March 24, 2015

CONTENTS

Proposal

March 24, 2015
J. Smith, President
Company Inc.
Address
Town, Province   N1H 1B5

Dear Mr. Smith,

Proposal for a Stage I Feasibility Audit for an ESOP at Company Inc.

We are pleased to present our proposal regarding the feasibility of an Employee Share Ownership Plan (ESOP) at Company Inc. (the Company) in a manner that meets your goals, your corporate vision and ensures that the ESOP is aligned successfully with your existing corporate culture and structure over the long term.

The purpose of the ESOP is to:

1. Reward valued current employees who remain with the company and provide an incentive to contribute to its future success and growth
2. Engage employees across the organization to be more consciously aware of the "Big Picture" at the Company
3. Create a business legacy for the current owners that will continue into future generations
4. Create a long-term, flexible succession plan for the current owners, giving them the maximum flexibility in ownership during the transition

Our mission statement is to make shared ownership a profitable reality. We are uniquely suited to accomplish this task for the following reasons:

1. ESOPs are our specialty and our company was established to deliver the design, communication and implementation of ESOPs.
2. We have eighteen years of experience using this Model, with a proven track record.

3. Clients are primarily small- and medium-sized privately held Canadian companies across a range of industries.
4. We offer national and international ESOP strategic partnerships and experience.
5. We can provide or source the necessary components for the ESOP including design, business valuation, tax planning and legal counsel.

Objectives of a Successful ESOP

- Create increased value for shareholders through higher employee productivity and morale and alignment of employee and corporate goals
- Achieve a high employee participation rate in the ESOP
- Integrate the ESOP into the corporate culture and incentive program
- Integrate the ESOP with corporate strategy
- Develop a flexible broad-based structure that potential acquirers or investors can accept

The ESOP Transformation Model©

The ESOP Transformation Model, which we have developed and used for the benefit of our clients, is transaction-oriented. Our goal is to produce the best available plan that meets owner, corporate and employee objectives with an economical investment and reasonable time frame.

The ESOP process is encompassed in two parts:

1. Stage I – Feasibility Audit
2. Stage II – Design, Communication and Implementation

Staffing

The overall ESOP diagnostic, design and tax components are provided by ESOP Builders Inc. The business valuation can be provided by one of our strategic partners or any Certified Business

Valuator (CBV) of your choice. The project will be managed by Perry Phillips (ESOP Builders president).

Stage I - Feasibility Audit

The purpose of this stage is to assess the goals and needs of all the stakeholders; the Owners, and the employees. We do this through:

1. a detailed discussion with the Owners assessing the specific ownership goals required to make the ESOP successful
2. private interviews with key employees and an optional detailed private questionnaire for employees to assess their knowledge of, and desire for owning shares in the Company.
3. review of company financials, corporate structure, tax structure (see Appendix 1)

You will receive a detailed Feasibility and Recommendations Report outlining:

- the various options available to you to achieve your goals
- the pros and cons of each option
- our implementation recommendation
- your investment to implement our recommendation, strategies for financing, and the critical path necessary to deliver the project on budget and in a timely manner

At this point, the Owners choose to proceed with our recommendations, modify the goals of the ESOP or stop the process, depending on the results of the feasibility audit.

Confidentiality

We confirm that all materials provided by you and your company are confidential and will be used solely in relation to the ESOP assignment. We will sign any confidentiality agreement pursuant to this representation.

Your investment and other expenses

Please note that the fee quote is only for the Stage I ESOP Feasibility Audit and is valid until September 24, 2015*.

At signing, we request the fee for the Feasibility Audit plus HST. [GST].

Should circumstances arise that might materially affect our time and cost, we will discuss the matter with you first and take direction accordingly.

In addition, we will bill all reasonable disbursements incurred separately at cost (including travel and accommodation). We will discuss the specifics prior to incurring any other significant expenses.

Your investment for Stage I is $X,XXX* plus HST. [GST].

If you wish to proceed, please sign this letter where indicated below.

Payment of **$X,XXX** can be made by cheque or by electronic funds transfer payable to ESOP Builders Inc.

When received, we will proceed with the assignment. We are also pleased to receive from you the necessary documentation listed in Appendix 1.

At the completion of Stage I, if you decide to proceed to Stage II (design, communication and implementation (Appendix 2)), your investment will be as follows:

ESOP Design, Education and Tax Strategy	**$X,XXX**
Business valuation	**X,XXX**
Legal document	**X,XXX**
Total	**$XX,XXX**

*This quote is effective for 6 months from date of this Proposal

Thank you for the opportunity to quote on this most important work.

Yours truly,

P Phillips

Perry Phillips CPA, CA, CBV
President

You are hereby authorized to proceed in accordance with the above terms of reference for the ESOP activities for Stage I:

Company Inc.

Per

_____   _____
Signature   Date

_____   _____
Name   Title

APPENDIX 1

Stage I Initial information and documents required for Feasibility Audit

The first 6 are required as soon as possible. The remainder are important (not time-sensitive) but help you create greater value.

1. Corporate and share ownership structure
2. Last 2 years of financial statements
3. Organization chart
4. Copy of employment contracts with two key individuals
5. Employee contact information for interviews
6. Copy of Unanimous Shareholders Agreement (if in place)
7. Contact names of external advisors
8. Details on profit sharing plans, incentive plans, benefit plans etc.
9. Key-man insurance and other relevant policies
10. Forecasts or budget financial statements
11. Industry background (competitors, public and private)
12. Any studies, reports or valuations done within the last 3 years on the company and/or industry
13. Details of any ongoing or planned management consultant studies and related activities

APPENDIX 2 – ESOP PROCESS STAGE I AND STAGE II

The deliverables involved in the ESOP process usually include:

- Delivery of the project on budget and in a timely fashion following a critical path (as in Appendix 3)

Stage I

- Interviews with owners
- Interviews with key employees
- Summary of feedback from interviews
- Review of financial statements, budgets and forecasts
- Feasibility and Recommendations Report

Stage II

- Meet with owner to finalize ESOP parameters
- Organization and co-ordination of an ESOP team of employees and advisers
- optional detailed private questionnaire for employees
- ESOP team meetings
- ESOP design and strategy
- Employee information session
- Business Valuation Report
- Blueprint (detailed description of the ESOP design)
- Tax review and Income Tax Summary document
- Review of legal documents
- Assistance in preparation of the Employee Information Package
- Final closing meeting – Town Hall meeting

APPENDIX 3 – DRAFT CRITICAL PATH MILESTONES

Stage I

WEEK 1   Sign engagement letter for Stage I
Send documents to ESOP Builders for review
Interviews with owners
Separate Interviews with each key employee

WEEK 3   Draft Feasibility and Recommendations Report
Review Report with owners
Decide to proceed to Stage II

Stage II

WEEK 4   Sign engagement letter for Stage II
Receive documents

WEEK 5   Initial meeting with owner
- Objectives
- ESOP Team members to be confirmed
- Scope ESOP design

WEEK 6   Contact ESOP Team
First meeting
- develop critical path
- allocate responsibilities
- communication strategy

WEEK 11   Draft Blueprint of ESOP

WEEK 12   Draft valuation

WEEK 13   ESOP Team meeting
ESOP information session

WEEK 15   Finalize Blueprint
Draft legal and tax documents

WEEK 17   Finalize all documents

WEEK 18   Information Package

WEEK 19   Town Hall meeting

WEEK 20   Close ESOP transaction

Completion of Stage I – 3 to 4 weeks. Completion of Stage II – 3 to 6 months. If the client chooses to extend the project beyond 6 months, additional charges may apply

APPENDIX 4 – NEWS ARTICLES ON ESOPS AND ESOP BUILDERS

[links]

A Piece of the Action: ESOPs can be a key succession planning tool

Why you should give your employees a piece of the company

Sharing: a path to prosperity

APPENDIX 5 – GLOBAL ESOPS STATISTICS

In Canada, 40% of PROFIT Magazine's 200 Fastest Growing Companies had ESOPs

[links]

The Economic Power of Employee Ownership in the U.S.

Employee Ownership in Britain 2014

APPENDIX 6 – STATISTICS ON HIGHLY ENGAGED WORKFORCES

Participative ESOP companies are known to have highly engaged cultures. A 10-year study of 200 Fortune 500 Companies with highly engaged cultures showed the following benefits:

- 314% higher profit growth
- 94% higher profit margins
- 116% higher total return on investment
- Recruiting: 3.5 times more job applications
- Productivity: 20% higher performance scores
- Absenteeism: significantly less
- Customer loyalty: 2X non-engaged workforces

APPENDIX 7 – CURRICULUM VITAE OF PERRY PHILLIPS

[As this sample is for illustrative purposes only, the 4-page cv has not been included here.]

APPENDIX III
XYZ MANUFACTURING INC.
QUESTIONNAIRE

INSTRUCTIONS

PLEASE COMPLETE THIS QUESTIONNAIRE... BY **DATE**

Your responses will be kept confidential. We will never use or disclose your responses together with your name.

This questionnaire may be completed online at surveylink.com.

If you return this form via email to Name@Adviser, please hilight or underline your selections and type in any of your written responses. You may send it as an attachment or as the email message itself. In either case we will never use or disclose the information on your email message together with your name.

Please make every effort to complete the questionnaire and respond as fully as possible where written responses are requested. (Do not include your name or names of others.)

Please mark the appropriate answer:

1. Do you understand what is meant by the following terms:

Employee Share Ownership Plans (ESOP)	**Yes**	**No**
Shares (stock or equity)	**Yes**	**No**
Shareholder	**Yes**	**No**
Stock options	**Yes**	**No**
Vesting period	**Yes**	**No**
Exercise price	**Yes**	**No**
Registered retirement savings plan (RRSP)	**Yes**	**No**
Self-directed RRSP	**Yes**	**No**
Capital gains	**Yes**	**No**

Strongly Agree: 1–2 / Agree Somewhat: 3–4 / Strongly Disagree: 5 / Do Not Know: 0

2. Share ownership (ESOP) would be a valuable financial benefit   1   2   3   4   5   0

3. An ESOP would be a competitive advantage for our company   1   2   3   4   5   0

4. I understand how companies like ours may change in value over the years   1   2   3   4   5   0

5. Owning shares would improve my perception of the company   1   2   3   4   5   0

6. Owning shares would improve my commitment to the company   1   2   3   4   5   0

7. Owning shares would improve the company's commitment to me   1   2   3   4   5   0

8. I would be interested in purchasing shares if I thought it a fair deal   1   2   3   4   5   0

9. I consider share ownership more valuable than bonus or profit sharing   1   2   3   4   5   0

10. Do you know the difference between:

    public and *private* companies?   **Yes**   **No**

11. Do you know how:

    public companies are valued?   **Yes**   **No**

12. 12. Do you know how:

    private companies are valued?   **Yes**   **No**

13. What is your opinion on the amount of corporate information that the company provides to employees?

    Too much information   **Enough information**   **Not enough information**

    If "not enough", what additional information would you like?

14. a. Please rank the following in order of importance to you (from 1 to 5):

    Very Important: 1 / Not Imporrtant: 5

a.	Bonus/profit sharing	1	2	3	4	5	0
b.	Education subsidies	1	2	3	4	5	0
c.	Flexible hours	1	2	3	4	5	0
d.	Subsidized Group RRSP	1	2	3	4	5	0
e.	Subsidized personal financial planning	1	2	3	4	5	0
f.	Fitness programs	1	2	3	4	5	0
g.	Stock equity (shares)	1	2	3	4	5	0
h.	Stock options	1	2	3	4	5	0
i.	Other (please describe other)	1	2	3	4	5	0

14. b. From the above list, list the top 3, by letter, that are most important to you:

   1.
   2.
   3.

15. Do you believe *all* future senior employees should be eligible to purchase shares?

Yes   **No**   **Do not know**

Please state your reasons:

16. Do you believe *all future* employees (employees below the senior level) should be eligible to purchase shares?

Yes   **No**   **Do not know**

Please state your reasons:

17. If offered shares in this company (and you had all the necessary information disclosed to you), would you purchase them?

Yes   **Probably**   **Probably not**   **No**

17. a. If "**Probably not**" or "**No**", please indicate your reasons for not joining the ESOP

17. b. If "**Yes**" or "**Probably**", how much would you likely invest on an *annual* basis?

$1,000 to $2,000   **$2,001 to $5,000**   **$5,001 to $10,000**

$10,001 to $20,000   **$20,001 to $30,000**   **Greater than $30,000**

18. What do you think would be the pros and cons of owning shares in the company?

19. What is the most important thing this company could do to make you want to be a shareholder?

20. Approximately how long have you been with the company?
    _____ **years**

21. How long do you currently view your career continuing with this company?

    Less than 1 year   **1 to 3 years**   **3 to 5 years**

    5 to 10 years   **greater than 10 years**

22. Think forward 5 years and imagine what could have taken place that would have made you glad you still worked at the company. Briefly describe:

Thank you for your attention and effort.

APPENDIX IV
FREQUENTLY ASKED QUESTIONS

(Some specific values and percentages have been used for illustrative purposes.) Outlined below is a list of the most common questions asked about ESOPs.

1. Is participation mandatory?

   A. No. Your position with the company does not depend upon your participation in the program.

2. Who are eligible for the shares?

   A. Generally, all full-time regular employees who were employed with the company up to [specify date] are eligible for the ESOP. Generally all full-time employees hired after that date would have a six-month waiting period before becoming eligible. The Board will determine whether employees who have satisfied these employment criteria are to be classified as a Designated Person, an Eligible Person or a New Eligible Person. The Board of Directors will also have the ultimate discretion as to whether anyone can be excluded from participation. Contract personnel are not eligible.

3. Who decides how many shares an employee can buy?

   A. The Board of Directors allocates shares for each employee and manages the program.

4. Is seniority a factor in the allocation of shares?

   A. Employees who have been employed prior to [specify date] get a one-time bonus allocation.

5. How do we know that the method of allocation is fair?

   A. The Board of Directors has used a salary formula for uniformity. The management also has to ensure that individuals who are key to the future success and value of the company are rewarded adequately. This has been done by developing different classifications with different share allocations.

6. Are we eligible to transfer shares or options into a RRSP or 40l (k)?

   A. The shareholders' Agreement does permit the transfer of shares to an RRSP, and you cannot hold options within an RRSP. For U.S. employees, the company shares can be transferred into your 401(k) but options cannot.

7. Can we use money other than our bonus if we choose to acquire shares under the Share Acquisition Plan?

   A. No. The Board wants to ensure that the employees earn the shares through the bonus program at this time.

8. Can we buy more shares than our bonus will pay for?

   A. No. You can acquire only up to the number of shares that have been allocated for you. This could be below or above your bonus amount. The company has allowed participants up to December 31 to use their bonus to acquire shares.

9. When will the company go public and on what exchange?

   A. Our current objective is to go public within the foreseeable future. However there are no guarantees. The exchange will probably be the

TSE but it could also be NASDAQ. You will be kept informed of our progress towards this goal.

10. How much of the share offering would be made available to the public?

A. This ESOP offering is for employees only and, no shares will be made available to the public.

11. Do our shares have any value before we go public?

A. Yes, but there are limited ways to realize the value, as detailed in the shareholders' agreement. For example, upon death, your estate would receive fair market value, and upon termination you would receive 75 per cent of fair market value.

12. How do I liquidate the shares if the company does not go public?

A. If the company does not go public or sell to a third party, you can sell shares only according to the special circumstances described in the shareholder agreement.

13. How long do we have to hold the shares after we go public?

A. That depends upon which exchange and their restrictions. Generally, you may have to hold them for a period of 0 to 365 days, or more in special circumstances.

14. How is the share price/option price determined?

A. The Board of Directors determines the fair market value of the shares and options through consultation with its accountants. The value will be generally determined annually by the Board of Directors.

15. What is the initial value of the shares and the terms to acquire them?

A. Each common share will initially be $100.00. Your bonus will be used to acquire common shares, which also entitles you to receive stock options. However, you do not have to pay anything for the stock options.

16. When are the shares/options offered and exercised?

A. This offer will be made on [date]. However, you can acquire your shares up to [date]. The options are immediately vested, and you have up to five years to exercise them. For new employees, shares with matching options will also be provided under this program.

17. Are the shares/options better than the cash equivalent? How do you compare them?

A. We are not qualified to give investment advice, and you must do your own analysis of the offer. However, Canadian employees acquiring shares do not pay tax on that amount until the shares are sold. You also receive a stock option. If you were to take a cash bonus instead of shares, you would have income tax withheld. However, as with any investment, there is a risk of losing your investment. U.S. employees receiving a cash bonus pay tax when receiving the cash benefit. When you receive shares or options the receipt of shares/options will be subject to tax before you receive the cash benefit from the proceeds of selling the shares.

18. What happens if a third party buys the company?

A. You would receive your pro rata portion of the proceeds of the sale.

19. How much financial information will be available before I decide to buy?

A. The company will provide a summary of historical and current results.

20. Will we see financial statements every year?

A. Yes, a summary financial report will be presented annually.

21. Can we cash out our shares at any time?

A. No. Your shares can be sold to the company only in certain circumstances, such as death or termination, based upon the shareholders' agreement.

22. Can we change the percentage of our bonus used to acquire shares?

A. No. The percentage of your bonus to be received in shares cannot be changed. Once you have acquired your elected amount of shares, the remainder of your bonus (if any) will be paid in cash.

23. What happens to our shares if we leave the company?

A. If you leave the company, it may purchase your shares at the company's option. If you leave as a result of death, disability, or retirement, you will receive fair market value (FMV). As a result of bankruptcy or termination, you receive 75 per cent of FMV. All stock options that are vested at the time of death, disability, or retirement must be exercised within 180 days of leaving the company, and the company has the right to buy back the shares. All stock options that are vested at time of termination must be exercised within 30 days of leaving the company, and the company has the right to buy back the shares.

24. Do the shares have voting rights?

A. All the shares are common shares with full voting rights.

25. Will we get dividends?

A. If dividends are declared on common shares, you will receive your allocation. However, since we are a growing company that needs to reinvest its capital in technology and staff, we will not likely pay dividends.

26. Is there a limit on the percentage of shares held by individuals?

A. There is a 5 per cent limit on individual ownership of shares.

27. What are the risks of investing in the company?

A. As with any investment, there is the risk of loss. The company could potentially go bankrupt, in which case your investment would be lost. The company is not public; therefore there is no liquidity to your shares. The company is relatively small and must compete against larger and better-capitalized competitors.

28. What proportion of my bonus can I use to acquire shares?

A. You may elect 0, 25, 50, 75, or 100 per cent of your bonus as cash with the dollar value of the balance used to acquire shares.

29. What if we go public before I acquire all my shares?

A. It is the company's intention to make all reasonable efforts to create the opportunity for all employees to have acquired all of their shares under the Share Acquisition Plan prior to going public subject to regulatory requirements.

APPENDIX V

ESOP BLUEPRINT

ESOP SHAREHOLDERS' AGREEMENT

The ESOP Blueprint is Schedule B of the ESOP Shareholders' Agreement. It is not included here.

To receive a free sample of the ESOP Blueprint, we invite you to visit www.esopbuilders.com/BookDownloads

MODEL ESOP SHAREHOLDERS' AGREEMENT

DATED AS OF •

PLEASE NOTE – this is a model agreement and some or all of the terms hereof will not be appropriate for use in every situation. Each ESOP shareholders' agreement must be designed to fit the specific facts applicable to each corporation, its shareholders and its ESOP design.

TABLE OF CONTENTS

ESOP SHAREHOLDERS' AGREEMENT

dated as of the • day of • , 201 • .
AMONG:

•, a corporation amalgamated under the laws of the Province of l (the "Corporation")

- and -

Every person executing Schedule A attached hereto, or being deemed to have executed Schedule A, from time to time (each a "Shareholder" and collectively the "Shareholders")

WHEREAS:

a. The Corporation has established an employee share ownership plan (the "ESOP") whereby certain employees of the Corporation will be eligible, from time to time, to acquire and hold certain [voting/non-voting] shares in the capital of the Corporation (the **"ESOP SHARES"**);

b. The parties hereto wish to make certain arrangements regarding purchase and sale of the ESOP SHARES and the administration of the ESOP further to the ESOP Blueprint annexed hereto as Schedule B (the "ESOP Blueprint"); and

c. The Shareholders wish to establish their rights, liabilities and obligations in respect of the ESOP SHARES now or hereafter owned by them, the sale of the ESOP SHARES in certain circumstances, and certain other matters as hereinafter set forth;

NOW THEREFORE in consideration of the foregoing, and of the mutual promises, covenants and conditions herein stated, the parties agree as follows:

1. DEFINITIONS AND INTERPRETATION

1. Definitions

Where used in this Agreement unless the context otherwise requires, the following words and phrases shall have the meaning ascribed to them below:

a. **"Accountants"** means such independent firm of chartered accountants as may, from time to time, be chosen by the Directors as auditors or accountants of the Corporation;

b. **"Act"** means the • Business Corporations Act, as amended from time to time, and every statute that may be substituted therefor, and in the case of any such amendment or substitution, any reference in this Agreement to the Act shall be read as referring to the amended or substituted provisions therefor;

c. **"Agreement"** means this ESOP SHAREHOLDERS' AGREEMENT including any and every amendment or supplement hereto and any and every instrument supplemental or ancillary hereto;

d. **"Articles"** means the certificate of incorporation of the Corporation, filed •, and as from time to time, amended or restated;

e. **"By-laws"** means any by-laws of the Corporation which are, from time to time, in force and effect;

f. **"Directors"** means persons who are, from time to time, duly elected or appointed directors of the Corporation;

g. **"Disposition"** has that meaning ascribed to it in Article ;

h. **"Disposition Date"** means, in the case of Article 10 the date that a notice is delivered exercising the Election or Obligation;

i. **"ESOP"** has the meaning ascribed to it in the first recital of this Agreement;

j. **"ESOP Blueprint"** means the ESOP Blueprint of the Corporation attached hereto as Schedule B;

k. **"ESOP SHAREHOLDER ADVANCES"** means, with respect to each Shareholder, all outstanding loans due and owing from time to time by the Corporation to such Shareholder;

l. **"ESOP Shareholder Interest"** means all the ESOP SHARES owned by an ESOP SHAREHOLDER plus all ESOP SHAREHOLDER ADVANCES owed to that ESOP Shareholder;

m. **"ESOP SHAREHOLDERS"** means all those persons who have executed Schedule A attached to this Agreement, or who are deemed to have executed it, from time to time, and ESOP SHAREHOLDER means any one of them;

n. **"ESOP SHARES"** means certain [voting/non-voting Common Shares] in the capital of the Corporation issued pursuant to the ESOP Blueprint and this ESOP SHAREHOLDERS' AGREEMENT;

o. **"fair market value"** means the highest price determined in an open and unrestricted market between informed prudent parties acting at arm's length and under no compulsion to act, expressed in terms of money or money's worth, as determined pursuant to ;

p. **"Minimarket"** means a sale of ESOP SHARES by Shareholders or to persons eligible to purchase ESOP SHARES pursuant to the ESOP Blueprint, such Minimarket being administered by the Plan Administrator appointed under the ESOP Blueprint;

q. **"Officers"** means persons who are, from time to time, duly elected or appointed officers of the Corporation;

r. **"Plan Administrator"** means an Officer appointed by the Directors and responsible for the approval of employee Share purchases and the administration of the ESOP;

s. **"Prime Rate"** means the commercial lending rate of interest which the Corporation's bank quotes as the reference rate of interest to determine the rate of interest it would charge to its customers for loans in Canadian dollar funds;

t. **"Shares"** means shares in the capital of the Corporation, and includes ESOP SHARES and shares that are issued to shareholders other than ESOP SHAREHOLDERS, including Common Shares and Preferred Shares;

u. **"Special Resolution"** means either:

  i. a resolution passed by not less than two-thirds of the votes cast at a duly constituted meeting of the Directors entitled to vote on such resolution, as the case may be; or

  ii. a resolution in writing approved by all of the Directors entitled to vote on such resolution, as the case may be.

2. Currency

Unless otherwise provided for herein, all payments contemplated herein shall be paid in Canadian funds, in cash or by cheque.

3. Invalidity

If any article, section or any portion of any section of this agreement is determined to be unenforceable, invalid or illegal for any reason whatsoever that unenforceability, invalidity or illegality shall not affect the enforceability, validity and legality of the remaining portions of this agreement and such unenforceable, invalid or illegal article, section or portion thereof shall be severed from the remainder of this agreement.

4. Headings

The captions and headings in this Agreement are for convenience of reference only and shall not affect the interpretation of any provisions in this Agreement or its scope or intent.

5. Applicable Law

This Agreement shall be interpreted in accordance with the laws of the Province of •.

6. Gender

Wherever the singular is used, it shall be deemed to extend to and include the plural and vice versa, and where one gender is used, it shall include all genders.

7. Severability

Any provision of this Agreement which is invalid or unenforceable may be severed and such severance shall not affect the validity or enforceability of any other provision or covenant herein contained.

2. PRECEDENCE OF THIS AGREEMENT

1. Supersedes Prior Agreements

The provisions of this Agreement apply to the ESOP SHARES and ESOP SHAREHOLDERS only and not to any other Shares of the Corporation, whether issued or not, and supersedes all former agreements, blueprints, executive summaries or other documents relating to the disposition of any ESOP Shareholder Interest, and all such agreements are hereby declared to be of no further force or effect whatsoever except to the extent, if any, that the substance thereof is incorporated into this Agreement. Without limiting the generality of the foregoing, this Agreement does not supersede any agreements, articles, options, provisions or entitlements of the Initiating Shareholders, as defined herein, as well as any Shares held by the Initiating Shareholders, or any of them.

2. Notice by the Corporation of Shareholder Agreement

The Corporation by its execution hereof, hereby acknowl- edges that it has actual notice of the terms of this Agreement, consents thereto and hereby covenants with each of the ESOP SHAREHOLDERS that it will at all times during the continuance hereof be governed by this Agreement in carrying out its business and affairs and accordingly, shall give or cause to be given such notices, execute or cause to be executed such deeds, transfers and documents and do or cause to be done all such acts, matters and things as may from time to time be necessary or conducive to the carrying out of the terms and intent hereof.

3. IMPLEMENTATION OF AGREEMENT

1. Deemed Consent

Each of the ESOP SHAREHOLDERS shall be deemed to have consented to any transfer of ESOP SHARES made in accordance with this Agreement and each covenants and agrees to waive any restriction on transfer contained in the Articles or By-laws in order to give effect to such transfers.

4. EMPLOYEE SHARE OWNERSHIP PLAN

1. No Guarantee of Continued Employment

Where a Shareholder is an employee of the Corporation, such Shareholder acknowledges that being a Shareholder does not guarantee his/her continued employment with the Corporation, nor will it have any effect on the terms of such Shareholder's employment with the Corporation. Each Shareholder also acknowledges that ownership of ESOP SHARES grants him/her no right to or interest in any other or additional ESOP SHARES, except as provided in the ESOP Blueprint.

2. ESOP Blueprint

Subject to section , each of the ESOP SHAREHOLDERS agrees the issuance of ESOP SHARES to employees of the Corporation under the ESOP, the administration of the ESOP, and other matters pertaining to the ESOP shall generally be administered in accordance with the ESOP Blueprint. If there is a conflict between the provisions of the ESOP Blueprint and this Agreement, this Agreement shall govern. If this Agreement is silent on any matter which is covered by the ESOP Blueprint, the ESOP Blueprint shall govern.

3. Alteration, Amendment, Suspension or Termination of ESOP

The parties hereto acknowledge that the Directors may, in their sole discretion, alter, amend, suspend or terminate the ESOP, including the ESOP Blueprint, in any manner, provided that such action does not materially and adversely affect any of the issued and outstanding ESOP SHARES of any Shareholder, without such Shareholder's consent.

4. Risks

Each Shareholder acknowledges and agrees that:

a. There is a limited market for the ESOP SHARES and there is no guarantee that the ESOP SHARES will ever have a market or that the Corporation will remain profitable or in business. Each Shareholder further acknowledges that he/she may only be able to sell the ESOP SHARES in certain and in limited circumstances.

b. If a Shareholder is required to sell ESOP SHARES to the Corporation, there may be tax consequences even if there was no gain in value.

c. The Corporation can issue new ESOP SHARES or other Shares in the future that could dilute existing ESOP SHAREHOLDERS' ownership and value.

5. RESTRICTIONS ON TRANSFER OF ESOP SHARES

1. Prohibitions

No Shareholder shall sell, assign, pledge, transfer, encumber or dispose of any ESOP SHARES or Shareholder Interest except in accordance with the terms of this Agreement or with the prior written consent of the board of Directors.

In no event shall any Shareholder be permitted to:

a. acquire, whether by purchase, transfer or otherwise, more than 5% of the issued and outstanding ESOP SHARES (unless approved by Special Resolution), subject to any ESOP SHARES held by ESOP SHAREHOLDERS in excess of that amount prior to the date hereof; or

b. purchase ESOP SHARES in excess of any limitations established at the discretion of the Plan Administrator, as determined by the Directors,

and the Corporation shall refuse to enter any such transaction in its books and records without the approval of the Directors as contemplated by Article c.

Subject to any approval required by applicable law or by this Agreement, the Corporation may make a decision about, take action on, or implement, without the approval of the ESOP SHAREHOLDERS, an initial public offering, whether on a treasury or secondary basis, resulting in the holding of equity of the Corporation, directly or indirectly, by the public, or a transaction giving rise to a stock market listing or over-the-counter quotation of equity of the Corporation, directly or indirectly, including an amalgamation, securities exchange take-over bid or other transaction having a similar result.

2. ESOP Minimarket

Notwithstanding any other provision in this Error: Reference source not found, the ESOP SHAREHOLDERS agree that the Corporation may, at any time, maintain and administer a Minimarket, which shall be maintained and administered in accordance with the ESOP Blueprint. In the event that the

Minimarket is established, the ESOP SHAREHOLDERS will be authorized to sell, transfer and assign a specified number of ESOP SHARES per Minimarket sale to any person eligible to purchase ESOP SHARES pursuant to the ESOP at a Minimarket in the manner contemplated by the ESOP Blueprint, subject to the restriction in Section 5.01(a) that no Shareholder may hold more than 5% of the issued and outstanding ESOP SHARES.

The purchase price for any ESOP SHARES being purchased or sold at a Minimarket shall be the price per ESOP SHARE determined pursuant to .

3. Condition of Transfer

Any Shareholder who is authorized to sell, transfer and assign ESOP SHARES to a person eligible to purchase ESOP SHARES pursuant to the ESOP shall, as a condition of such sale, transfer and assignment make it a condition precedent of the transfer that the person acquiring such ESOP SHARES indicate his or her intention to be bound by this agreement by executing Schedule A hereto (unless such person has previously executed such Schedule A). If such condition precedent is not satisfied, the board of Directors shall be under no obligation to consent to the transfer of ESOP SHARES nor to record the transfer on the books and records of the Corporation.

4. ESOP Shares

The provisions of this Agreement relating to ESOP SHARES shall apply mutatis mutandis to:

a. any ESOP SHARES or securities into which such ESOP SHARES may be converted, changed, reclassified, redivided, redesignated, redeemed, subdivided or consolidated;

b. any ESOP SHARES or securities that are received by the ESOP SHAREHOLDERS as a stock dividend or distribution payable in ESOP SHARES or securities of the Corporation; and

277

c. any ESOP SHARES or securities of the Corporation or of any successors or continuing companies or corporations to the Corporation that may be received by the ESOP SHAREHOLDERS on a reorganization, amalgamation, consolidation or merger, statutory or otherwise.

5. Consent Procedure

Any act prohibited by this Error: Reference source not found will be permitted and will not constitute a default under this Agreement, nor will it constitute a Disposition, provided that it is approved by a Special Resolution, and all conditions attached to such approval are met.

6. Certificate Endorsement

Certificates for all ESOP SHARES shall be endorsed with the following legend:

> "The ESOP SHARES represented by this Certificate are subject to the provisions of the ESOP Shareholders Agreement dated as of • made among [insert name of the Corporation] and its ESOP SHAREHOLDERS, and such ESOP SHARES are not transferrable on the books of [insert name of the Corporation] except in compliance with the terms and conditions of such Agreement."

7. Manner of Holding ESOP SHARES

Employee ESOP SHAREHOLDERS may hold their ESOP SHARES personally, or in a Tax Free Saving Account ("TFSA"), or in a Registered Retirement Savings Plan ("RRSP"), or a combination of the foregoing.

6. TAG AND DRAG ALONG

1. Tag Along Option

If at any time, shareholders controlling the Corporation (the "Initiating Shareholders") receive a bona fide offer (in this Article called the "Offer") from one or more persons dealing at arm's length with the Initiating Shareholders to purchase all, or any part of, the Initiating Shareholders' Shares, which is acceptable to the Initiating Shareholders, the Corporation shall at least thirty (30) days prior to the date specified for completion of the transaction of purchase and sale contemplated in the Offer give written notice (in this Article called a "Disposition Notice") to the ESOP SHAREHOLDERS (in this Article the "Remaining Shareholders") stating that each Remaining Shareholder has (and each Remaining Shareholder shall then have) the option (the "Tag Along Option") to sell to the purchaser(s) making the Offer all, or the corresponding part, of such Remaining Shareholder's ESOP SHARES, simultaneously with and conditional upon the completion of the transaction of purchase and sale contemplated in the Offer and at the same price per Share and on the same terms as are contained in the Offer.

2. Exercise of Tag Along Option

The Tag Along Option shall be exercised by written notice (in this Article, an "Acceptance Notice") by a Remaining Shareholder stating the number of his/her ESOP SHARES that he/she wishes to sell, up to the maximum number permitted, delivered to the Initiating Shareholders not later than fifteen (15) days after the Disposition Notice is given to the such Remaining Shareholder. If a Remaining Shareholder gives an Acceptance Notice, then:

a. The Remaining Shareholder shall be obligated to sell the portion of his or her ESOP SHARES specified in his or her Acceptance Notice upon the terms specified in the Offer to the proposed purchaser(s) under the

Offer, conditional upon and contemporaneously with the completion of the transaction of purchase and sale contemplated in the Offer; and

b. the Corporation agrees with the Remaining Shareholder that it shall not permit the transfer of any of the Initiating Shareholders' ESOP SHARES in the Corporation under such Offer unless payment for the portion of the Remaining Shareholder's ESOP SHARES being sold are to be included in such sale is made in accordance with the terms of the Offer.

3. Drag Along Obligation

If the Offer is conditional upon the sale of all of the ESOP SHARES in the Corporation, or the same percentage of the Shares owned by the Initiating Shareholders and ESOP SHARES owned by the Remaining Shareholders, the Disposition Notice shall state that each Remaining Shareholder shall be obligated (the "Drag Along Obligation") to sell all or the applicable percentage of the ESOP SHARES owned by each such Remaining Shareholder upon the terms specified in the Offer to the proposed purchaser under the Offer, conditional upon and contemporaneously with the completion of the transaction of purchase and sale contemplated in the Offer, and each Remaining Shareholder shall accept and complete such Offer and the Drag Along Obligation in accordance with its terms.

4. Outstanding Payments to Former Shareholders

If the Initiating Shareholders sell all of their Shares, any former Shareholder who is still receiving annual payments pursuant to the provisions of   shall be entitled to accelerate all outstanding amounts owing to them thereunder and all such amounts shall be payable to said former Shareholder on the same date as the closing of the sale by the Initiating Shareholders of all of their Shares. It is further agreed that the former Shareholder shall not be entitled or required to accept the purchase price applicable to the sale of Shares by the Initiating Shareholders.

7. SALE EVENTS

1. Disposition

For the purposes of this , "Disposition" means:

a. where any one or more of the following occurs in relation to a Shareholder:

   i. the Shareholder has died;

   ii. the Shareholder is petitioned into bankruptcy or makes an assignment for the benefit of his or her creditors;

   iii. the Shareholder is judged insane or incompetent to handle his or her own affairs by a court of competent jurisdiction;

   iv. an order is made by a court of competent jurisdiction purporting to deal with the Shareholder's Shareholder Interest pursuant to the Family Law Act of • or other similar legislation;

   v. the Shareholder's Shareholder Interest is seized or attached in any way for the payment of any judgment or order;

   vi. the Shareholder has made or purported to make a sale, transfer or assignment of his or her Shareholder Interest in contravention of this Agreement;

   vii. the Shareholder has defaulted in the payment of any sums due and owing by him or her to the Corporation and such default continues after thirty (30) days from the date of notice of such default having been given to him or her by the Corporation indicating an intention to exercise the Election provided for in this ;

   viii. a default by a Shareholder of any provision of this Agreement, and such default continuing after thirty (30) days from the notice of such default having been given to him or her by the Corporation;

   ix. if the Shareholder is an employee of the Corporation, and the Shareholder, through bona fide illness, physical or mental, shall be unable to devote the time and attention to the affairs of the Corporation required of him or her, such disability shall have continued for twelve (12) months and such Shareholder having received, while still disabled, a written notice from the Corporation demanding the Shareholder sell the ESOP SHARES of the Corporation beneficially owned by him or her;

x. if the Shareholder is an employee of the Corporation, and the Shareholder, through bona fide illness, physical or mental, shall be unable to devote the time and attention to the affairs of the Corporation required of him or her, such disability shall have continued for twelve (12) months and such Shareholder having delivered, while still disabled, a written notice to the Corporation demanding the Corporation purchase the ESOP SHARES of the Corporation beneficially owned by him or her; or

xi. if the Shareholder is an employee of the Corporation and that Shareholder voluntarily resigns as an employee and such resignation does not meet the criteria for a "retirement", as defined under xiii;

xii. if the Shareholder's employment with the Corporation is terminated for "just cause", including without limitation, if the Shareholder commits theft, fraud, embezzlement or financial misappropriation or other similar criminal act with respect to the Corporation;

xiii. if the Shareholder's employment with the Corporation is terminated without "just cause"; or

xiv. if the Shareholder is an employee of the Corporation, and that Shareholder retires. For the purpose of this Agreement "retire" or "retirement" means that the Shareholder is over the age of 65 on the date he or she terminates his or her employment with the Corporation and ceases employment completely, and does not reduce his or her employment from full-time status to part-time status. For the purposes of this Agreement any employee Shareholder who works more than half the hours and less than all the hours specified by the Corporation from time to time as the standard for full time employees, shall be considered part-time, and even though he/she is over the age of 65, he/she shall not be considered to have "retired" for the purposes of section 7.05 hereof, unless his/her hours are less than half the standard.

b. For the purposes of Articles vii and ix above, the period of disability for any employee Shareholder shall be deemed to commence on the first working day that such Shareholder does not attend to the affairs of the Corporation in the manner required of him/her, statutory holidays and vacations excepted. In calculating the period of disability, unless and until such Shareholder shall have returned to attending to the affairs of his/her employer in the manner required of him/her for thirty (30) consecutive normal working days, the said period of disability shall be deemed to have continued without any interruption whatsoever.

2. Minimarket, Election and Obligation

a. Upon the occurrence of any Disposition with respect to Shareholder (in this Article referred to as the "**Vendor**") referred to in Section , and at any time thereafter (provided the event creating the Disposition has not been cured, to the extent it can be cured), the Vendor shall sell his or her ESOP SHARES in the Minimarket (should one have been established at that time), and if no Minimarket has been established, the Vendor shall sell his/her ESOP SHARES to the Corporation in accordance with the Election and Obligation described below. The decision to established Minimarkets from time to time shall be in the sole discretion of the Directors. Following the sale of ESOP SHARES in the Minimarket (if any), any remaining ESOP SHARES of the Vendor shall be sold to the Corporation in accordance with the Election and Obligation described below. In such event, any limitations on the sale of ESOP SHARES described in Section shall not apply.

b. Subject to Section 7.02 , upon the occurrence of any Disposition with respect to a Vendor referred to in subsections 7.01(a)(ii), (iv), (v), (vi), (vii), (viii) and (xi), and at any time thereafter provided the event creating the Disposition has not been cured (to the extent it can be cured), the Corporation may elect to purchase, and to require the Vendor to sell, the Shareholder Interest of such Vendor in accordance with this (each respective right in this Section referred to as the "Election").

c. Subject to Section 7.02 , upon the occurrence of any Disposition with respect to a Shareholder (in this Article referred to as the "Vendor") referred to in subsections 7.01(a)(i), (iii), (ix), (x), (xii), (xiii) and (xiv), and at any time thereafter provided the event creating the Disposition has not been cured (to the extent it can be cured) the Corporation shall have the obligation to purchase, and the Vendor shall sell, the Shareholder Interest of such Vendor in accordance with this   (each respective right in this Section referred to as the "Obligation").

3. Notice to Exercise Election

The Election may be exercised by the Corporation at any time after the occurrence of the Disposition described in Subsection a for so long as the event giving rise to the Disposition continues by providing thirty (30) days' written notice to the Vendor. The notice shall state the date of the occurrence of Disposition and its particulars. On the expiry of the thirty (30) days' notice (and provided the event of Disposition is not cured before the expiry of such date) or on such earlier or later date as the Purchasers and the Vendor mutually agree, the Vendor shall sell and the Corporation shall purchase, the Shareholder Interest of the Vendor. If the event of Disposition is cured on or prior to the expiry of the thirty (30) days' notice (and provided the transaction did not close earlier by the mutual agreement of the parties), the notice shall be deemed terminated and neither the Vendor nor the Purchaser shall have any obligations to the other of them in connection therewith.

4. Exercise of Obligation

The Obligation shall be exercised in the same manner as the Election.

5. The Purchase Price

The purchase price shall be determined in accordance with Article 9.

Upon the occurrence of any Disposition with respect to Triggered Shareholder referred to in subsection a, viii, ix or xiii any time after five (5) years have passed since such Triggered Shareholder acquired his/her ESOP SHARES, such Triggered Shareholder will immediately sell his or her ESOP SHARES to the Corporation for fair market value determined in accordance with . Notwithstanding the foregoing, Triggered Shareholders referred to in subsection xiii may continue to hold his or her ESOP SHARES for up to five (5) years following the date of his or her retirement, and not later than the expiry of such five (5) year period, such Triggered Shareholder shall sell his or her ESOP SHARES to the Corporation in the manner described herein.

6. Condition - Solvency of the Corporation

Notwithstanding any other provision of this , the Corporation shall not be obligated to purchase any Shareholder Interest if doing so would result in there being reasonable grounds for believing that the Corporation is, or would after the purchase be, unable to pay its liabilities as they become due, or if doing so would cause the realizable value of the Corporation's assets after the purchase to be less than the aggregate of its liabilities and stated capital of all classes. However, the Corporation shall purchase such portion of the Shareholder Interest as they are able to purchase without breaching the foregoing sentence. In the event that any remaining portion of the Shareholder Interest that is to be purchased by the Corporation is not purchased by it as a result of this Article, the obligation of the Corporation to purchase such portion shall be delayed until such time as the board of Directors determines the Corporation is able to purchase the Shareholder Interest without breaching this Article .

7. Suspension of Election and Obligation

Notwithstanding any other provision of this , if a Disposition Notice is delivered pursuant to after an Election or Obligation is exercised, but before the transaction contemplated by such

Election or Obligation closes, the closing of such Election and/ or Obligation shall be suspended until after the transaction contemplated by the Disposition Notice closes or the Offer affiliated therewith is withdrawn, expires or is otherwise terminated.

8. Redemption of Preferred Shares

Notwithstanding any other provision of this , each Shareholder acknowledges that the Corporation has the right to redeem any or all of the issued Preferred Shares for the redemption amount of • Dollar ($•.00) per share pursuant to the provisions of the Articles of the Corporation.

8. ADDITIONAL TERMS OF SALE

1. Closing Date

Any transaction arising out of   hereof shall be closed at the office of the solicitors for the Corporation on such date (in this Article referred to as the "Closing Date") as shall be agreed between the Selling Party (as hereinafter defined) and the Purchasing Party (as hereinafter defined) and, in default of agreement, as specified in Section 7.03 (respecting Article 7). Notwithstanding the Closing Date, the closing shall be effective as of the Disposition Date.

2. Terms Applicable to All Sales

Whenever a sale of a Shareholder Interest or portion thereof occurs pursuant to the provisions of   hereof, the following terms and conditions shall apply to such sale:

a. the party selling the Shareholder Interest (in this Article referred to as the "Selling Party") shall covenant with and warrant and represent to each of the parties purchasing the Shareholder Interest (in this Article referred to as the "Purchasing Party") as follows:

i. That as of the Closing Date, the Selling Party will be the sole beneficial owner of the Shareholder Interest and hold a good and marketable title thereto, free and clear of all mortgages, liens, charges, pledges, security interests, encumbrances and other claims whatsoever (excepting those securing obligations of the Corporation) and that the Selling Party is entitled to transfer the Shareholder Interest in accordance with the terms of this Agreement without restrictions; and

ii. all necessary steps and proceedings shall be taken to permit the Shareholder Interest to be duly and regularly transferred to the Purchasing Party or its nominee;

b. there shall be delivered at the Closing Date to the Purchasing Party by the Selling Party:

i. a complete release by the Selling Party of all claims against the Corporation;

ii. a release by the Selling Party of all claims against the Purchasing Party arising out of or with respect to the Shareholder Interest of the Selling Party except with respect to the terms incidental to the purchase and sale of that Shareholder Interest;

iii. if applicable, the resignation as Director and Officer by the Selling Party or its nominee holding office with the Corporation; and

iv. the share certificates representing the ESOP SHARES comprised in the Shareholder Interest included in the purchase with the transfers thereon duly endorsed in favour of the Purchasing Party.

3. Terms Applying to Certain Sales

a. The purchase price applicable to any purchase of ESOP SHARES or a Shareholder Interest by the Corporation shall be paid in equal annual instalments of not less than 20% of the purchase price commencing on the Closing Date over a period not to exceed five (5) years.

Notwithstanding the foregoing:

i. If the purchase price is less than $•, the purchase price shall be payable in full within 90 days of the Closing Date; and

ii. Upon the occurrence of any Disposition with respect to Triggered Shareholder referred to in subsection a, the purchase price shall be payable in full within 180 days of the Closing Date .

The principal amount of the purchase price from time to time outstanding shall bear interest at a rate per annum, calculated annually, not in advance, which is equal to the Prime Rate on the date the transaction is consummated, with interest on overdue interest at the same rate. Such interest shall be payable at the same times as payments of principal, the first of such payments of interest (if any) to become due and payable one year after the Closing Date, with interest at the aforesaid rate computed from the Closing Date.

Notwithstanding the provisions of this Article , the Corporation shall have the privilege at any time and from time to time to prepay any amount due, without notice or bonus. Further, the aggregate payments to all ESOP SHAREHOLDERS during any financial year of the Corporation shall not exceed the maximum amount (the "Annual Pay-Out Cap") determined by the board of Directors annually for that financial year (if any) having regard to the financial condition of the Corporation as a whole, its obligations under the Act, its lenders and/or other arm's length third parties, its cash flow, and such other matters as the board of Directors considers relevant. If the amount to be paid to those ESOP SHAREHOLDERS in such year exceeds the Annual Pay-Out Cap, each such Shareholder shall be paid his or her pro rata share of the Annual Pay-Out Cap (based on the number of ESOP SHARES being sold by such Shareholder compared to the total number of ESOP SHARES to be sold in that financial year), not to exceed his or her respective purchase price, and the payment schedule contemplated by this Article shall be extended by as many annual payments as are necessary (but limited by each Annual Pay-Out Cap) to pay the respective

Shareholder the purchase price, together with interest thereon, in full., Notwithstanding the foregoing Annual Pay-Out Cap, in no circumstances shall the five (5) year payment period referred to above be extended by more than a further five (5) years. Any such payment to any subject Shareholder will only be made after all distributions have been paid in full to any Shareholder whose payment is coming due within the time period described in the foregoing sentence.

b. In the event of a purchase of all or a portion of a Shareholder Interest pursuant to an Election which has been exercised as a result of a Disposition by the Selling Party pursuant to Article 7, the Purchasing Party shall use reasonable efforts to obtain the release of the Initiating Party from any guarantee made by such Initiating Party with respect to indebtedness of or the performance of obligations by the Corporation or the Corporation failing which each of the Purchasing Parties shall, jointly and severally, covenant and agree, in proportion to the portion of the Shareholder Interest purchased by them, to indemnify and save harmless the Selling Party and their respective representatives and successors from and against all claims, liabilities, costs, charges and expenses, including legal costs on a solicitor and own client basis sustained or incurred by the Selling Party after the Closing Date and in any way arising out of any guarantee from which the Selling Party has not been released.

c. With respect to any purchase of a Shareholder Interest or portion thereof pursuant to   where the Purchasing Party is not the Corporation, there shall be delivered at the Closing Date to the Purchasing Party by the Selling Party an assignment by the Selling Party to the Purchasing Party of the ESOP SHAREHOLDER ADVANCES forming part of the Shareholder Interest purchased upon payment in full by the Purchasing Party to the Selling Party of the amount agreed to be paid in respect of the ESOP SHAREHOLDER ADVANCES so purchased plus accrued but unpaid interest thereon, if any.

d. With respect to any purchase of a Shareholder Interest or portion thereof pursuant to   where the Purchasing Party is the Corporation, the

ESOP SHAREHOLDER ADVANCES shall be repaid to the Selling Party on the Closing Date.

e. If a Shareholder fails to complete the subject transaction of purchase and sale required of him or her by this Agreement, the President of the Corporation shall have the right, without prejudice to any other rights which the Corporation may have, upon payment of the portion of the purchase price payable to such Shareholder contemplated by the transaction, to execute and deliver, on behalf of and in the name of the Shareholder, such deeds, transfers, share certificates (if any), resignations or other documents that may be necessary to complete the subject transaction, and the Shareholder hereby irrevocably appoints the President of the Corporation as his or her attorney in accordance with the Powers of Attorney Act and in accordance with the said Act, the Shareholder declares that this power of attorney is a continuing power of attorney and may be exercised during any subsequent legal incapacity on his or her part. The power of attorney hereby granted is a power coupled with an interest.

4. Additional Terms - Sale to Outside Party

A sale or transfer of a Shareholder Interest or portion thereof to a person or corporation not already a Shareholder shall not be effective, and the Selling Party shall not be released from his obligations under this Agreement until the Purchasing Party acknowledges in writing that it is bound by the terms of this Agreement.

9. VALUATION

1. Definition

In this Article, "ESOP Anniversary Date" means a date determined annually by the Plan Administrator appointed under the ESOP for the annual valuation of the ESOP SHARES, provided that the following ESOP Anniversary Date shall not be more than twelve (12) months and not less than ten (10) months after the last ESOP Anniversary Date.

2. Valuation Date

Where this Agreement requires the ESOP SHARES to be valued in accordance with this , the fair market value of the ESOP SHARES at any particular date is the price per Share established on the ESOP Anniversary Date and applies until the next ESOP Anniversary Date.

3. Valuation

a. The value of each issued and outstanding Preferred Share shall be
   • ($•.00).

b. The value of each issued and outstanding Common Share shall be determined by the Directors, in their sole discretion, as of the most recent ESOP Anniversary Date, considering the independent valuation referred to in Article b. Said value shall be the applicable purchase price for all Common Share transactions until the next ESOP Anniversary Date. Such purchase price may only be changed prior to the next ESOP Anniversary Date if there is a material change in circumstances that in the reasonable opinion of the Directors requires a material change to the then prevailing purchase price.

c. The independent valuation of each Common Share shall be based on the valuation of the Corporation performed at least once every three years by a chartered business valuator selected by the Directors. Said valuation shall establish the fair market value of all the Common Shares including the ESOP SHARES for the year in question, and shall set out a formula prepared by such valuator for use by the Directors in each of the subsequent two years. Each year, the valuation shall be based upon the annual financial statements for the most recently completed fiscal year and forecast future financial results of the Corporation. The Directors shall update the formula used to evaluate all the Common Shares including the ESOP SHARES at least once every three (3) years. Each year that a valuation is not performed, the Directors shall update the most recently completed valuation based on subsequently completed annual financial statements of the Corporation.

10. RESTRICTIVE COVENANTS

1. Non-Solicitation

Each ESOP SHAREHOLDER covenants and agrees with the other parties bound hereby and with the Corporation that he/she will not (without the prior written consent of the Corporation and the other parties bound hereby), so long as he/she is an ESOP SHAREHOLDER and for a period of one (1) year thereafter:

a. divulge to any person the name of any customer or client of the Corporation;

b. knowingly solicit, interfere with or endeavour to entice away from the Corporation any customer, client or any person in the habit of dealing with the Corporation; and

c. interfere with or knowingly entice away or otherwise attempt to obtain the withdrawal of any employee of the Corporation.

The Corporation may apply for or have an injunction restraining breach of threatened breach of the covenants herein contained.

2. Severability

The covenants made in section   hereof are made by each ESOP SHAREHOLDER acknowledging that they have specific knowledge of the affairs of a Corporation. If any of the covenants therein contained shall be held unreasonable by reason of the duration or type or scope of service covered by the said covenant, then the said covenant shall be given effect to in such reduced form as may be decided by any court of competent jurisdiction. Each ESOP SHAREHOLDER hereby acknowledges that all restrictions hereinbefore contained are reasonable and valid and all defences to the strict enforcement of all or any portion thereof are hereby waived. If any clause or portion of any such covenant should be unenforceable or declared invalid for any reason whatsoever, such unenforceability or invalidity shall not affect the enforceability or validity of the remaining portions of the covenant or of this agreement and such unenforceable or invalid portion shall be severable from the remainder of this agreement.

3. Confidentiality

All confidential records, material and information and copies thereof, and all trade secrets (and without restricting the generality of the foregoing, including inventions, discoveries and methods of processing and production) concerning the business or affairs of the Corporation (collectively, "**Proprietary Information**") shall remain the exclusive property of the Corporation. While a shareholder of the Corporation or at any time thereafter, the ESOP SHAREHOLDER(s) shall not divulge the contents of such Proprietary Information to any person (except the Corporation, the Corporation's qualified employees or the Corporation's accountants), and the ESOP SHAREHOLDER(s) shall not, at any time, use the contents of such Proprietary Information for any purpose whatsoever, except for the exclusive benefit of the Corporation.

For the purposes hereof, "**confidential records, material and information**" includes information known or used by either of the Corporation in connection with its business including, but not limited to, any formula, design, prototype, compilation of information, data, program, code, method, technique or process, information relating to any product, device, equipment or machine, information about or relating to the Corporation's customers and the Corporation's markets and marketing plans, present and future, information about or relating to the Corporation's potential business ventures, financial information of all kinds relating to the Corporation and its activities, all inventions, ideas and related material, but does not include any of the foregoing which was known to the ESOP SHAREHOLDER prior to his/her becoming a shareholder of the Corporation or which is or becomes a matter of public knowledge.

4. Nature of Business

For the purpose of this c, the nature of the business of the Corporation is •.

11. POWER OF ATTORNEY FOR VOTING

1. Power of Attorney

Each of the ESOP SHAREHOLDERS agrees that the President of the Corporation from time to time (in this Article 11, the "**Attorney**") shall be entitled:

a. to vote all of the ESOP SHARES in the capital of the Corporation beneficially owned or controlled by each Shareholder on all matters for which the holders of such ESOP SHARES would be entitled to vote at all meetings of the ESOP SHAREHOLDERS or of the holders of a class of ESOP SHARES of the Corporation, for whatever purpose called, in such manner as the Attorney shall from time to time, in his sole and absolute discretion, consider necessary or advisable, and the parties hereto acknowledge that in exercising his discretion in the voting of such ESOP SHARES, the Attorney may act arbitrarily and notwithstanding any actual, potential or perceived conflict of interest on his part; and

b. to take part in and consent to any corporate or Shareholder action wherein the vote or written consent or resolution of the ESOP SHAREHOLDERS of the Corporation may be authorized or required by law, in his sole and absolute discretion, and the parties hereto acknowledge that in exercising his discretion, the Attorney may act arbitrarily and notwithstanding any actual, potential or perceived conflict of interest on his part.

c. The power of attorney hereby granted is a power coupled with an interest. For greater certainty, this power of attorney shall remain valid during any period of mental incapacity of any Shareholder.

2. Subject Matter

The matters, or corporate or shareholder actions, to which the power of attorney granted by Article   are limited are as follows:

a. consenting to the exemption from the audit requirements contained in the Act; and/or

b. taking any action on behalf of the Corporation in connection with its rights, duties, obligations and responsibilities under [prior agreements].

3. Further Assurances

For the purposes of implementing the intent of this , each of the ESOP SHAREHOLDERS hereby agrees to execute and deliver from time to time, whenever requested by the Attorney, such further powers of attorney in favour of the Attorney or his or her designee with respect to the power of attorney granted by Article in such form as may be reasonably requested by the Attorney.

4. Limitation

Each of the ESOP SHAREHOLDERS agrees that the Attorney shall not be liable or responsible for any action taken or suffered or not taken with respect to the power of attorney contemplated by this .

5. Enurement

For greater certainty, the provisions of this Article 11 shall enure to the benefit of the heirs, executors, administrators, successors and assigns of the Attorney.

12. ARBITRATION

1. Application

Any matter of dispute among the parties to this Agreement or matter of interpretation with respect to this Agreement shall be referred to arbitration which shall be conducted in the manner set forth in this .

2. Initiation

The party initiating the arbitration may institute the proceedings by delivering to the other ESOP SHAREHOLDERS and the Corporation a notice (in this Article referred to as the "Arbitration Notice") containing the name of three (3) persons proposed as arbitrator, together with their respective addresses and callings and a copy of their respective consents to accept the appointment, from which the other ESOP SHAREHOLDERS may choose one (1) to serve as arbitrator. If the ESOP SHAREHOLDERS receiving the Arbitration Notice do not agree with any of the arbitrators proposed and fail to propose to the party initiating the arbitration an acceptable alternate within thirty (30) days thereafter, the party initiating the arbitration shall apply to a court of competent jurisdiction on notice to the other ESOP SHAREHOLDERS and the Corporation, for appointment by the court of a single arbitrator.

3. Scope

The arbitrator shall determine the issues of fact falling for determination by the arbitration proceedings, including any necessary interpretation of provisions of this Agreement, within a period of thirty (30) days after confirmation of his appointment as arbitrator. The arbitration shall be conducted in accordance with the *Arbitrations Act,* [insert name of province] and the decision of the arbitrator with regard to any matter properly before him/her shall be final and binding upon the parties hereto whether they have entered into the arbitration or not.

4. Costs

Any costs arising out of arbitration proceedings hereunder shall be borne by those parties in the amounts determined by the arbitrator.

5. No Appeal

The parties hereto covenant that they will not apply nor will they have any right to apply by any means to any court to challenge any decision of the arbitrator on a matter properly before the arbitrator.

13. GENERAL

1. Amendments

No modification or amendment of the Blueprint or the ESOP is binding unless it is executed in writing by the Directors or the Plan Administrator. No modification or amendment of this Agreement shall be effective unless it has been approved in writing by ESOP SHAREHOLDERS holding not less than two-thirds of the issued and outstanding ESOP SHARES.

2. Undertakings

The parties hereto undertake and agree to execute and deliver such further and other documents and assurances as may be necessary to give effect to all of the terms and conditions of this Agreement.

3. Enurement

This Agreement shall be binding upon and shall enure to the benefit of each party hereto as well as the heirs, executors, administrators, successors and permitted assigns of such party.

4. Notice

a. All notices, requests or demands to or upon the parties hereto shall be in writing and delivered or sent by registered mail postage prepaid, by delivery, or by email addressed, to the Corporation and to the address of the president of the Corporation for the time being, with a concurrent copy to the registered office of the Corporation, and if to the ESOP SHAREHOLDERS, to the addresses set out in Schedule A attached hereto, or to such other address as may be specified by one of the parties hereto to the other in a notice given in the manner herein provided.

b. Any such notice, request or demand sent as aforesaid shall be deemed to have been received by the party to whom it is sent on the third business day following the mailing thereof if sent by registered mail, on the day of delivery, if delivered, and on the business day following the transmittal thereof, if sent by email; provided, however, that in the event normal mail service or email service shall be interrupted by strike, slowdown, force majeure or other cause, then the parties sending the notice, request or demand, shall take whatever steps are necessary to ensure prompt receipt of such notice, request or demand by the other parties.

5. Merger

In the event of a sale of ESOP SHARES by a Shareholder to another Shareholder, the provisions of this Agreement shall not merge with but shall survive the closing of that sale.

6. Execution in Counterparts

This Agreement, including Schedule A attached hereto, may be executed in several counterparts, and delivered in the original, by fax or by email attachment in Portable Document Format (PDF), each of which when so executed and delivered shall be deemed to be an original and such counterparts taken together shall each constitute one and the same instrument and, notwithstanding their date of execution, shall be deemed to bear date as of the day and year first above written.

7. Time

Time shall be of the essence of this Agreement.

8. Non-Waiver

No provision of this Agreement shall be deemed to be waived unless such waiver is in writing. Any waiver of any default committed by any of the parties hereto in the observance of the performance of any part of this Agreement shall not extend to or be taken in any manner to affect any other default.

9. Duration of Agreement

This Agreement shall continue in full force and effect until terminated by agreement amongst the ESOP SHAREHOLDERS and the Corporation.

10. Independent Legal Advice

Each of the ESOP SHAREHOLDERS acknowledges and agrees that:

a. he or she has read and understood this agreement; and

b. he or she has been given the opportunity to obtain independent legal advice in connection therewith and has either done so or has freely chosen not to do so.

SIGNATURE PAGE FOLLOWS

IN WITNESS WHEREOF the parties hereto have executed this Agreement as of the date and year first above written.

[INSERT NAME OF THE CORPORATION]

Per: _____

    Name: •

    Authorized Signing Officer

Per: _____

    Name: •

    Authorized Signing Officer

SCHEDULE A
SHAREHOLDER EXECUTION OF ESOP
SHAREHOLDERS' AGREEMENT

RECITALS:

1. There exists a shareholder agreement dated as of •, (the "SA") amongst the Corporation and its employee shareholders.
2. Each of the undersigned is or has become a shareholder of the Corporation, has received a copy of the SA and is required to execute and deliver a counterpart of the SA to the Corporation and its shareholders.

EACH OF THE UNDERSIGNED HEREBY COVENANTS TO AND WITH THE CORPORATION AND ALL OF ITS ESOP SHAREHOLDERS that he, she or it is bound by the SA as if he, she or it was an original party to the SA and that his, her or its address for notice is that address recorded opposite his, her or its name.

Shareholder	Signature	Date	Address for Notice

SCHEDULE B
ESOP BLUEPRINT

APPENDIX VI
ESOP ASSOCIATIONS AND HELPFUL WEBSITES

ESOP Association Canada

ESOP Association Canada is a non-profit organization founded in November 1990 for the purpose of promoting the concept of employee ownership for business in Canada.
Website: http://www.esop-canada.com/

National Center for Employee Ownership (NCEO)

A non-profit membership organization providing unbiased information and research on broad-based employee stock plans. The NCEO publishes news on legal, regulatory, and financial developments; ideas, tips, and reports on management practices in employee ownership firms; technical articles by employee ownership experts; research and case studies; a one-page pullout for rank-and-file employees; and company, media, and resource information.
Website: http://www.nceo.org/

The ESOP Association United States

The ESOP Association is the largest employer sponsored advocacy and education association focused on retirement savings in America, is a national non-profit membership organization, with 18 local Chapters, serving approximately 2,800 employee stock ownership plan (ESOP) companies, professionals with a commitment to ESOPs, and companies considering the implementation of an ESOP.

The ESOP Association publishes the ESOP Report, covering the latest regulatory and case law updates, Capitol Hill briefings, technical and managerial advice from ESOP professionals, tips on winning ESOP companies and employee owners, and association news.

Website: www:esopassociation.org

Employee Ownership Association United Kingdom

Non-profit and politically independent organization that works in close partnership with its members to champion, promote and provide insight into the business case for employee ownership in the U.K. Association website has case studies, research and frequent blogs about employee-owned companies. The association has a mandate for 10% of U.K. GDP to be delivered by employee-owned businesses by 2020.

Website: http://employeeownership.co.uk/

The Employee Share Ownership Centre U.K.

A non-profit subscription based organization founded to inform, lobby, and research in the interest of developing all forms of broad-based employee share ownership plans in the U.K. and Europe.

Website: http://www.esopcentre.com

Employee Ownership Australia and New Zealand

Membership association engaging with and helping companies that have or want to implement employee ownership or employee share plans.
Website: www.employeeownership.com.au

International Association for Financial Participation (IAFP)

IAFP is the international association of companies, academics, and individuals in the European Union, Asia, Eastern Europe and the Americas which supports financial participation for employees as a means of increasing productivity and fostering worker satisfaction. The IAFP website provides a global perspective on ESOPs, related research and government incentives.
Website: http://www.aipf-association.fr/en

Aon Hewitt

A global management consulting firm specializing in human resource solutions. Compensation surveys, research papers, and other publications are available on their website.
Website: http://www.aon.com

PricewaterhouseCoopers Stock Plan Reporter

The Stock Plan Reporter provides general due diligence information regarding taxation and regulatory issues associated with equity compensation offered to foreign-based employees. The site covers general issues associated with stock options, employee stock purchase plans, restricted stock and restricted stock unit plans, performance stock and performance stock unit plans, and finally both stock and cash settled SARs in over 75 countries. This data is particularly useful for companies to anticipate opportunities

and barriers before expanding their plans to new countries and to provide regular updates once the plans have been implemented.
Website: http://www.equityplanner.pwc.
com/HRS/EquityPlanner/EPv1.nsf

The World at Work

The World at Work is a non-profit human resources association for professionals and organizations focused on compensation, benefits, work-life effectiveness and total rewards. Provides thought leadership in total rewards disciplines from the world's most respected experts and a community of fellow practitioners.
Website: www.worldatwork.org

International Foundation of Employee Benefit Plans (IFEBP)

A non-profit, non-lobbying, educational association serving the employee benefits field. Website includes industry news and a listing of publications.
Website: www.ifebp.org

The National Association of Stock Plan Professionals

In the US, provides opportunities for education, networking, and information exchange through its national office, local chapters, and national and local conferences. Members are professionals whose responsibilities are related, directly or indirectly, to stock plan administration and design.
Website: www.naspp.com

The Financial Accounting Standards Board

In the US, establishes and improves standards of financial accounting and reporting for the guidance and education of the public, including issuers, auditors, and users of financial information.
Website: www.fasb.org

APPENDIX VII
PROFESSIONALS

Please note this list is not exhaustive. These are organizations and individuals known to the authors.

ESOP Builders Inc.

ESOP design, implementation, communication; cross-border ESOPs

Contact:
Perry@esopbuilders.com,
Camille@esopbuilders.com,
info@esopbuilders.com
1 (877) 995-ESOP (3767)
4646 Dufferin St., Suite 6
Toronto, Ontario M3H 5S4
http://esopbuilders.com

National Benefit Services Inc.

Assisting employers since the early 1980s with the design, administration, and communication of their ESOPs, stock options, and broad-based employee share programs; Cross-border ESOPs

Contact: Jerry Kalish, National Benefit Services president
jerry@nationalbenefit.com
National Benefit Services, Inc.
300 W. Adams Street, Suite 415
Chicago, IL 60606
Ph. 312-419-9080
www.nationalbenefit.com

Kalex Valuations

Established in 1996, Kalex Valuations Inc. has grown to become a leading boutique provider of independent business valuations, dispute support, tax dispute and transaction advisory services.

Contact: Melanie Russell, Kalex Valuations founder
melanie@kalexvaluations.com
http://www.kalexvaluations.com

Maarschalk Valuations Inc.

Paul Maarschalk's varied career has largely focused on corporate finance and corporate financial planning. He has worked in Canadian and international companies in financial services, value added agriculture, mining, mineral exploration, marketing, software and banking.

Contact: Paul Maarschalk, founder,
pmaarschalk@shaw.ca
http://valuationsandplanning.com

Canadian Institute of Chartered Business Valuators

Maintains registry of members

Contact:
https://cicbv.ca
(416) 977-1117

Dale & Lessmann LLP Canadian Counsel

For more than 20 years Dale & Lessmann have been advising clients on ESOPs.

Contact: David E. Clark, Dale & Lessmann LLP partner
dclark@dalelessmann.com
416-369-7808
www.dalelessmann.com

Chartered Professional Accountants of Canada (CPA Canada)

Each province has its own institute which maintains a registry of members by specialty, including tax.

Contact:
https://www.cpacanada.ca
(416) 977-3222

Ownership Thinking Canada

Using Ownership Thinking processes – education, measures, and incentives – can create a true sense of ownership among all staff members and accountability for the business and financial objectives they work on every day. Employees can think and act like owners to improve the bottom line.

Contact:
The Ownership Thinking program is facilitated by TAC.
http://ownershipthinking.ca

The Achievement Centre (TAC)

TAC provides professional development programs, coaching, and strategic planning to organizations around the world and has developed a reputation for delivering results by focusing on the people side of business. Through TAC's paced-learning programs, organizations initiate behavioural changes, helping employees reach their full potential.

Contact: Marc Lacoursiere, The Achievement Centre president
marc@tacresults.com
www.TACresults.com

Tyson & Associates Limited

Management consultants specializing in compensation, including profit sharing

Contact: David E. Tyson, Tyson & Associates Limited president
tyson.consult@sympatico.ca
Suite 210, 83 Elm Avenue, Toronto, Ontario M4W 1P1
(416) 966-1379
http://www.compensationcanada.com

Canadian Western Trust

Owned by **Canadian Western Bank**, which administers corporate loans to employee-owners, CWT registers TFSAs and RRSPs for ESOPs. Big enough to provide world-class service but local enough to know their clients by name, with people and personal relationships at the heart of everything they do.

Contact: Matt Steele, business development manager
matt.steele@cwt.ca
Website: http://www.cwt.ca

APPENDIX VIII
ESOP LEGISLATION IN CANADIAN PROVINCES

BRITISH COLUMBIA

Visit: http://www.mit.gov.bc.ca/icp/esop

1. Tax Credits

The Employee Share Ownership Program provides employees with a 20% tax credit for making investments in their employers' businesses. There is no lifetime limit on the amount of the tax credit, although there is a $2,000 tax credit limit per person per calendar year (corresponding to an investment of $10,000).

If the employee investor sells his or her shares prior to the end of the 3-year hold period, they will be required to repay all or part of the tax credits received on the shares, depending on the selling price.

2. Cost Sharing

The Government of British Columbia will reimburse the company, or an employee group, 50% of the eligible costs of a professional advisor used in the establishment, registration or ongoing administration of an ESOP plan. This reimbursement is limited to $2,500 per calendar year.

Who is eligible to apply for cost sharing?

Any company with fewer than 150 employees or any group of employees no matter what the company size is eligible to apply.

SASKATCHEWAN

Visit http://www.economy.gov.sk.ca/employeeinvestment

Employees receive a 20% provincial tax credit on the first $5,000 they contribute each year.

Employees are also eligible for a federal tax credit until March 1, 2017 (investments are eligible for the 2016 tax year). The federal tax credit is 10% in 2015 and 5% in 2016. Under this program, employees working with their employer can set up and invest in an LSVCC fund, which in turn invests into their company of employment.

MANITOBA

Visit: http://www.entrepreneurshipmanitoba.ca/
programs-services/363/employee-share-purchase-tax-credit

Employee Share Purchase Tax Credit

Employees who participate in a registered employee share ownership plan can qualify for a 45 per cent tax credit. Investments made through an employee's RRSP or TFSA will also be eligible for the credit.

The maximum tax credit that may be earned in a year is: $202,500 (on a $450,000 investment) if the ESOP was established and registered to facilitate succession planning for a family business or to facilitate an employee buyout or takeover designed to create and maintain employment in Manitoba; or $27,000 (on a $60,000 investment) for shares acquired under any other registered ESOP.

The credit is partially refundable up to $27,000. Any credits earned in excess of that amount are non-refundable. An additional restriction provides that only $67,500 may be claimed as a credit in any one year, but excess credits can be carried forward 10 years or back three years.

To be eligible to issue shares under this program, a corporation must be a Canadian-controlled private corporation with a permanent establishment in Manitoba and must pay at least 25% of its total wages and salaries to Manitoba residents. The corporation and its affiliates must have no more than $25 million in gross assets and $10 million in net assets, all or substantially all of which must be used in carrying on an active business. In addition, the revenue of the corporation and its affiliates must be derived principally from an active business and not from property and/or prescribed activities.

NOVA SCOTIA

Equity Tax Credit

Personal income tax credit to investors (including employees) investing in eligible businesses.

For investments made after December 31, 2009: calculated at 35 per cent of investment made by individual to a maximum annual investment of $50,000 (maximum annual credit of $17,500, includes current year and the carry forward or back amounts).

ABOUT THE AUTHORS

PERRY PHILLIPS

From helping Canada's fastest growing companies implement engagement strategies to supporting business owners exiting on their terms, Perry Phillips is recognized as one of Canada's leading experts on employee share ownership plans (ESOPs).

Perry is the president of ESOP Builders Inc., founder of the ESOP Association Canada and co-author of *The Ten Trillion Dollar Opportunity: Designing Successful Exit Strategies for Middle Market Business Owners: A Guide for Professional Advisors – Canadian Edition.*

CAMILLE JENSEN

Camille is the vice-president of ESOP Builders, Canada's leading designer of employee share ownership plans for private companies. In addition to helping companies implement ESOPs, Camille is an active volunteer with the ESOP Association Canada. Camille was a key organizer and chair of the first Canadian Employee Ownership Conference held in June, 2015 and writes frequently on ESOP issues.

CPSIA information can be obtained
at www.ICGtesting.com
Printed in the USA
LVOW10s2045040518
576041LV00007B/13/P